SO MANY MEN IN ONE

To the Greeks, he was Joseph, stolen from his family by the Turkish oppressors and raised to be the cruelest and most savage of soldiers.

To the Turkish Sultan, he was Youssef, the only one the supreme ruler could trust to aid him in a desperate game with the fate of a vast empire at stake.

To the women in his life ... the volcanic Selina ... the icily-elegant Olga ... the defiant Katerina ... and the others ... he was a lover whose desire came hand-in-hand with the threat of death—as he moved through a world where intrigue and violence reigned and where raging passion burned across all boundaries. ...

WINDSWEPT

Big Bestsellers from SIGNET

- ☐ **THE GIRL IN A SWING** by Richard Adams.
  (#E9662—$3.50)*
- ☐ **DMITRI** by Jamey Cohen. (#E9663—$2.75)*
- ☐ **BRASS DIAMONDS** by Berent Sandberg. (#E9665—$2.50)*
- ☐ **ROADWORK** by Richard Bachman. (#E9668—$2.25)*
- ☐ **HUNGRY AS THE SEA** by Wilbur Smith. (#E9599—$3.50)†
- ☐ **MAGGIE'S WAY** by Martha Barron Barrett. (#E9601—$2.75)*
- ☐ **MASQUERADE** by Cecilia Sternberg. (#E9603—$2.75)
- ☐ **SALEM'S DAUGHTER** by Maggie Osborne. (#E9602—$2.75)*
- ☐ **KEY WEST CONNECTION** by Randy Striker. (#J9567—$1.95)
- ☐ **THE DEEP SIX** by Randy Striker. (#J9568—$1.95)
- ☐ **THE VISITOR** by Chauncey G. Parker III. (#E9562—$2.75)*
- ☐ **THE BOOKS OF RACHEL** by Joel Gross. (#E9561—$3.50)
- ☐ **THE 81st SITE** by Tony Kenrick. (#E9600—$2.75)*
- ☐ **SHANGHAI** by Barth Jules Sussman. (#E9563—$2.75)*
- ☐ **EMPIRE** by Etta Revesz. (#E9564—$2.95)

* Price slightly higher in Canada
† Not available in Canada

Buy them at your local bookstore or use this convenient coupon for ordering.

THE NEW AMERICAN LIBRARY, INC.,
P.O. Box 999, Bergenfield, New Jersey 07621

Please send me the SIGNET BOOKS I have checked above. I am enclosing
$_____ (please add 50¢ to this order to cover postage and handling).
Send check or money order—no cash or C.O.D.'s. Prices and numbers are subject to change without notice.

Name _____

Address _____

City _____ State _____ Zip Code _____

Allow 4-6 weeks for delivery.
This offer is subject to withdrawal without notice.

WINDSWEPT
A Historical Novel

Athena G. Dallas-Damis

A SEQUEL TO
Island of the Winds

A SIGNET BOOK
NEW AMERICAN LIBRARY
TIMES MIRROR

PUBLISHED BY
THE NEW AMERICAN LIBRARY
OF CANADA LIMITED

Publisher's Note

This novel is a work of fiction. Names, characters, places, and incidents are either the product of the author's imagination or are used fictitiously, and any resemblance to actual persons, living or dead, events, or locales is entirely coincidental.

NAL BOOKS ARE AVAILABLE AT QUANTITY DISCOUNTS WHEN USED TO PROMOTE PRODUCTS OR SERVICES. FOR INFORMATION PLEASE WRITE TO PREMIUM MARKETING DIVISION, THE NEW AMERICAN LIBRARY, INC., 1633 BROADWAY, NEW YORK, NEW YORK 10019.

Copyright © 1981 by Athena G. Dallas-Damis

All rights reserved

First Printing, March, 1981

2 3 4 5 6 7 8 9

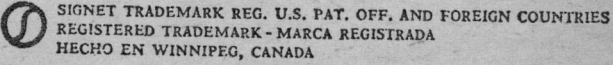

SIGNET TRADEMARK REG. U.S. PAT. OFF. AND FOREIGN COUNTRIES
REGISTERED TRADEMARK - MARCA REGISTRADA
HECHO EN WINNIPEG, CANADA

SIGNET, SIGNET CLASSICS, MENTOR, PLUME, MERIDIAN and NAL BOOKS are published in Canada by The New American Library of Canada, Limited, Scarborough, Ontario
PRINTED IN CANADA
COVER PRINTED IN U.S.A.

*To my son, Peter Dallas, and our
windswept journey together . . .*

PROLOGUE

THE RAIN FELL in a steady drizzle. It penetrated the dusty earth that thirsted in the August sun. A miracle—rain was unheard of this time of year. Perhaps the heavens pitied the town, the whole island of Chios which shriveled in the heat, trying valiantly to survive.

It was four years since the holocaust of 1822—of the massacre that brought rivers of blood, ashes and scarred bodies, death and desolation. The hills, once green with pine, now lay barren and empty—black and gray ashes along the mountainsides. Here and there a bit of green appeared, where the villagers, full of hope, tried to rebuild what once was. The sword and flame of the conqueror, the once-friendly Ottomans, had cut down life and all that sustained it. Four years—thousands dead, thousands sold in the slave markets of Constantinople and North Africa and thousands exiled, rushing to safety in the neighboring islands. From these last, life trickled back to Chios the following year, and the next, and the next. Until once again the island breathed . . . not the free air it had hoped and fought for, but at the least, breathable air. The cruel Ottoman governor was replaced by a kindly one who ruled Chios more humanely, more leniently, trying to forget the bitterness and hatred that had spewed from the sudden revolt of these island people who had been the Sultan's favorites. And so the Chiotes set to work rebuilding their homes and gardens, their shops and schools. And slowly, some were able to buy back their families from bondage—gold coins paying for the release of human slaves.

The rain continued. It beat down on the strange-looking tombstones with their marble turbans—twenty-four markers on this Greek spot reserved for the Turkish dead. Joseph stood transfixed, ignoring the water that had soaked through his clothing. He stared at the Moslem inscription on the largest of the stones: *KARA-ALI, Grand Admiral of the Navy of Sultan Mahmud. Killed in battle, June 7, 1822.* Joseph winced as he recalled the great naval commander he had admired, and that scene on the flagship four years ago. He remembered how he was torn between his duty and the strange feeling that engulfed him when he looked at the two women prisoners he had escorted to the ship for Kara-Ali's pleasure. Somehow he had felt, from the first moment he saw the Chiote woman and the girl, that they would change his life. As indeed they had—Helena, the mother he had never known, and young Joanna, who carried his brother's child inside her womb. And then the explosion had blown the ship apart, and with it his whole life. And the great Moslem admiral gasped his last breath on shore where his men had tried to revive him. The Greek Kanares had repaid the Ottomans for the bloody massacre that destroyed his island, even though he had snuffed out the lives of his own countrymen as well—over a thousand Chiote prisoners in the ship's hold went down in the flaming waters. But the Sultan was not to be satisfied with this. He ordered further retaliation, and the second massacre followed on the near-devastated island of Chios. Joseph remembered Jason's lifeless body on the ground . . . Jason, the brother he was to acknowledge, too late, after a lifetime of separation.

"My brother," he whispered aloud now, recalling that final moment.

"My brother Jason," he repeated the last words he had spoken to his twin, "you were a Greek and you died a Greek . . . but I am a Turk and nothing can change this . . . praise Allah!"

Yet *was* he a Turk? Could he deny that his bloodline was Greek? That this woman, Helena, bore him and nurtured him? That he was abducted as a child . . . torn from loving arms to be raised as a Moslem, a Janissary whose life was dedicated only to the Sultan? His tormented mind whirled as tiny voices buzzed inside his head: "Turk! Greek! Turk! Greek!" over and over until he thought it would explode.

"Allah," he cried out, praying with all his might, "Allah, help me . . . help me . . ." He caressed the wet granite and clutched the stone as a wave of blackness swept over him.

A loud thundering explosion ripped the sky; lightning flashed over the graves and the wind rose and twisted as though to uproot them. Startled, Joseph looked up. As the lightning flashed again, he closed his eyes and a knowing smile crossed his face.

"Praise Allah," he shouted as the rain caressed his face and washed away his doubts. "Praise Allah!" His voice grew louder as the wind subsided. Allah had heard and answered him.

The rain continued to fall. Joseph knew now what he must do. Nothing and no one could change his mind. Not his mother, nor Joanna, nor even little Jason, for whose sakes he had tried so hard to conform. Joseph's heart, his duty, were in Constantinople with the Sultan he had sworn to love and protect. The sixteen years of indoctrination had done their work well—they had conquered the law of the blood. The Christian child Joseph, who had become Youssef the Turk would remain Youssef always, until he died. For a while, he had allowed his heart to rule him. But now that Joanna was gone there would be no more pleading, no more tears. He was no longer afraid of breaking this woman-child's heart—and she *had* been a child, with a woman's passion, not yet twenty in her last days. He had loved her in his own way—as best he could. He had taken this girl who had lost her home and the man she loved, his brother, and given her his name, his heart, security to her unborn child. But as the months passed, Joanna had sensed the restlessness within Joseph. She had tried so hard to please him, desperate to keep him near her. And she had almost succeeded those three short years they were together. But now it was over—the lovely Joanna could not hold him now . . . she was dead. A painful smile crossed Joseph's face.

Only moments ago he had gone to the small cemetery of St. John's. He stood beside the freshly dug grave and remembered the laughter of Joanna's voice, the way she had clung to him when she sensed his yearning for the only homeland he cared to acknowledge. Slowly, patiently, she had eased his pain with her love. As he looked at the earth that covered her, Joseph relived those moments, and told her, finally, what he could not tell her when she was alive . . . "I must go back—the Moslem life is the only life I want." He hoped Joanna would understand and forgive him.

But Helena? What of his mother? Would she understand and forgive too? She had known so much tragedy in her life, this still-beautiful woman with the brave heart. The thought of what his decision would mean to her dimmed his newfound excitement in Allah's reply. And what of little Jason, the child he had taken on as his own? Did he not owe him an obligation? Yet what kind of father could he possibly be to this Christian child when he, Youssef the Janissary, was first and foremost the servant of Allah and the Ottoman Sultan—when the lure of Constantinople beckoned, and the only life he remembered, the only life he could consider his own, called out to him? No, it was better for the child, for everyone, that he go back—that he remain his own man. Youssef consoled himself in the thought that Helena would have little Jason, her grandchild, to comfort her. She would raise him and love him for both her lost sons.

Youssef turned from the graves and hurried to the fortress wall where his horse waited. With a mixture of joy and sadness he rode back to Thymiana.

Part I

CHAPTER 1

Constantinople ... 1826

THE MOON REACHED its peak and began to descend over the palace. Mahmud II, Grand Ruler of the Ottoman Empire, opened his eyes and turned to the sleeping girl beside him. In the moonlight spilling through the windows of his bedchamber, he noticed the long brown lashes against her white skin, the blonde hair that lay disheveled on the silken pillow. The brocade that covered her naked body had slipped to expose one of her white breasts, and he stared, transfixed, at the sight.

She looked no more than sixteen—eighteen at the most—and he pondered her age and the circumstance of her being here. She was just another slave girl who arrived with others, months ago—bounty from an uprising in the Slavic provinces. He had hardly noticed the girl until Besma, his Sultana, suggested he choose her from those who paraded before him in the customary ritual of his selecting a bed partner for the night. The Sultana, a former bath attendant who gave Mahmud love and many sons, was deeply concerned at the Sultan's despondence of late, at his disinterest in their conjugal bed, and his other beds for that matter. And so she had tried her best to bring him added pleasures and new excitements, hoping, with each group of new slaves that arrived in the harem, to arouse her Sultan's waning desires.

Mahmud stared at the sleeping girl and smiled bitterly as he thought of the past few hours with her. Such a beauty, he thought—and I have done nothing, nothing! She had been brought to him bathed and scrubbed by the virgin slaves, perfumed and pomaded, her nails painted and her body-hair shaved —all this, the customary preliminaries for such occasions. Like every Sultan since the reign began, Mahmud learned to accept these nightly rituals in bedding a slave or concubine with little complaint. For the lusty, warm-blooded Sultans it was indeed a trial on their nerves, not to say their patience. But Mahmud had found the wait exciting . . . once. Now, at the age of fifty-six, it was suddenly a monotonous, tiring ritual devoid of the old longings.

Ah, Mahmud, he thought as the girl stirred, what lusty nights you have known, what glories of carnal prowess you have realized. But now you are tired, Mahmud, you are a weary, aging emperor who passes up such flowers as this for the demands of an empire. And indeed, affairs of state had taken their toll on his energies. The Empire was in a state of upheaval and revolution, with danger mounting in the Christian provinces. From within, the Janissaries were in constant rebellion, and the Sultan's life was in jeopardy. The situation grew worse each day, and Mahmud was forced to take stark measures. Just recently he had sent for Mehemet Ali, the military genius who ruled Egypt, the Empire's most thriving province. He was Mahmud's only hope in subduing the treacherous Greeks who, of all his subjugated peoples, were giving him the most trouble. The Greek Revolution which had erupted in 1821 was going badly for Mahmud. No wonder I have become impotent, he bewailed, shuddering at the thought. Here I am beside the most ravishing of beauties, and all I can think of is the meeting of the Divan (the Turkish Council of State). But it was an important meeting—his life and the Empire lay in the balance. Months ago he had called home the Janissary units scattered in the various provinces throughout the Empire, determined to settle the matter. For Mahmud knew his days were numbered in the wrath of his once-loyal troops. Who would have believed that the very guardians of the Empire would one day turn their mania for killing against the one they had sworn to protect?

The girl sighed and continued her deep sleep. She's tired, he thought, ashamed of his unresponsiveness to her playful efforts. His mind wandered again . . . yes, the only solution was the elimination of the Janissary unit—Mahmud had already put forth his plan; secretly he had begun to gather a separate army that would deal with the Janissaries. The annihilation of his cherished soldiers saddened him, for they were the elite unit of his army reserves—the toughest, fiercest fighters in the Ottoman Empire—comprised of young men abducted as children from the Empire's Christian provinces and raised in strict indoctrination. By the time they were ready to assume their military duties, they looked forward to slaughtering the Christian "infidels" who revolted against the Sultan. For the soldiers believed as they had been told, that they were the chosen sons of Allah whose Moslem parents were killed by the Christians. They were prepared, at all times, to give their lives for their Moslem God and for the Sultan himself . . . until the unrest began. The first rumblings were in response to Mahmud's attempts to westernize the Empire. His liberal ways irked and dissatisfied the soldiers who saw his methods of progress as detrimental to the Empire. As the years passed and new changes took place, discontent grew among the Janissaries and soon the turbulence brewed the first of many rebellions to come. Now it had reached dangerous proportions. But Mahmud was determined to win—the Janissaries would rue the day they dared to turn against their ruler. Only Youssef would be spared. The thought of Youssef pleased him and the Sultan pondered the days with the young soldier who had saved his life and had become more dear than his own sons. Reluctantly, Mahmud had allowed Youssef to remain in Chios and serve in the Moslem army there, to be with his Christian wife and the mother he had found in the days of the massacre. Mahmud remembered his own mother, the only human being besides Youssef who had brought out any tender instincts in him. And because she had loved Chios, the Sultan showed benevolence to the Chiotes, forgiving them their revolt, and allowing them to rebuild the island his soldiers had laid in ruin. Chios was still under Ottoman domination and would remain so for years to come.

Mahmud wondered if Youssef would return. Surely he knew the Sultan would not have called him home if it were not important. He knew that the great ruler loved him like a son and wanted his happiness. Once back, Youssef would realize that Constantinople was where he belonged. Mahmud would make him stay—he would appoint him a Vizir, a

Minister, anything. If he was still unhappy, let him send for his family—they would be made welcome here. Mahmud smiled with pleasure at the thought of Youssef beside him again ... someone to trust, one who would lay down his life for him. It was a warm, secure feeling and he stretched the thought in his mind as the hours moved slowly on.

Finding sleep impossible, Mahmud rose quietly so as not to wake the girl. His bath would be prepared at dawn, by the attendants in the quarters nearby— a three-roomed suite in white marble, with golden hangings encrusted with pearls and with water gushing in through fountains. According to custom, the Sultan always rose first in the morning to have his bath while his concubine went through his clothing to take whatever money was in his pockets, legally hers to keep. It was only a few hours past midnight ... the night would be long for Mahmud. He knew that even at dawn there would be no cause to take the customary bath—he would have neither the need nor the mood for it. He fumbled about not knowing what to do with himself.

The girl sighed and he turned back to her. The coverlet had slipped from her body and she lay naked to the waist. He saw her shiny skin still gleaming from the oils they had applied. It was smooth and fair, and he noticed the ruby they had placed in her navel. By Jove, he thought, all that work for nothing. He watched her intently and she fidgeted on the bed, pouting and squirming, perhaps from an unpleasant dream. Sultan indeed, he opined, I can imagine how disappointed she must be in her master. He suddenly craved the old pleasures and regretted not having made more of an effort these past hours. Perhaps it was not too late. He rang for the servants and ordered an aphrodisiac. It was a long time since he had felt desire—he decided to make another attempt.

The slaves returned with the cups of warm brew. The girl was awakened, and hardly knowing what was happening, drank from the gold cup they held to her lips. When she swallowed the sweet tea, she turned to the Sultan and smiled. She was in no need of an aphrodisiac, but the tingling feeling pleased her. The hours she had spent here had been a puzzlement; she had been told to expect great things as the Sultan's chosen, and was disappointed when he lay there instead, staring at the ceiling until he fell asleep, or pretended to. Having had little experience, she did not know what to do when her attempts to arouse him failed, so she simply lay beside him, her thoughts wandering, as Mahmud snored. The minutes passed and she tried to console herself—after all, the change of scenery in itself was worth leaving the *haremliki* where she lay, bored and frustrated, day after day, on those silken pillows, chewing mastic or bathing and whiling the day doing nothing. It was dull and infuriating, and she had waited eagerly for something exciting to happen. At times she watched the more daring slave girls prepare for their stolen moments with the eunuchs, knowing well this was punishable by death. Though she would never risk her life for this, she watched the lovemaking in awe and some excitement, pitying at the same time those poor castrated beings who were used as women in the sex play. There were a few of these men who still had sexual feelings, not having been castrated completely, but they were unable to perform, and it was pitiful to watch them in their agony. As for the slave girls who made love among themselves, to break the monotony of their boredom, it had shocked her at first, for she never dreamed such things existed. And though she soon accepted it as daily routine in the other girls' lives, she refused to take part in such activities. She was not a difficult person and was proud of her ability to adjust to life's changes . . . breaking the law was not one of them. Besides, she was certain that something better awaited her if she were only patient. One day soon, she kept telling herself, the Sultan would notice her . . . they would have a wonderful night together, he would be dazzled with her beauty . . . and then she would never have to return to this dull corner of the palace. She would bear him a son and become a *kadin*, and, as a semi-official wife of Mahmud, this position of honor would allow her to live in her own suite and have her own retinue. And so the girl waited, trying not to think of her home and her parents, the rebellion and the slaughter of her people and that last moment before she was taken from her village. It was a humiliating, degrading experience, and she would never completely forget it as long as she lived, but she told herself it was gone, past, and there was nothing she could do but concentrate on her own future.

Now a feeling of peace and euphoria swept over her and she wondered if she had not drunk a different brew from the Sultan's. He began to move in a nervous, spastic manner and his eyes were glazed. But whatever it was, the sensation it brought pleased her and she turned toward Mahmud who came at her on the bed. She closed her eyes and waited.

The pounding on her body startled her and as she

looked at the man panting above her, another scene, another body flashed before her eyes. She tried to push it away but it persisted.

She was in her home again, in Serbia, in the town of Visegrad near the River Drina, and the screaming Ottoman soldiers had broken down the door. Swinging their sabers they leaped to where she and her grandfather sat beside the fireplace. The Turkish lieutenant grabbed her and tore off her clothing as another soldier lopped off the old man's head. She screamed, watching the head roll on the floor beside the rocker where his body had slumped. She remembered the glowing embers in the fireplace as the lieutenant fell upon her and then ... fire seemed to penetrate her. The pounding of his sweaty body sickened her, her flesh cringed at his touch, and she tried to scream, but nothing came out. For a while she thought she was dead. And then she heard her parents being dragged from the other room. A feeling of nausea and revulsion engulfed her as she saw the lieutenant leap upon her mother, spend himself on the sturdy, peasant body, and then mutilate it with his sword. Her father was allowed to watch this final humiliation before his own bloody death. The girl, horrified at the sight, finally found her voice and screamed, pleading with the soldiers. But the Ottomans were not interested in bargaining. These Slavic infidels had revolted against the Empire and they must pay. She would be spared, as all young girls, for the slave markets.

In Constantinople, she was not put up for sale with the others. It was decided that such beauty must be set aside for the Sultan. And indeed, she was a striking picture among the dark slave girls and even darker Ottoman women. She was fair, with blue eyes and golden hair, a nose and lips that seemed to have been sculptured . . . tall and slim, unlike the large-boned, muscled peasant girls of her village. For days she was in shock, pale and wan, and they left her undisturbed in the harem to recover. Weeks went by and she lay cold and numb in the *haremliki*—months of pain and loneliness, of shame, frightened thoughts, and bittersweet memories. Slowly the girl managed to erase the past—it was her only chance of keeping her sanity. She knew she must forget what happened, both the good and the bad, and pick up whatever life was left. For life was sweet and worth saving. As for the ravaging of her body, the terror of her first experiences slowly subsided as she watched the gentleness in the girls' loveplay, so different from the lust of the brutal lieutenant who had violated her. She soon longed for affection from a man, though why she should expect such a thing often confused her— even the men of her village rarely showed signs of tenderness. She passed her days dreaming of the day the Sultan would take her to his bed—perhaps he would caress her and whisper in her ear, touch her until she reeled with ecstasy, like those around her. Thus she whiled away the hours with her romantic fantasies.

The pounding over her continued and she realized that Mahmud was battling his own devils. Sweat had covered his body and rubbed on hers, and she found it offensive, not at all what she had expected this moment to be. Mahmud grunted and groaned, and finally rolled off the girl, sick at heart and body, furious at what he had become. He turned his face away and felt, at that moment, like a child who needed his mother so he might cry in her lap. But Aimee, the French Queen Mother of the Ottoman Empire, was not here to comfort her son. Actually, it was since her death that Mahmud's sexual appetite disappeared. He could not explain this, but there was a certain joy to the ritual of bowing low before the Queen Mother before making the selection of his bedmate for the night. Perhaps he missed this, and the way she always smiled and nodded her approval at his choices. Now she was gone, the Empire was going, and so, he felt, was Mahmud.

"Allah, Allah . . ." he whispered between clenched teeth, "give me strength . . ."

Mahmud suddenly realized that what had come to bore him, what seemed unimportant since the death of his mother, was now an obsession, a symbol of the declining ruler. Sexual fulfillment became, at this moment, the key to his successes and failures. He must conquer his aging body if he was to conquer the opposing forces in his life. He refused to listen to Besma, who often told him that his excessive drinking had ruined his virility . . . the thought never entered his mind, not now or in the past few years of his decline in the bedchamber.

The girl watched him as he lay, his back to her, breathing heavily. She sensed his humiliation and at his whispered plea to Allah, felt a strange sadness for him. This man has killed my family, she thought . . . I should hate him, I should seek revenge. But tonight there was no fighting spirit within her. Her body was soft and anxious to receive its awakening

... the fantasies she had lived these past months struggled to take life. She wanted to help him in his crisis—she was intrigued by the challenge. Let Mahmud pay for his sins at a later time—now she would venture with him to a new world—she would open herself to womanhood. In the awakening of her calculating female mind, she evaluated the situation. She knew the old memories would find their way back to her—the bloodshed, the tears, even the "peaceful," coexisting days under Moslem occupation. They had been treated worse than animals, deprived of the right to speak out, to hope, to plan for a future. Revolution was seething among the Slavs, and they secretly planned for the day of liberation. Neighboring Greece was on her way to freedom—soon Serbia, too, would rise. Her heart beat quickly—she was about to play her most important role.

She leaped from the bed and ran to the other side, kneeling to the floor, her head beside Mahmud's, on the pillow.

"Forgive me, oh great one, for being so forward as to speak this way." She watched him for signs of anger, and seeing none, continued. "It was my fault, mighty Sultan, you are not to blame. I have had no experience in the bed—a proper bed that is, such as yours."

His eyes showed interest.

"You see ... I was raped."

Mahmud's dazed mind cleared—he was not moved by the statement, but she was beguiling in her manner. He motioned her to go on.

"I was raped by one of your soldiers ... in my village ... and it was not a pleasant experience."

Mahmud made a grimace and chewed his teeth. The lucky man, he thought.

"I will try to be more responsive . . . great Sultan," she went on, "please allow me to make amends."

His eyes glinted as she stood up, her nakedness glowing through the sheer strip of silk tossed casually over her body. He wanted her now, as he did before, but he knew it was of little use to command his body when it refused to obey.

"Great Sultan . . . come." She suddenly took command, and he was pleasantly amused, almost forgetting his predicament. "Let me prepare a potion that works miracles. Do I have your permission to call your servant?"

Mahmud smiled approval and with increased daring she gently shoved him to the anteroom of the bathing quarters. She was faring well.

"Let them rub your tired body, and ease your mind—I will prepare you a sumptuous bed." She winked, her audacity going beyond propriety. Her heart pounded with anxiety and fear—a tiny fear that surfaced—but Mahmud was not annoyed. He hurried to his bath with rekindled hope.

The girl turned to the door and opened it. Besma stood there. She had seen no burning tapers in the room and was anxious to learn the results of the evening. When the two concluded their whispered conversation, Besma took the girl's hands and pressed them.

"I am grateful beyond words for whatever you can do for my Sultan," Besma told her. "You will be amply rewarded."

She turned away, hurrying to do the girl's bidding, but in her heart she doubted that much could be done for him. She firmly believed the Sultan had sopped himself with drink for so long, he was rendered useless. When my son becomes ruler, she promised herself, I shall see that he never touches a drop—I will personally destroy every bottle of liquor in the palace. And with this, she hurried to send back what the girl had requested.

When Mahmud emerged, oiled and massaged from the next room, the girl was standing over a small brazier of burning coals, holding a small copper pot. It contained a boiling liquid to which she added herbs and peculiar objects from a small package wrapped in linen brought by the servant. When the girl saw Mahmud, she handed the pot to the slave girl beside her and hurried over to him. She smiled as she grasped his beard and yanked off a few hairs. Then she scraped a piece of skin off his hand and, ignoring his cry of pain, proceeded to drop them into the boiling pot. As she went about her work—Mahmud was amused at her intensity—musicians from behind the screens began to play softly. And since it was hours before dawn, the tapers were relit for the ceremony that was to take place. She sat down with the Sultan and explained to him that she had prepared a gypsy love potion certain to arouse the weakest of spirits, to send men soaring to the clouds, and to make his body respond to his mind's every whim.

"This tea will be accompanied with prayers to our Christian God," she said. "He will help you . . . but you must believe . . . our God is merciful."

Merciful indeed. Why a Christian God would

want to help a ruler who killed off His followers was beyond Mahmud's comprehension, but in his present state he would accept anything without question.

The brew was very strong for it contained every herb the girl could muster. It was topped off with a touch of *raki*, the powerful liqueur made from the famous mastic of Chios that kept Mahmud's troops—and Mahmud himself—in a state of constant stupor. There was just a drop here, merely for the taste, and mixed in this strange potion, she assured him, it would have the desired effect—it would turn him into a tiger. If not, she knew it would mean the *haremliki* for her again. She poured the brew through a cloth strainer and set the cup on a small table.

"A tiger . . . a mightly bull, great Sultan. . . ."

She mumbled various Slavic phrases above the cup, made the sign of the cross, twisted her head about and looked fixedly up at the ceiling.

"My God is merciful, great Sultan . . . he will hear me." And she began murmuring every prayer she could remember. Lord help me, she added softly to herself.

They were alone now, and she walked with him to the bed. As they lay down she began to kiss him, to gently caress his body. Then she went on, childishly tickling his belly and jabbing his stomach until he giggled ridiculously. She seemed to be doing all things at once—she rubbed the back of his neck, hummed Slavic love songs in his ear, and yanked his hair playfully when he least expected it. Before he could recover from the surprise of this strange onslaught, she poured the liquid down his throat and began to praise the virility she insisted lay within him.

"Oh, great Sultan, what a handsome form is yours . . . what a youthful body . . . we will make it live again."

Her lips moved down over his flesh and she tasted the sweet scent of lilacs rubbed over his body. She felt him tense and she kissed him harder, whispering words of praise, of his famed prowess both on the battlefield and in the bedchamber. She cooed sweetly as she manipulated his body and he swelled with pride and strength. And then, pleased with the proper staging of her play, she climbed on top of the bulging frame. Drunk with lust and power, Mahmud exploded in a torrent of lovemaking long forgotten to him. Indeed, Mahmud performed as he had not done in years—he went on for hours, starting and stopping, bellowing one moment, whispering the next. He was rejuvenated and he drank of his new virility.

When dawn appeared, he was taking his third encore. The girl was exhausted but showed no signs of it. She sighed at the right moments and groaned with an ecstasy that seemed genuine, although it was the most tiring work she had ever performed, surpassing even the long hours of plowing their fields in Serbia. But she gathered added strength for the ultimate results, and the handsome reward that would follow. And, too, she enjoyed her new power over the Sultan. The more he took of her, the more he wanted. In his new virility Mahmud wondered if her God had truly taken an interest in him. Was He so benevolent, he wondered, or was He merely stupid? But Mahmud did not care what it was . . . at this moment he felt he could conquer the world and every bed in it.

Hours later, the musicians stopped playing; the candles flickered and were doused by the discreet slaves who entered and exited without a sound. Mahmud lay spent and happy beside the girl. Soon, he was snoring in a contented sleep he had not known for months, while she, every bone in her body aching, sighed with relief . . . and congratulated herself. She knew that after tonight, she would never have to go back to the *haremliki*.

The sun climbed in the sky as Mahmud returned from his bath. He was fully dressed and would be meeting with his Council in a few hours. As the servants came in with breakfast trays, he grinned proudly and grabbed the girl, squeezed her to him, and bit her neck. Then he produced a pearl necklace and placed it in her hands. She shrieked with delight, secretly calculating the rewards of her efforts. Besma, too, would have a substantial gift for her. She put the pearls around her neck and sat beside him to partake of the food.

"You are a gem," he said between mouthfuls. "What is your name, girl?"

"Selina, your excellency . . . and I have something to tell you," she answered shyly. Then, taking on courage, she added, "There is something I must explain . . ."

She began to feed him sweet grapes and figs from the basket before her.

And, carried away with her cleverness, she told him the truth about his "rejuvenation"—that she knew nothing about the brew she had concocted, other than hearsay from the village women. There was no prayer to a Christian God for new strength.

(How could she have possibly asked God . . . it would have been pure anathema!)

"It was you, great Sultan, who convinced your body that it was young and vigorous as before . . . it was all in your mind. I merely helped you regain that marvelous strength you once possessed."

He looked at her in surprise, frowning in an attempt to grasp the full meaning of her words. Had she made a fool of him?

"Silly man." She laughed provocatively and kissed his ear. "You had it all the time."

She rubbed his stomach and he squeezed her against him, his face a blank. He rose slowly. So, his strength did not come from her potion, or her miserable Christian God. All those chants and prayers . . . she had merely told a tale . . . and he had believed it. Annoyance came and went quickly . . . he finally smiled and let out a triumphant shout.

"By Allah!" He began to laugh loudly as he summoned the servants. "By Allah, you fooled the great Sultan. . . ." His voice bellowed throughout the chamber.

Seeing her stand quietly, half smiling before him, he grabbed her and lifted her from the floor. Then he sat her on the silken pillows and caressed her hair, kissed her on the neck gently while she shrieked, not from pain, but in nervous relief. She had been terrified of his wrath. But there was only joy in his mood. Her heart skipped at the tenderness of his touch—it was the gentleness she had hoped for. Together they ate, eyeing each other with satisfaction. She felt a new happiness—the life she had dreamed of was opening up for her.

"You will be moved to other quarters, my pet,"

he said to her between mouthfuls, "and you will be available to me every night—every night I can possibly spare."

He smiled and took her in his arms again.

"Little Serbian gypsy," he whispered, "Selina . . . I will see you tonight."

He walked out smiling contentedly.

CHAPTER 2

Chios ... 1826

"I HAVE TO go ... please try to understand."

If he could only make her see ... there was nothing holding him now—nothing. Joseph shook his head in frustration at the look on her face.

"Don't you see? I belong there ... the Sultan needs me."

His words meant nothing to Helena and she would not accept them. She looked sternly at him, waiting for a further explanation.

"Can't you understand? I'm a Moslem soldier ... a Janissary ... I cannot be anything but that." He looked at her intently. "It's what I *want* to be ... the only thing."

Helena controlled the anger that rose in her, the crushed disappointment in the son she had tried so hard to win over. When she finally spoke, her voice was calm.

"No matter what you say ... what you do ... you are a Greek ... do you hear me, Joseph, a Greek! My blood flows in you ... our family's blood. ... Nothing can change that."

She watched for his reaction but his face showed

no emotion as he stared at her. She knew she was losing the battle and she was desperate.

"You were taken from me by those murderers who raised you to be like them...."

Realizing she was making no impact on her son, her tone softened. She was pleading now.

"Won't you think about it a little longer ... before you decide?"

But in her heart she understood his reasoning. How could she, after all, expect Joseph to feel loyalty for a home and a family he never knew? How could she expect him to prefer her and Chios to the Sultan and the Empire that took a child, educated it, pampered it, and made it a fanatically loyal Ottoman soldier? And yet she had hoped for a miracle, prayed his instincts would win out in the end. But he was a grown man set in the ways he was taught ... she could not hold him back. Yet she still refused to give in.... One more effort, she would make one final, desperate effort to keep him near her.

"It's because you lost Joanna that you feel this way, son. You know you were happy these past three years with her ... with us...."

Yet she knew his happiness had been bittersweet, a forced emotion. He had tried valiantly to make the best of things, to adjust to his new life ... but it was useless.

"Happy?" He smiled bitterly. "Three years with these damn Chiotes? I hate them and their smug ways."

He saw the startled look in her eyes, the pain that flashed in them ... but she quickly regained her composure. He admired her spirit but he could not stop ... he wanted to hurt her.

"You talk about my Greek blood . . . I know nothing about Greek blood, *Kyra* Helena," addressing her as "Madame."

She winced at his words.

"I am your mother, Joseph, your mother, not *Kyra* Helena. Is it so hard for you to say the word?"

He felt sorry for her . . . and guilt at himself . . . but his anger won out. His voice was cold in reply.

"I have no mother . . . I never heard the word. I have no father . . . no one except Sultan Mahmud . . . no home but the palace. . . . And you expect me to feel love . . . for this?"

He looked around the room as though he hated it. His voice rose, and she noticed the veins throbbing at his temples.

"This is not my home . . . these are not my people. I have no feeling for them. . . ."

His voice broke . . . he was sorry he said the words the moment he saw the pain they inflicted. Suddenly he was not Youssef the Janissary, but the lost child Joseph, whom Helena had found and was losing again. He had the sudden urge to be in her arms, to lean on her shoulder. For a moment he almost understood how she felt and wished he could feel differently about leaving.

"Except for you . . ." he went on, his voice gentle now. "Yes, for you I *do* have feeling . . . a feeling inside I cannot explain."

He wanted to say, I love you, Mother, I love you in spite of all this, but the words stuck in his throat. He wanted to confess to her that he was torn inside, that one part of him wanted to stay with her, here, but the other part kept pulling him away. Helena felt his anguish and her heart twisted. She put her arms around him and held him like a child, silently, lovingly. What could she say to comfort this tormented part of her flesh?

"Oh, my son, my beloved son Joseph."

She pulled him down to her and kissed his forehead. She realized she could not condemn him for what he believed, for what was not his fault. He held onto her as though for dear life, afraid to say anything lest he weaken and remain. He must go where he belonged—with the Sultan who needed him, who awaited him. Joseph knew about the unrest within the palace, of the Janissary rebellions that had increased. He could not remain in Chios while the Sultan was in danger.

Helena led Joseph to the sofa on the other side of the room. They sat down and he stared at the dainty crocheted lace on the arms, knowing her hands had woven the intricate patterns. He looked from it to her and back again. After a slight pause he spoke in a near-whisper.

"I cannot change what I am . . . what I was brought up to be." His eyes were pleading now. "And so I must do what I must . . . please don't try to stop me."

She shook her head, and he wondered whether this meant she would not stop him, or that she would not accept his decision. He did not know that she had finally resigned herself to defeat.

A whimpering sound came from the bedroom. Joseph smiled sadly.

"You have little Jason, your own lost Jason who came back. . . . *He* is your real son . . . your only son."

No, no, she wanted to cry out. Jason is gone, *you* are my only son now . . . please don't leave me. But she said nothing . . . she merely looked at him,

WINDSWEPT

and in her own wise way remained silent. She would accept his final word. There was a difficult, unsurmountable road in Joseph's future tightly intertwined with that of the past. She would not confuse him further, would not destroy whatever feelings of love and loyalty existed inside him, though they were for another person, another land. It was against everything she ever believed in, but she knew she was fighting for Joseph's survival. This was the only stable emotion he might ever feel, his only hold on life. So be it, Helena, she thought, accept what cannot be changed. She nodded and smiled at her son, who watched her carefully, wondering what she was thinking. Was she hating him . . . disowning him? It would disturb him if she were. . . . He wondered why it mattered. When he looked deep into her eyes he saw only love . . . the undemanding, unbending love of a mother.

"You are a remarkable woman, Ky . . . ra . . . Helena. . . ." He smiled sadly and held her hand, "And I will always remember you."

"Will you come back sometime . . . to see us?"

He thought awhile.

"Yes," he said slowly, "yes, I think I will want to come."

He secretly vowed to take care of Helena and the child. He would see that they never lacked for material things. He wanted to do this, and the thought was of some comfort now.

Joseph was startled to see tears fill Helena's eyes. In the four years he had known her, he had seen her cry only twice. At Jason's death . . . and Joanna's. She was otherwise always composed. He thought of his twin brother now and the irony of his death, only minutes before amnesty was proclaimed by the

Sultan. Joseph had often wished he was the one to have died . . . he had so much less to lose than his brother. Knowing the happiness Jason had brought his family, and the pain Youssef had brought, he wished more than ever that the sword had cut him down instead.

Gently, without thinking, he wiped the tears from Helena's face, and was surprised at the smoothness of her skin. She's at least forty-five years old, he thought, a woman who has suffered deeply, yet she is fresh and young, as though grief has never touched her. The village women of that age looked old, wrinkled. . . . he was suddenly very proud of her.

She smiled and put her hand over his, pressing it to her cheek. He turned away in embarrassment and walked over to the window where she could not see his face.

The child waddled into the room rubbing his eyes. At sight of his grandmother's face, he looked anxiously from one to the other. Then he ran to Helena, and she took him on her lap and kissed him. Joseph turned and faced them. Slowly he walked to the boy and patted his head. The child looked at him resignedly. Little Jason was never quite relaxed with this man he called Father, as though he felt something was not quite right. There was a coldness, a hesitation between the two—Joseph was reserved, almost cautious when he confronted little Jason. And the child was shy and withdrawn in the man's presence. Only with Helena did he feel comfortable, as a child feels with its parents. He was happy and content when she was around, while Joseph was never missed. The child hugged her now, glancing uneasily at Joseph's drained face.

"I'll go and gather my things."

There was not much to gather, but Joseph needed some excuse to leave the room. The ship would be sailing tomorrow. Why did he feel so guilty? He was annoyed with himself as he stood rooted there, unable to move.

Helena tried to smile but could not manage it.

"I baked fresh bread today . . . and there's almonds and figs . . . I'll fix you a basket. . . ."

Now that she knew it was impossible to change his mind, she was determined to make it less difficult for him. She touched his shoulder, hesitated a moment, then turned toward the kitchen so he would not see her fresh tears.

The child followed his grandmother as Joseph hurried to his room.

CHAPTER 3

THE RAIN HAD stopped and vesper bells sounded. Helena took little Jason and set out for the hilltop near her home and the chapel of the Prophet Elias, to light her customary candle. Although her favorite time of day to visit the Prophet was at dawn, her moments of meditation, she often went in late afternoons, too, especially when she was troubled or in need of strength. Today the ship had sailed for Constantinople with her son aboard. It was another death, another piece of her life torn away. And so she had come to find solace with her favorite saint. The Prophet Elias has been near me through so much, she thought, he has been my anchor, my hope. She climbed the hill hurriedly, the still-wet earth sinking under her footsteps. The brush and overhanging pines of the past were gone . . . burned during the massacre. Now there were only ashes and stumps . . . the once beautiful hills of Chios were gray and mourning.

The child stumbled in his efforts to keep up with Helena and she stopped to pick him up. She reached the summit out of breath, and hurried inside the chapel where she lit a candle before the icon of the Prophet. His elongated face and deep-set eyes looked down at her compassionately.

"Oh, Prophet Elias," she whispered, "you have known so much of my intimate life . . . give me strength once again to face this new loss . . . help me."

The child watched her every move with a seriousness that belied his age. He was only four years old but he carried an almost adultlike wisdom. He's exactly like Jason, Helena thought, and her heart twisted with pain and longing for her dead son. Oh, Jason, if only you had lived . . . you were all the world, my hopes, my strength, my reason for living. But Jason was dead and his child remained—this child she must raise to follow in her son's footsteps. If only Joseph had stayed . . . if only there were hope of his changing. But no, the years of indoctrination had been too strong, too effective.

Joseph had been torn from her arms when he was only six. The Turk would have taken her other son, too, but a knife in his belly altered his plans and Helena had escaped with Jason, leaving, reluctantly, her other son behind. The young boy was taken to Constantinople and raised a Moslem, inducted into the dreaded Janissaries where the gentle Joseph was transformed into Youssef the fanatic killer, taught to hate all Christians, to lust for Christian blood. When Chios revolted, the Turks sent him to fight his own people, and in her irony, Fate played one of her many games. In the holocaust of the Chian slaughter, the twin brothers came face to face. Moments before the cry of amnesty filled the air, the twin fighters rushed to each other, arms outstretched in greeting. But it was too late . . . Jason was struck from behind by another Moslem sword. In the weeks that passed, Joseph came to know his mother and Joanna who carried his brother's child. And he married the young girl, loved her, arranged to serve in the Moslem unit in Chios to remain with her. As for Helena, though he never formally acknowledged her as his mother, there were moments when she saw his heart reach out to her, when she felt his pain and frustration at what he was and what he was trying to be. Helena had tried, too . . . they all had tried to make Joseph feel welcome, to make him a part of their family. But Joseph was of the Moslems, the Sultan's favored one, and the years of careful teaching against all Christians could not be erased.

The realization that Helena had truly lost her only remaining son brought a pain that was almost unbearable, and her breath caught for a moment. The child tugged at her dress, frightened.

"Grandmother, what's the matter?"

"Your . . . father . . . is gone, Jason. . . ." She half sobbed, and as she looked down at him she remembered another little boy, exactly like this one, who tugged at her dress so many years ago. And the tears came, streaming down the face of the woman Fate had marked for tragedy.

"Please don't cry, Grandmother . . ." the child pleaded gently and hugged her skirts. "Please don't cry . . . we have each other. . . ."

It all came back so clearly . . . was it really twenty-one years ago? A deep sigh escaped her and she knelt down beside the child and hugged him to her.

"Yes, my darling," she said through her tears, "yes, we have each other. You will be my comfort . . . the sons I lost. Oh, Jason, you've come back. . . ."

Little Jason stayed in her arms, not moving,

feeling far more than a child can, the pain of this woman who was both parents to him. His mother Joanna was a pleasant memory that drifted in and out of his daily life. And Joseph was a stranger who never really belonged with them. The woman and child walked out of the chapel, hand in hand, as dusk began to fall.

Suddenly, they heard a sound—footsteps—and looked up to see the tall figure of Captain Petros approaching. His rugged face was lined—worry and deep concern were written there. He looked at Helena anxiously.

"I couldn't wait for you to come down . . . I had to see you . . . now . . . here."

He knew this was a very special place to her—that she had spent many happy hours here with Jason while he was growing up. She ran to him and he took her in his arms. The child watched them silently, his brown eyes inquisitive.

"Cry," Petros said, "for heaven's sake, cry . . . you deserve to. . . ."

He held her as she buried her face over his heart. This is where you belong, his heart whispered, but she did not hear. She was caught up in these endless twists of Fate. Why, her own heart whispered, why? Is there no end to this?

"I'm here, Helena," he tried to comfort her, "I'll face this with you."

She wiped her eyes and looked at him with gratitude. How good it was to have the comfort of his presence, his quiet love. He had suffered too, having buried a wife and daughter, loving Helena but keeping his distance all these years. Thank God, Helena thought, that he never found out about Maria and

Ali Bey—his wife's indiscretion would have crushed him.

"I'm tired," she whispered, "I'm so tired . . . I don't want to fight anymore."

"Let him go, Helena," Petros reasoned. "Joseph's a man. Let him find his way . . . you can't keep him near you, no matter what you believe."

She shook her head.

"I know, I know. . . ." The tears welled up again. "But I had him for so little time. They took him away and I never knew, all those years, how he was growing up, what he was feeling . . . and then to find him and lose him again so quickly . . . you don't understand the pain. . . ."

"And yet you let him go, Helena . . . and you smiled and kissed him and wished him well. Because you are what you are too, and you know that love is to let go . . . to not hold tightly. . . ."

He took her face in his hands.

"Perhaps that's why I love you so . . . you don't hold on . . . and it makes me want to stay forever."

She smiled and he took courage. "Marry me, Helena," he begged, "marry me and let's make a life together . . . now, before it's too late."

"You know I'm not free to marry you."

"But you are . . . he's been gone twenty years. By law you are free. Divorce him . . . no one can blame you."

She shook her head. Divorce? How could she bring such disgrace to her family name? She had married Stratis for better or worse, and though she would never sleep with him again after the humiliation he had caused her, she must resign herself to her fate.

"We can live in Constantinople if you like . . . and you'll be able to see Joseph."

He was bribing her now, knowing well that after fighting in Chios's first rebellion he would not be welcome in Constantinople, his former headquarters. But he would have done anything to convince Helena. For years he had resigned himself to the situation, trying to smother his desire for Helena while his love burned slowly, like an ember. Now it leaped into flame, perhaps because he knew that time was against them. He did not want his life to end without fulfilling this love, and though he had settled for her companionship, he was now determined to take advantage of the present situation . . . and of the few good years left them.

"Helena, we've wasted so much time . . . please." He would convince her—he must—perhaps Joseph's leaving was a blessing in disguise.

"I may be able to resume my shipping business in Constantinople. It's a beautiful city, Helena, and you'll have the best of everything there."

He knew material things meant little to her but he could think of nothing else to say, to persuade her. He felt like an adolescent pleading with his first love and was annoyed at the position in which he had placed himself. But he loved Helena . . . it was all worth it if he could spend his remaining years with her. He took her hand and she looked at him sadly, wanting desperately to do as he asked, but hesitated, frightened at such a move. My poor, dear Petros, she thought, you have no one. Maria and Joanna are only a bittersweet memory . . . and our little grandson is more mine than yours. She loved him, loved him all these years, knowing she could never belong to him.

"We are all that are left, Helena . . ." Petros whispered, echoing her thoughts, his eyes pleading. "You and I . . . and little Jason. Please, let's not waste any more years. Can't you see it was meant to be? Why else would it have ended like this?"

She stared at him, confused, anxious. Could a life together be possible for them after all? Would she see Joseph again? If only she dared take this chance for happiness.

He wiped her eyes with his handkerchief, and the child, who seemed to be busy playing with pebbles and branches nearby, glanced at them furtively. As the three began to descend the hill, a ray of hope entered Helena's heart, making it pound with anticipation. Oh, God, she prayed, please guide me in doing the right thing. She looked below to the waters and saw the ship sailing out into the horizon.

"Godspeed my beloved son . . . my Joseph," she whispered. "God keep you safe . . . and bring us together again."

CHAPTER 4

At Sea

YOUSSEF LEANED AGAINST the mast and polished his saber. From time to time he glanced up at the waves and far out into the horizon. He sat purposely at the stern of the ship so he would watch Chios disappear behind him. His pangs of guilt left him in the excitement of this voyage he had long awaited. But he was not to be free so easily—soon the thought of Helena and Joanna began to gnaw at him. He seemed to see shadows of their faces in the waves, sometimes from behind a cloud. Everywhere his gaze fell, he was haunted by the two women he was trying to put out of his life. And each time he saw Helena's face, he remembered her pained expression, the way she hugged him to her for the last time. He could curse himself for his weakness—why should he care? He had no other choice but to leave that wretched island. Joanna was gone and she had been the only thing that kept him there. He was a stranger among the Chiotes and would always be. He had missed his young wife more each day and regretted not being more affectionate with her. But she knew that he loved her . . . he was always good to her, and their moments of love were passionate, tender ones. Youssef was never able to speak of his feelings, and torn as he had been with desire to return to Constantinople, he had often resented this love. He wondered now if Joànna thought he had stopped loving her—she had not fought to live those days of childbirth—he winced as he remembered the tiny body that was taken from her before it could breathe its first breath. Had she given up, too? No, it was Kismet—Fate that her time had come, that was all. Youssef believed that Joanna understood him . . . or did she? The more he thought of it, the more confused he became. He pushed the thought from his mind and tried to concentrate on his future and the return to his old life. Excitement raced through him again—now he would do what he was meant to do.

The days at sea dragged by—Youssef thought they would never end. He avoided the others and spent his time thinking, planning his future, taking walks about the deck, polishing his sword until he could see his face in the blade. But the nights—the nights were endless. He lay on the deck and watched the stars, counting them, outlining the constellations. But even here he seemed to stumble into outlines of women's faces. He was afraid, at one moment, that his mind might be affected.

And then the dreams began—over and over, every night, until he was afraid to fall asleep. He was walking in a wilderness, lost and anxiously looking about for a face, a voice, anything. Suddenly two figures appeared in the distance. He shouted and ran toward them, and as he approached, he saw that one wore a long, black cape, its hood covering a woman's head. And when she turned to look in the distance, as though she, too, were searching for someone, he saw that it was Helena. The second figure, the girl beside her, was Joanna—there was no doubt of that. He shouted with joy and called out to them, but they did not seem to hear. He began to run toward them and just as he was about to reach them, they turned, looked at him curiously, and walked away, as though they had not seen him . . . walked away and disappeared into the fog.

The dream occurred every night, exactly in the same manner. Youssef would wake up in a cold sweat, calling their names, and he would look about him frightened, and realize he was on the ship. Often he would not be able to fall asleep again, and he would lie there and wonder about the meaning of this dream.

On the seventh night the dream changed. When he ran to the two figures, they did not disappear. Helena put her arms around him and hugged him—oh, the joy of it. Youssef bent his head and laid it on her shoulder with relief, grateful to have reached his destination at last. Then he turned to Joanna, embraced her and hugged her to his heart, kissing her, over and over. The women laughed—a musical tinkle in the air—and as he held them to his side, he cried, "Praise Allah, I found you!"

But as he uttered the words, he felt the women slipping through his arms, melting slowly, like candles. He watched them horrified, and as they turned their faces up to him, pleading for help, they were not the faces of Helena and Joanna. He had never seen these women before. The older was fairer than his mother, and she had gray, almond-shaped eyes. The girl was Joanna's age and had her coloring, but her face was the most beautiful face he had ever seen. His breath caught at sight of her deep, blue eyes framed in the longest lashes, the whitest skin. In moments, they were gone—just a pool of blood at his feet. He stared at the puddle terrified, and screaming, he ran through the wilderness, miles and miles of wilderness, without a soul, or a voice, or a human cry to answer him.

Finally, exhausted, he stopped at the sound of a man's voice.

"Land ho!"

He woke to the watch's signal, and realized he was on the ship again, and that it had all been a dream. For two weeks the dreams came every night, in the same order—five or six days when he wandered lost and alone, desperate for a human voice or a touch, staggering through the unending wilderness. His pain went deep then—he felt as though he were the only living human on this earth. And then, on the seventh day, when the second dream appeared, he would wake screaming with terror.

The ship passed through the Dardanelles into the Sea of Marmara. Youssef was grateful that soon they would be in Constantinople. As he thought of the palace, a sense of uneasiness mixed with his anxiety—his joy and anticipation had dulled, and he felt a strange foreboding.

CHAPTER 5

Constantinople

THE MEETING WAS about to begin. Mahmud looked around the assembly room, at the political and religious leaders—members of the Divan—gathered here, and pondered the task of winning them over without letting them know of his plans to annihilate the Janissaries. Watching these men, some of whom did not support his policies, he concluded, confidently, that he would succeed. A new self-assurance was his, and he credited it to Selina and his newly returned manhood.

The Sultan knew he was within the bounds of law in what he was about to propose . . . and the Divan would have no idea it would provoke the Janissaries into revolting one final time.

"Men," he shouted as the assembly fell silent, "you know that our Janissaries have been beaten consistently by the Greek rebels. I believe this proves they are not the soldiers they once were." He paused and looked at the faces around the room. "Do you agree?"

"Yes, *effendi*." Their voices rose in unison.

"Yet the Greeks could not beat the Egyptian forces led by our Mehemet Ali."

"True, true!" The members of the Divan could not deny this.

"In other words," continued Mahmud, "the Egyptians have proved that soldiers trained in the European method are superior to ours."

Mahmud still bristled at the price he had paid for this Egyptian victory. Mehemet Ali, Pasha of Egypt, had saved the situation in Greece with his Egyptian troops. But the sly one had agreed to fight for Mahmud only if the Sultan extended Ali's pashalic to include Syria, Damascus, and Crete. Mahmud had been infuriated at this blackmail, but having no choice, he relented.

"Ali's troops stormed into Greece and surprised the *giaours*."

"Indeed," came a voice from the audience, "the *giaours* were expecting the Janissaries and knew only their tactics. . . ." He burst out laughing.

Mahmud did not mind the interruption and waiting for the laughter to stop, shouted for all the Divan to hear.

"Yes . . . and because of this we Turks won back most of the cities those infidels had taken from us."

He had the attention of every man in the room.

"This is a lesson we cannot ignore."

"Indeed, *effendi*," Selim Bey called from the audience, "especially now, with the new reversals."

"May Allah bless you," replied Mahmud, "and they are indeed serious reversals. The recent interference of Britain and Russia is abominable—they are threatening to send new forces to help the Greeks."

"We are doomed," called out a voice.

"We cannot allow this to happen." A murmur rose from the crowd.

"Yes, *effendes,* that is why we are gathered here—first we must clarify our fighting strength from within—then we must decide what stand to take regarding the great powers. We are facing a crisis!"

The men shouted agreement and their booming voices bounced against the great walls of the assembly.

"Change tactics . . . we must change tactics. . . ."

The cry came from one of Mahmud's supporters who had spread the word among other sympathizers and now looked to them for support.

"The Janissaries . . . we must decide on the Janissaries." Other voices picked up the cry. The men had given careful thought to the logics of the discussion. There was reason in Mahmud's words . . . even his opposers could not deny this. The problem of the Janissaries must be solved quickly.

"But how can we change tactics without offending the troops?"

Mahmud turned to the inquirer, careful not to mention his secret plan. He proceeded with care.

"I propose that we take a part of the New Army we had formed by Selim—say about a quarter of the men—and incorporate it with the Janissary units. They can begin training our men in the European fashion."

The assembly pondered the suggestion as a buzz filled the room.

"The result can only mean better fighters, more disciplined soldiers," he added, watching for their reaction. Some of the men's faces showed signs of agreement.

"I ask for your approval in this matter, *effendes*. Give me the power to make this incorporation."

They all began to talk at once, and finally a voice rose above them.

"Suppose the troops refuse, great Sultan?"

"The matter will be handled with great diplomacy," Mahmud replied, "so there will be no reason for the Janissaries to object. After all, they will still be in command—it is the others who will be incorporated into their unit."

Mahmud made no mention of the personal army of fourteen thousand artillerymen he had amassed, drilled, and trained by Kara Djehennem, an officer of unscrupulous devotion, for just such an emergency.

The assembly took only minutes to reach a decision. They granted Mahmud the formal power to act, and he was pleased—now he could make his next move . . . it would have to be in the next week. As he folded his hands and silently praised Allah, a servant approached his aide with a message, passed on quickly to Mahmud's ear. The Sultan's face lit up and a cry of joy escaped his lips.

"Ah, Allah is good . . . more joyous news . . . bring him in."

He turned to the assembly and raised his hands for silence.

"*Effendes,* share in my joy. My most devoted soldier has returned from abroad. He is the one, true Janissary, to be trusted by us all, once having saved my life. I have considered him the most loyal and obedient servant of the Empire."

Youssef was ushered into the room and hurried to Mahmud's side. He knelt before the Sultan, kissed his hand, and looked up at his smiling face. Youssef's heart beat fast at the misty eyes of the Sultan, the warmth of his welcome. I am home where I belong, he thought, and sighed in contentment.

"You came when I needed you, Youssef," the Sultan whispered, "just in time . . . praise Allah . . . I shall not forget this."

All things were going Mahmud's way again. . . . He was convinced it was Selina who had brought him this good fortune. Perhaps it *was* a gypsy potion he had drunk. He smiled again and patted Youssef's head, motioning for him to sit beside him. Youssef sank down on the silken pillows and looked from the Sultan to the Assembly, his glance taking in the large room with its rich tapestries and gold hangings, the Persian rugs and gold-encrusted statues. The opulence pleased him . . . he felt so much at home.

"And now that our current business is ended," the Sultan announced, motioning to the servants, "we shall eat and drink, and partake of the joys of life."

A gong sounded and dancing girls appeared as the servants carried in trays laden with food and fruits, nuts and delicacies from the Ottoman kitchens. Youssef found himself in a world he had thought lost to him. As he ate, the Sultan watched him with pleasure, embracing him from time to time as they drank toasts to his return.

"Eat! Drink, Youssef . . . and later we will talk." The Sultan nodded, "There is much I have to say to you."

He looked from the dancing girls to Youssef's drawn face.

"You are tired from your journey, my boy . . . take a day to rest. The matters of state can wait twenty-four hours. Now let us celebrate."

He pointed to the dancers who swirled wildly to the sensuous Eastern music.

"Choose a beauty for tonight . . . whomever you want, Youssef."

The young soldier felt very tired—what he really wanted was to sleep, but the thought of those dreams changed his mind. And, too, he wanted to please the Sultan—he decided to try to enjoy the festivities as best he could. Glancing at the dancers, his eyes paused at an olive-skinned Amazon—a tall, curvaceous beauty, who seemed most tempting for his bed. Perhaps, he thought, if I am occupied for the night, the dream will not appear.

The hours passed in merriment and he became lightheaded from the *raki* and the loud music. He wanted to stop drinking but Mahmud prodded him on.

"Drink up, my boy, we have much to celebrate tonight."

Mahmud downed his own cup, feeling light and carefree. This was, indeed, a night for feasting. He motioned to a servant.

"Have Selina taken to my quarters . . . I will be there shortly." And then to Youssef, "Go on, choose your mate, my boy, and let's be off."

The early-morning hours found the men sprawled in drunken stupor. Mahmud had left hours ago to join Selina, but Youssef had remained, pondering a decision. Finally he was led to the sleeping chamber, his chosen following close behind. He welcomed this pleasant distraction—praise Allah, he would not spend the night alone. His mind was now a swirling mass, and visions of Helena and Joanna kept flashing before him. Curse it, he thought, will they give me no peace? As they entered the chamber, he turned to the girl beside him.

"What is your name?"

"Roxelana."

"Well, Roxelana"—he smiled and bowed drunkenly—"welcome to my bedchamber."

She smiled and tossed her head back playfully. . . . He grabbed her waist and pulled her to him. Then, turning with her still in his arms, he looked at the luxurious bed the servants had prepared for them, and his fears vanished.

Their bare bodies slipped between the silken sheets and he felt an exhilaration—his heart began to race wildly at the soft touch of the girl beside him. Joanna flashed before his eyes, but only for a second—he took Roxelana in his arms. The girl looked at him with a seductive smile that quickly turned to a frown—Youssef had fallen back in a wave of dizziness. She wanted to pound him but smiled instead and shook her head knowingly—she was used to drunken males in the palace—it was a part of the evening's merriment. But Youssef excited her more than the others—she wanted him awake, alive. She began to kiss him, and, running her fingers over his body, she whispered all the words she knew men want to hear at such moments. Youssef opened his eyes as she pressed against him, turned to her in his stupor, and began to make love—hungry, yearning, pained love, that mercifully released the frustrations and agonies of the past weeks. Roxelana was soft to the touch and wild in her passion, haughty and proud in her movements. You're all alike, he thought amused, humble or proud, my dears, you women are all alike in the bedchamber. And yet he found a great satisfaction in this lovemaking. He had had no other girl since Joanna, and he welcomed the release, the luxurious smell of a slave girl, the suppleness of her body. The room spun as he hungrily drank of Roxelana—it was an ecstasy he had almost forgotten.

When he finally lay back, he felt a soothing peace and the desire to sleep for days on end. He closed his eyes and sleep came quickly, eager to accommodate him. But a few hours later, the girl woke and nudged him impatiently.

"Come now," she whispered, "a young, stalwart soldier like yourself is not going to waste the night on sleep."

She was thrilled at his lovemaking—his animal passion was not as violent as the other soldiers'—there was a gentleness in his lust. She wished he had not drunk so much *raki*, for she wanted to make the most of this time with him. She wondered if she would have other evenings with him—there were so many other girls waiting. Yet she knew she pleased him. She nudged him again and he stirred, opened his eyes slightly and turned the other way. Roxelana leaped from the bed and ran to the other side—there she shook him and he looked up to see her standing in her nakedness. He half smiled—these girls are tireless, he thought, and no wonder, they have nothing to do all day but sit around waiting. He pulled her down to him and they resumed the loveplay, his desire to sleep quickly disappearing in the joy of their game.

"Now, my beauty," he said when it was over and

he had pulled the silk coverlet over her body, "now you will let me sleep."

Pretending he did not notice her disappointment, he fell back in a deep sleep from which he did not awaken until late the next afternoon.

The curtains were pulled back and Youssef squinted at the sun's rays that spilled into his room. A servant had brought a message from the Sultan. He was to rest another day—Roxelana could remain with him. They would meet tomorrow after the noon hour. Youssef pondered Mahmud's consideration, his generosity to him. How kind of the Sultan to understand the labors of his trip, the emotional turmoil of his sudden change of life. He wanted Youssef to have a clear mind, an alert body, to be refreshed and vibrant when they sat down to discuss important matters of state. Mahmud looked forward to sharing his confidences with this man who was like a son to him. Besides, the great Sultan was quite exhausted from his own night games with Selina—he, too, needed another day to fortify himself for the tasks that lay ahead.

Youssef lay back and watched the servants bring food, while a smiling Roxelana emerged from her bath fresh and perfumed. She sat on his bed and placed a gold cup of almond nectar to his lips. They ate together, although he was not hungry. The food soothed his stomach but his head needed more time to clear. He had drunk a great deal of *raki*, but it was not the liquor that dazed him—as a Janissary he was used to excessive drinking. He frowned as he reminded himself that the powerful drink was made of Chian mastic—will that island never leave my thoughts, he wondered. Yes, he knew it was not the *raki* that made him dizzy . . . it was the intoxication of all that had happened in the last month. At least, he thought comfortingly, the dream did not appear last night. He felt a great relief—perhaps it had vanished because he had taken another female to his bed . . . perhaps now the fates would let him be. He pulled Roxelana to him and kissed her hungrily, and they began the new day with more passionate lovemaking than before.

On the noon hour of the second day, Youssef emerged from his bath fresh and exhilarated. He felt cleansed in both body and mind, and looked forward to the day's events. Roxelana had returned to the harem, and word had arrived that the Sultan awaited Youssef in his private quarters within the hour. The young soldier dressed, took a glass of wine, and walked out to the balcony. The sun had peaked in the sky and he stood there pondering the pleasures of the past hours with Roxelana. He felt reborn and took a deep breath as he looked past the houses and *tekes* of the city, to the horizon. And then he frowned again, for he realized he was facing west, toward Chios. I wonder what Kyra Helena is doing, he half whispered. What he really wondered was how she had taken his departure. Was she all right? And then it occurred to him that she was too strong and vital a woman to be easily bent. She would survive and continue her life, for she had the child, little Jason, to raise—it would occupy her time and give her hope for the future. He made a mental note to send her something as soon as he was settled here. The fact that he thought of Chios at all annoyed him—why should he, when he had wanted to leave so much, to get back to this exciting life. He smiled as he thought of Helena again—how surprised she would be to know he thought of her at all . . . and pleased, too. The notion warmed his heart.

"*Effendi.*" The soft voice made him turn in the direction of the adjoining balcony. "You must be the one from Chios," it went on.

His eyes came to rest on the most beautiful girl he had ever seen in his life. He stared unbelievingly, curiously, at the deep pools of blue, the white skin, and the long, golden hair that crowned her body. There were many beauties in the palace from all parts of the world, but none could match this creature. He looked closely at her—there was something familiar about her . . . but he was sure if he had seen such a face before, he would have remembered.

"Welcome," she said and smiled. "I heard much about you in the palace."

He did not reply . . . all he could do was stare.

"I am happy you are here . . . because my Sultan is happy." She smiled, wickedly this time. "You know, you and I . . . the two of us . . . have brought much joy to Mahmud with our presence."

It is an omen, she thought, that we both should have come to Mahmud at this time. She wanted to tell this handsome stranger of her feeling, but his coolness silenced her.

Youssef seemed to have lost his voice and felt ridiculous standing there, but outwardly he was composed, and Selina did not guess his confusion. In fact, she mistook it for hostility. She pouted at his seeming rudeness—she had, after all, merely wanted to be friendly.

"I am Selina," she persisted, "and I am new to the Sultan's quarters . . . but I heard him speak of you. Last night in his sleep he even whispered your name. . . ."

She giggled. "He whispered *my* name, too . . . but that was different, of course."

She saw that he was not amused.

"I make you welcome, Janissary Youssef . . ."

Would this girl not give up?

". . . and I offer my friendship to you."

She bowed and her long hair fell over her head in a cloud of gold.

Youssef finally gathered his wits and moved nervously toward her. A tiny smile crossed his face—so she wanted to be friends . . . and she was new in Mahmud's bedchamber. The girl must be mad, he thought.

"How long have you been in the palace?" Where had he seen this face before?

"Over four months . . . four very lonely months . . . but it is only three nights I have been with the Sultan."

"Well, my beauty," Youssef said, mocking her, "you won't be with the Sultan for long if you go around offering friendship to other men."

He saw the hurt expression on her face, but continued.

"You'll pay with your head, you know . . . and such a lovely head . . . if you go around chattering to strange men. . . . Don't you know the laws here?"

She glared at him.

"I am from the province of Serbia. We do not cut off heads there."

"Now that's a clever statement. . . ." He laughed and the sound delighted her in spite of her anger. "You are not in Serbia, my beauty, you are in Constantinople."

He leaned over the ridge, so close he could touch her. His voice was serious now.

"Look here, if you are the Sultan's property, you are *only* the Sultan's . . . both in the bed and everywhere else. And don't you forget that!"

He looked in her eyes, surprised at their blueness, and turned away to avoid the distraction.

"You do *not* speak to soldiers—any soldiers," he added, "especially not to Janissaries . . . at *any* time!"

She blushed at his reprimand and a deep red covered her face. Her eyes filled with tears and she turned away abruptly and disappeared through the gold-framed doors.

Youssef shook his head and set out for his meeting with Mahmud. As he walked along the corridor he wondered if she had spoken to other men in the palace. The fool, he muttered under his breath, the little idiot . . . but she is so lovely, so vivacious, she dazzles the senses. He thought of her as he hurried on to the Sultan.

CHAPTER 6

MAHMUD LIFTED HIS cup and turned to Youssef. They were alone in the Sultan's private quarters, except for the servants who went about quietly taking care of their needs.

"To the Empire . . . and to our successes together."

He gulped down the wine with satisfaction, admiring the young man. He is serious, intelligent, loyal, Mahmud pondered—a fine specimen of the Ottoman soldier. I am pleased, indeed.

"Now tell me about your life in Chios . . . I want to know everything."

He listened intently as Youssef tried to span the period with as few details as possible. He spoke of his brother Jason and the irony of fate that killed him moments before their reunion. Without quite knowing the reason, he began to detail the horrors of the massacre—the rivers of blood, the fire and devastation. He was aware that Mahmud knew all this, yet he seemed bent on bringing back that day that had shocked the world.

The Sultan's somberness turned to anger.

"They were fools, Youssef, traitors . . . and they deserved what they got. The Chiotes had everything."

Mahmud did not want to be thought of as a barbarian.

"You know they were my favored ones. What other occupied region did as they pleased, ran its own government, its own schools? None, by Allah! The other Greeks were treated like the dogs they are—but this is where I made my mistake. I was too benevolent, too generous to the *giaours* on Chios. . . . They should never have had those privileges . . . the ungrateful wretches . . . they brought the destruction upon themselves." He ran out of breath, and his face puffed up in fury.

Mahmud had no intention of apologizing for the slaughter he had ordered in retaliation of the Chian revolution, but he wanted Youssef to know he had no alternative but to act as he did.

Youssef nodded in agreement. "Yes, they brought it on themselves."

But the words did not ring as true as he wished them to. Did the Sultan notice? He was furious at himself. Youssef, what is happening to you, that small voice warned him. He decided to move on to better things. He told Mahmud of the island's slow rise again, how the new Ottoman governor contributed to the rebuilding of the villages, how peaceful the Chiotes were again, more subservient than before. Youssef had hated this about them, but he made no comment now.

"I was not happy there, great Sultan," Youssef added. "I never belonged . . . my heart was always here in Constantinople, in the palace, with you."

Mahmud was pleased.

"This is your home, Youssef. It will always be your home, my son." He poured another cup of wine. "You had a wife, I understand?"

The memory was painful and Youssef wanted to skim over the subject quickly.

"She was a good female . . . a loyal wife," he said, hoping he showed little emotion. "She married me in my own faith . . . but she died . . . at childbirth. . . ." The words came out in spurts. "Only twenty . . . she was only twenty. . . . The child . . . it was a boy . . . died, too."

He did not want the Sultan to know of his pain. After all, pain was a sign of weakness, and Youssef had been hardened, taught to feel no emotion.

"Wives and sons are plentiful, my boy. You will have others. . . ."

Mahmud tried to be kind, but Youssef knew he could not understand this kind of loss, and he did not reply. Instead, he moved on to the subject of Helena. And for the first time, to his surprise, he referred to her as his mother. Mahmud noticed the admiration, the pride in Youssef's voice as he told of her courage, how she had fought man and the elements, even Fate, to survive.

To this, Mahmud could certainly relate. Now he felt on equal emotional grounds with Youssef. For the Sultan's love for his own Christian mother had been an extraordinary one. A deep sadness fell over him.

"You can always take another wife, Youssef . . ." Mahmud's eyes looked far away . . . "but a mother . . . ah, there is only one . . . she can never be replaced."

Youssef had always found the Sultan's love for his mother annoying—a sign of weakness. This feared ruler of an empire who had ordered the slaughter of mothers everywhere, who hanged Christian patriarchs and put children to the sword, was made limp at mention of his mother. Youssef remembered the Sultan weeping like a child at the Queen Mother's deathbed. He had almost hated him then, for his vulnerability. But now, Youssef began to understand. He remembered his first glimpse of Helena in the British Consulate on Chios. And later, when she held him to her, his heart turned with a feeling he could not explain. Now, at mention of her name, something stirred inside him. . . .

"Great Sultan," he said, trying to change the subject, "I have tired you with my tales."

"You are like a son to me, Youssef," Mahmud replied and touched him fondly on the shoulder, "you have not tired me at all. Tell me more of your mother . . . perhaps we can bring her here one day."

Youssef rose from his seat.

"No . . . I beg you, *effendi* . . ." He took a few paces, a calm gravity masking his turmoil. ". . . No, let her be."

Mahmud watched him carefully, silently questioning Youssef's reaction.

"She . . . she does not understand our way of life . . ." he tried to explain, "she is a Greek, a Christian. . . . It would be disruptive to me . . . to all of us."

"I see," Mahmud spoke gently. "Very well, we can discuss that later. Sit down now, Youssef."

He tried to look into the young man's soul. What lies hidden there, he wondered. What confusion has scraped the hard veneer of my Janissary friend?

"One final word, Youssef, before we go on to matters of the Empire."

He looked straight into the young man's eyes. "My boy, where a mother and a son are concerned, there is no Christian or Moslem, no Greek or Ottoman. There is only mother and son." He paused a moment. "Do you hear me, Youssef? Only mother and son...."

Youssef heard Mahmud as though in a fog. Of course he would say that, the Sultan's own mother had been a Christian, the French Catholic Aimee Dubucq de Rivery. Captured by pirates, this cousin of the Empress Josephine was brought as a gift to Abdul Hamid, who fell madly in love with her and took her as his favorite. And she set aside her faith for her husband, Mahmud's father, and lived in grandeur the rest of her life. Helena would never have done that.... Youssef could not help comparing the two women. And yet, in the end, the Queen Mother had begged her son Mahmud for a priest. Youssef remembered the scene so well. He was called to her chamber, and Mahmud, the fierce enemy of all Christendom, sent Youssef to Galata to bring back Father Chryssostom to give his mother the last rites. The Sultan did this, knowing it was another weapon for his enemies to use against him. And indeed, it had strengthened their reasons for calling him "the Christian Sultan."

Even Youssef had thought less of the Sultan for condescending to such an act, although his loyalty to him never wavered. There were many things Youssef could see more clearly now.

Mahmud decided it was time to move on to other matters—and well he must, for there were matters of dire urgency.

"And now, my boy, the Empire.... First, the question of the Janissaries."

Mahmud was once again the fierce ruler bent on revenge against traitors. Youssef was greatly disturbed at the chasm his comrades had built between themselves and the Sultan, the man they had pledged to defend against all enemies. He had hoped they might change, for though he knew of the constant rumblings through the years, he never quite believed that in the end, they would grow to such proportions.

"There is no solution but to eliminate them," Mahmud said as he walked the floor, twisting his beard. "Each day brings me closer to death by their hands; it is certain they are planning to take over the Empire."

"Are there none loyal to you? Must they all be disposed of? How will you do it?"

The questions tumbled out of Youssef so quickly that it startled them both. Although Youssef seemed outwardly composed, his words showed deep anxiety.

"They have all joined against me in this conspiracy . . . everyone of them, Youssef. There is no doubt of this. You are the only one who has remained true."

Youssef's sudden concern for the traitors irritated the Sultan.

"What do you mean 'must they be disposed of'?" he shouted angrily. "What do you expect me to do? Sit back and let them take over the palace?"

He was losing his patience. What is the matter with this boy, he wondered. A sense of uneasiness came over him. Although he trusted Youssef explicitly, he wondered if the hardness, the callousness bred in him was wearing down. Mahmud could not afford a trusted guard who had grown weak and concerned of others, be they Greek or Ottomans. The Sultan should be Youssef's only concern and the concern of all the Ottoman soldiers. Mahmud paused in his thoughts, realizing he was letting his suspicions cloud his mind. After all, the boy showed no definite signs of sympathy or weakness. It was only natural that he would make some statement about the actions of his fellow Janissaries, that he would ask about his plans for them. He watched Youssef carefully, waiting and hoping to hear him shout, "Death to the traitors" . . . death to all of them, as he had shouted that foggy day he sailed for Chios with the Sultan's troops, itching for blood and revenge.

Youssef suspected Mahmud's thoughts, but he remained silent. The thought of killing the unit which had been his life was not a pleasant one, but he would not hesitate to defend Mahmud, not for a moment. And yet he wished the slaughter of his comrades could be averted.

The Sultan was annoyed at Youssef's hesitation. "You are silent, Youssef. Do you perhaps believe they should be spared? Spared to kill your Sultan?"

"No, great ruler," Youssef replied, and his voice was sincere, convincing. "My only hesitation is in evaluating the circumstances. I know that it grieves you, too, to have to carry out such a decision—as in all things, I agree with you and share your sorrow at this turn of events."

By Allah, the boy is brilliant, Mahmud thought, he can read my mind, my heart.

"I know only this, great Sultan," Youssef continued, "that I stand by you on this decision and any other decisions you make."

And by Allah, he meant it—in spite of the emptiness inside him, he meant to be true to Mahmud. He was glad that the Sultan could not see deeper into his soul, for he would see that the old fire, the old fervor had greatly diminished.

I was foolish to doubt him, Mahmud scolded himself silently, I should have known I can trust my life to this man—has he not proved it in the past? It is just that Youssef was gone for so long, and in five years much can happen to one's beliefs. And yet, Mahmud reassured himself, had Youssef not returned the moment he learned I needed him?

"It may be that we will not have to kill them all." Mahmud decided to leave a slight opening. "If they accept my edict they shall not be harmed."

Youssef knew the pride of these soldiers—they would never stand for the insult of incorporation with other units. And he knew that Mahmud knew, but he said nothing. The Sultan offered Youssef more wine, and as they drank together, they felt more the comfort of each other's presence. I am here where I belong, Youssef repeated as the wine warmed his bowels and mellowed his thoughts. How could I have possibly doubted this? He promised himself he would forget those nagging thoughts and concentrate on the task before him.

CHAPTER 7

AT DAWN OF the next day the Janissaries received the official proclamation. They rose up, enraged, screaming in fury, and stormed into the kitchens where they set about upsetting all the kettles—the customary sign of rebellion.

"By Allah," they shouted, "what manner of trick is this? Never! Never, will we add outsiders to our unit!"

The Sultan waited patiently for their answer, confident his plan would succeed. The next day the Janissary units assembled in the Hippodrome. En masse, and carrying banners, they marched into the streets, shouting.

"Death to the Christian Sultan!"
"Death to the *giaour* ruler!"
"Save the Empire!"

But still the Sultan was determined to remain within the law. He dispatched four officers with a flag of truce to meet with the rebels and offer pardons to all the Janissaries if they dispersed and returned to their barracks. Hoping to reason with his comrades, Youssef begged to be allowed to go.

"I cannot risk that," the Sultan replied, "they would kill you on sight."

And he was right. The Janissaries not only

spurned the Sultan's offer, but immediately put to death the four messengers. They then set out, marching in a body, to the First Court of the Grand Seraglio, where they planned to overpower the Sultan. But to their surprise, Mahmud suddenly appeared before them riding a white stallion saddled with a cloth of gold. He held a gold harness in one hand, and the green Standard of the Prophet Mohammed in the other. And as he unfurled the banner, he shouted to the oncoming rebels, "I call on all the true believers to rally around their ruler. Do so and I, Mahmud, the Sultan of the Ottoman Empire, will pardon your transgressions and take you to my fold again!"

But the Janissaries were adamant—they proceeded to advance. And then, as though from nowhere, Mahmud's secret army, led by Kara Djehennem, appeared and opened fire. The Janissaries quickly retreated to the Hippodrome, but there too, gunfire awaited them—Djehennem had cleverly posted soldiers there. Hundreds were killed as the Janissaries bolted the door and waited for the siege to begin. But Djehennem was not about to fight by the rules. No indeed, there would be no classic warfare here. Instead, he gave orders to set fire to the buildings, and as the barracks went up in a blaze, the rebels were pummeled with shellfire. Mahmud waited in a small room over the main gate of the Seraglio. And Youssef, who had hoped this destruction might be averted, had now joined the fight, manning the guns with fury.

"Death to the traitors," he shouted as he fired, "death to every curséd one!"

The old excitement of battle overtook him and he felt, once again, like the Youssef of the past.

And then came the final stage. Those who managed to escape the fire in the barracks fled to the great well near St. Sophia, a huge underground lake that supplied water to the people of Constantinople. And as the splashing forms were overtaken, the murky waters became a battlefield. Hand-to-hand fighting ensued, and the Janissaries fought to the last man. Over ten thousand were killed—some later said it was closer to twenty thousand. And the greatest fighting unit of the Ottoman army, the troops the world had feared for four hundred years, were no more—cut down, destroyed by order of their own Sultan.

Youssef was with Djehennem's troops fighting inside the well. And as he cut down his old comrades, the old lust for blood raged, and he forgot who these men were—he knew only that they had betrayed the Sultan and must pay. Like the Chiotes, he thought, here in the darkness, as he remembered another black night of battle on a Chian mountaintop. And at one moment while he pinned a soldier to the edge of the well, ready to pierce his body, he saw a look of recognition on the soldier's face. And he remembered Jason, and the look of recognition in his brother's eyes as Youssef aimed his blade at him, in Anavatos. He was shouting, "I am your brother ... Joseph, I am Jason, your twin!"

Youssef now paused with his sword in midair, just long enough for the other man to grasp his own fallen sword and leap forward. Youssef sidestepped and the blade fell across his shoulder, exactly where he had cut Jason. All these details came back to him in the holocaust of this battle. His own shoulder wound was a minor one but it seemed to have pierced his heart instead. Before the second thrust could touch him, Youssef ran his sword through the Janissary's belly and stood over him, watching him gasp his last breath, as the blood oozed from his body.

When it was over Youssef stood pale and shaken, holding his wound as he looked around at the bodies, smelling the stench of death, waiting for the exhilaration he should feel. But it did not come. The battle was over—and the enemy was dead. But a part of him was dead, too. He turned to leave and stepped over the bodies, looking at the faces frozen in death. He had fought side by side with these men against the enemies of the Empire. They had eaten together, drunk together, divided spoils of war together. Youssef was glad the Sultan was safe, but there was emptiness inside him, and he realized that victory can have its own personal defeat. It was not always so, for him. He knew that now he had a greater understanding of life, and he suddenly realized he was not free . . . had never been free. He was pledged to the Sultan. It was a loose, luxurious yoke, but a yoke nonetheless. Yet . . . had he ever hoped for more? Why should it matter now?

They found him later, collapsed from loss of blood, and rushed him to his bedchamber, where Mahmud ordered the best medical care for him. When Youssef finally opened his eyes, Mahmud was standing at his bedside, a frown of concern on his face.

"You will be fine, my boy." Mahmud smiled with relief. "It's only a surface wound."

But they both knew it had gone deeper than the surface—it had touched Youssef's soul. The Janissaries were gone—and Youssef had been one of them. Still another tie had been cut. He looked at the Sultan and tried to speak, to tell him he was glad to see him alive and well, grateful that he was able to serve him again.

"I know . . . my boy, don't talk . . . it has ended, Youssef, we are at peace," Mahmud said to him.

Youssef closed his eyes and smiled wryly. Yes it had ended, and for him it was the end of an era, the end of a dream. It would never be the same again.

He recovered slowly in spite of the finest care in the palace. Mahmud visited him often and Besma and Selina stopped several times to see him. One afternoon while he slept heavily, the two women entered his room and stood beside his bed. The old dream had returned, and he was in that wilderness, clutching the figures of Helena and Joanna to him. And they had begun to slip through his arms and, like always, were slowly melting like candles at his feet. And, again, as they turned their faces up to him, he saw that they were no longer Joanna and Helena, but strangers—faces he had never seen before, except in this tormenting nightmare. He screamed and opened his eyes, to see Besma and Selina standing over him, grave concern on their faces. He was glad to see them, glad he had awakened from the dream that had begun to torment him again.

Mahmud sent him Roxelana to nurse his body and spirit, knowing well that, in a virile young man, both needed careful attending. And to Youssef's great relief, the dream disappeared the night Roxelana returned to his bed. In the morning light he lay pondering its meaning again. Was it indeed an omen?

Mahmud was pleased at Youssef's recovery. Peace reigned in the palace again, and with the demise of the Janissaries—the thorn in his side—Mahmud felt a new sense of security. It was time to move on to other matters of state. The situation with the Great Powers had worsened. Britain was uncooperative and antagonistic toward the Empire since the Chian Massacre, and there was danger of the Russians descending upon them to seize the Dardanelles in reprisal for his war with the Greeks. Those cursed Greeks, he muttered to himself, they have turned the whole world against us. He wished he could have every last one of them put to the sword, but foreign countries were shouting "barbarian" at him, and the time had come for more civilized maneuvers. He would begin with the Russians—he must convince them the Ottomans were not barbaric. Every effort must be made to win them over to the side of the Empire. Mahmud decided to send a new Foreign Minister to St. Petersburg. He would set about immediately to appoint one and select the proper entourage. As he recounted his trusted men for this important mission—Kashim Bey would make an excellent Foreign Minister—a thought occurred to him. He was concerned with Youssef's future . . . and he wanted to show his gratitude. At the same time, it would be most convenient to have a trusted servant who could report to him the various moves of his minister in Russia . . . one could never be too careful. He pondered the idea of placing Youssef in the diplomatic service—perhaps at first as a secretary, an assistant to Kashim Bey. If he liked the work it entailed, he could progress to a higher position. Youssef is intelligent, thought Mahmud, and he is personable, with his handsome looks and serious manner. He can read and write and knows mathematics; and above all, he is trustworthy—I must speak to him immediately. Yes, Mahmud was delighted with his idea—Youssef would become an ideal representative of the Empire. The fact that he was a Christian Greek by birth would definitely be to their advantage. Ah, he mused, and then perhaps I will give him one of my daughters in marriage—there must be one for his age. He tried to remember from the mass of children he had sired, which might be the one, and his joy grew at the thought of making Youssef his son-in-law. Indeed, this was a most fruitful day. . . . He set out to prepare for evening prayer.

CHAPTER 8

THE MUZZEIN'S CALL rang from the minaret and reverberated throughout the city. Immediately, all activity ceased and the Moslems fell to their knees and prayed to Allah. On the west balcony of the palace, Youssef knelt too, and his prayers, though fervent as before, were now mixed with doubts and questions to his Moslem God. The massacre of the Janissaries had left a deep scar within him. He knew they deserved their fate, yet he was confused at his feelings. Why should it matter so much? They were traitors and received their just rewards. What was the matter with him? He felt a slow change taking place within him, a disillusionment . . . he was frightened. This is all he had . . . if he lost this, where would he be? What would he have? He would be alone . . . alone in a wilderness . . . like the dream. He shuddered, remembering it.

"Tell me, Allah, am I weakening?" he whispered. "Why do I feel this way? Make me as I was before—glad and willing to shed the blood of traitors. Let me believe as I once believed. I am in your hands, Allah, I have no one else now."

He rose to his feet, the doubts still clouding his mind and his spirit, and stared out into the horizon, remembering another evening such as this, years ago, when as a twenty-one-year-old recruit he had first received his Janissary's uniform. He had stood proudly on this very balcony after evening prayers, caressing the silk of his uniform, the sword that hung at his side. He remembered staring into the horizon, anxious to be sent to whichever of their western provinces rebelled against the Sultan, to cut down infidels who were enemies of the Empire. And he remembered, too, being drawn to that place in the west that silently called out to him. It was something he could not understand, then. He knew now that it was Jason and Helena who called out . . . that the power of their love for him had drawn his spirit. How could he have known what lay ahead? So much had happened—he had gone to Chios, to those Helena said were his people. But she was wrong. Who *are* my people, he wondered now. When he was in Chios he knew the Chiotes were not his people—he was certain it was the Ottomans . . . that the Janissaries were his family. But now he was not certain at all. For he had stood with sword in hand, cutting down those who had been with him since childhood. He was a Janissary soldier . . . but there were no more Janissaries. Only the Sultan and the palace were left for him. Were these his people, then? They must be—they *had* to be. At least, with Mahmud he felt that he really belonged. Perhaps I have no people, he whispered, and a fear came over him. He gripped the ridge of the balcony until his hands turned white. . . . He had never known fear before, yet this had nothing to do with being heroic. It was the fear of being alone in the world, something that had never crossed his mind before. In fact, once he had enjoyed solitude, being apart from everyone and everything. His hands became numb and he released his hold, twisting them as he watched the color return.

Youssef always had a protective wall between himself and the world. Now he felt it slowly crumbling. Would it all eventually crumble? He needed that wall—it was his means of survival.

"Allah," he cried, "am I going mad?"

Once again he was confused, tormented—as though he had never left Chios.

Roxelana, who had grown tired waiting inside, stepped out into the balcony. She saw Youssef's face drained of color.

"What is the matter, *effendi?*" she asked, puzzled. "You should be happy with your new position. Do you realize you are to become a diplomat?"

She watched his somber face carefully.

"I'm the one who should be crying . . . I'm the one who has been cheated. I will be losing you, *effendi* . . . I will miss your strong arms around me. . . ."

She took his arm and leaned her head on his shoulder. And she began to cry. "Take me with you . . . please . . . *effendi.*"

Youssef looked at the girl and tried to hide his annoyance. The females in this palace are exasperating, he muttered under his breath. They cling like mollusks on a cliff.

"I wish I could take you with me, Roxelana," he said, suddenly feeling sorry for her, "but I'm afraid that's impossible. The diplomatic service does not provide such luxuries."

"You'll find someone there." Her dark eyes gleamed with disappointment and pain.

Youssef leaned over and kissed her.

"We have another month, yet," he said and playfully slapped her bottom. "Now, let me attend to my business."

Mahmud sat alone in his quarters, deep in thought. He had sent his announcement of the newly appointed Foreign Minister to the Czar in Russia, and awaited his reply. He hoped that by the time it arrived, Youssef would have forgotten the unpleasantness of recent events, and would have become immersed in his diplomatic studies. Kashim Bey had readily agreed both to the new assignment—he considered himself most fortunate—and the taking on of Youssef, whom he promised to teach thoroughly and to help in every way. And so, thought Mahmud, all Youssef needs is some responsibility. A few weeks of study with Bey, relaxing at night with Roxelana, and he will be a new man. His new assignment would strengthen Youssef's ties with the palace. And on his return from Russia, Mahmud planned to bestow upon him the title of Vizir, which carries with it wealth and social position. Oh yes, Mahmud would make Youssef richer and more powerful than Vizir Sokolli, the Christian from the Serbian provinces. If Youssef adapts himself to the diplomatic service, he will climb to brilliant heights. Mahmud's thoughts ran on. Ah, and his mother . . . we must then bring his mother from Chios. Then, Youssef would marry. He reminded himself to check with his concubines on the daughters available. Mahmud greatly enjoyed this game of human chess.

The weeks passed and Youssef threw himself into the task of learning the ways of the diplomat. In addition to Bey, he was given another teacher, a retired official who was both wise and experienced. He answered Youssef's questions patiently and listened with interest to his views on the matters they discussed. The old man found Youssef a capable and willing student and reported to Mahmud that his gift of pen and fine composition, his attractive appearance and quick mind more than qualified the young man for his appointed task. The Sultan was pleased that he had chosen well.

"Only his somberness . . ." the old man told Mahmud. "Youssef is too rigid . . . too serious . . . but I am certain he will relax when he meets the exuberant and volatile Russians."

Mahmud liked to tease Youssef about his somberness.

"Come now . . . smile, my boy." And as Youssef obliged him, often feeling like a puppet, Mahmud would slap his shoulder.

"That's it, relax . . . relax and enjoy it. You have a great future ahead of you."

Youssef learned quickly. He drove himself, as though time were never enough. But he was anxious to lay the past aside, to fall into the forgetfulness of this new project, of what seemed a new life. Allah, once again, had answered his prayers—a new optimism rose within him. Mahmud saw this and was pleased . . . he had great faith in this Janissary, the last of the living legend. He felt that all Youssef needed was experience and the chance to meet other cultures—on good terms, not by the saber as before. Youssef, too, looked forward to Russia and the people of this strange land.

It was early evening and Mahmud had just completed his review of state affairs. His aides had left him and he drank the rest of the *raki*, yearning suddenly for Selina. But he remembered that this was the night Besma was to visit him. He should not create problems, and he resigned himself to an evening of good conversation and peaceful sleep. Unless, of course—he grinned wickedly as he looked at his reflection in the mirror—unless his desire so overwhelmed his good manners that he would be forced to send Besma away with a kiss, and have the servants rush in the Serbian beauty to his bed. He laughed aloud and fondled his beard.

Selina paced the floor in boredom. She looked around her luxurious quarters, at the silks and jewels, the rich hangings and rugs, all she had dreamed about those months in the *haremliki* when she had almost stifled with boredom. She had held on for the day she would reach the Sultan's bed, certain it would be different then. And it was . . . at first. . . . Yes, at first it was all the magic she had dreamed it would be . . . exotic, luxurious, pulsating, wicked. She reveled in the glory . . . but in less than two months, all the excitement had gone from her nights with the Sultan. She was annoyed with herself, but she could not help it. The lusty, once-desirable ruler now seemed old, fat, unappealing to the young Slavic girl. And she knew why—the figure of that handsome Janissary on the balcony would not leave her. She was haunted by his dark eyes—almost black, they were—with eyelids slanted as though they were half closed. Such sad eyes . . . they made her want to kiss them. Tall and regal, like a tree, he stood that day on the balcony . . . and those broad shoulders, the narrow waist. She had grasped every detail about him in that short time they spoke. And he had hardly noticed her . . . she was infuriated. If only she could see him again, talk to him. She had plotted such a move all week, and finally tonight, she was going to carry out her plan. Roxelana would not be in his room—Selina's sources of information were quite accurate. Selina knew the dangers in what she was planning. If the Sultan discovered her, she would be put to death before she could offer any explanation . . . they would both be put to death. But in her state of infatuation, she preferred death to this anxiety.

"I am young and he is young," she whispered as she paced the floor, "and we belong together. . . . It is only right, Nature decrees it."

And again, as in her harem days of boredom, she lived with fantasies. This past week she had clasped her hands in longing, aching for the joy of his young body against hers. How wonderful it would feel . . . she yearned for this new dream, forgetting the other that was realized when she took her place of honor in the Sultan's bed.

In the days that passed her first meeting with Youssef, she had tried several times to strike up a conversation with him, pretending to run into him in the hallways or the balcony. Once she even entered his rooms, pretending the tray of sweets she brought was left at her quarters by mistake. Of course he had seen through the ruse—with an annoyed look he took her hand and led her sternly to the door.

"Go away, foolish child," he had said, humiliating her, "or we will both be dead."

Her striking beauty was difficult to ignore, but Youssef would never, under any circumstances, betray his own Sultan. He was strong-willed and knew he could fight any temptation. He tried to be gentle with her.

"Don't tempt Fate . . . you belong to the Sultan."

She drew her hand away angrily.

"I don't want the Sultan . . . he's old . . . and fat. . . ."

Youssef clamped his hand over her mouth.

"Idiot! The servants will hear you!"

She felt the heat of his palm on her lips and suddenly wrapped her arms around his neck. He was so surprised that his hand fell from her mouth.

"I don't want the Sultan," she whispered, and he felt her heart pounding as she pressed against him, "I want you, Youssef."

With all the fervor she could muster, she looked at him with the deep blue pools that were her eyes, and Youssef found himself drowning in them.

"Can't you hear my heart," she murmured softly, "it's going to burst!"

Her lips came against his and at that moment he forgot the Sultan, the palace, his will power . . . everything. He held her, taking the sweetness of her mouth, almost reeling from its effect. The power of her touch was uncanny—this had never happened to him before. But his logic quickly intervened. He pushed her away, almost knocking her to the floor.

"Don't ever come here again," he managed to say, trying to sound angry but not quite succeeding. "For both our sakes, forget this."

His heart had dropped inside him and was now falling, falling into a ravine. The effect of this girl was electrifying—it was not only her beauty, there was a magnetism, something else that drew him against his will. He felt that somewhere, perhaps in another world, she had touched his life. He closed the door behind her and stood there for a moment until he stopped trembling.

The days passed and the nights brought only turmoil and tempting thoughts. On this Saturday night Youssef tossed and turned in his bed, unable to sleep. The moon was hidden behind a cloud but myriad stars shone in the heavens—tiny flickering lights that hypnotized him as he lay there and stared through the window across his bed. A thousand things crossed his mind, but the most real, the most disturbing was that incident with Selina. He was shaken by her kiss, her touch, and he tried to remember that last sight of her as she stormed out of his chamber. He had not seen her since that day . . . and he did not want to see her. The very thought of taking up with her was madness. He would be cheating his own father . . . and of course he knew the law—death was the penalty for touching another's woman.

And yet, at this moment, he would have given his life for one night with Selina. He seemed to remember her saying the same thing . . . he shook his head as though to shake away the thought. You're a fool, Youssef, he scolded himself, to let a woman upset you, rule your feelings. You dare think to covet what the Koran prohibits! He had his choice of any female he wanted, outside of Mahmud's, and

Roxelana was one of the most beautiful of the lot. He tried to concentrate on the statuesque beauty who had brought pleasure and forgetfulness to Youssef's bed. But Roxelana faded before Selina's loveliness, her naive sensuality. Selina was fine enamelware compared to clay pottery. The desire to hold her swept over him and his body ached for her. He leaped from his bed, angry at himself.

"Curse the little bitch," he muttered aloud, "curse her a thousand times. She is not satisfied with what she has, but must destroy others to get her whim."

He poured a cup of wine and walked to the window, ruing the day he set eyes on her. For a long time he stood there, and soon the moon reappeared from behind the clouds. It was a beautiful night and he heard the strumming of ouds from the other parts of the palace. It was a night for love and many were enjoying it. He shrugged in resignation and returned to his bed where he tossed for hours and finally fell asleep . . . a disturbing sleep that brought the dream again. He was running, running after Helena and Joanna, and just as they turned to him, he felt a soft hand on his lips, and a slight figure slipped between the bedsheets, pressing against him. He sat up with a start and looked down at the small face framed in gold—it was Selina, curled up and smiling, like a child caught in a naughty act.

"You're mad!" he hissed. "Get out of here before they find you."

He tried to be firm as he looked at her half-naked body. By Allah, he thought, this is too much for any man to bear. The sheer silk barely covered her breasts and he could see the nipples standing, poised for his touch. He had resisted temptation many times in the past, but now, for the first time, his will was deserting him. He felt drawn to her, like a magnet to steel—it was useless to fight. He would have her and damned be it all. He threw caution to the winds and grabbed her to him, holding her as though he would never let go. She shrieked in delight and surrendered to the first real passion she had ever known.

"You are my only love . . . my only love . . ." she whispered over and over, as they coupled frantically through the night. "I knew it from the first moment I saw you."

She could not believe the miracle of this feeling. With Youssef she did not have to perform, to stimulate, to pretend love. She had only to lie in his arms and look at him, to tell him only the truth in her heart . . . and they were both on fire. How different this was. . . . She sighed in contentment . . . how wonderful, how exalting. At last she was a woman.

Long before dawn appeared she slipped away, and it was as though a part of Youssef went with her. For he knew he would not see her again. How could he face the Sultan now? What if their deceit were discovered? He must leave for Russia immediately, or he would not be responsible for his actions. Remorse overwhelmed him, erasing the ecstasy he had felt with Selina in his arms. He slept quickly and dreamed the dream again. And as the young girl melted from his arms into that pool of blood that was now so terrifyingly familiar, she looked up, and he recognized the strange, beautiful face. He screamed and sat up in bed, wide awake. So that was where he had seen Selina! She was the strange girl in his dream, the one who melted into a pool of blood at his feet. Now he was certain the dream was an omen—a dark, dangerous sign of what lay ahead.

Part II

CHAPTER 9

St. Petersburg, Russia

THE SNOW FELL unceasingly all day and by early evening a white blanket lay stretched along the Neva River. It was cold and the winds blew fiercely, carrying the snow along in all directions . . . and still the ground remained covered. It seemed that all the snow in the world had settled in St. Petersburg. The carriages arrived at the entrance to the Winter Palace in a steady stream and Youssef looked out his small window at the wonderland of white, staring in awe. He had never seen snow like this before. The palace was brightly lit to welcome the nobility for the Czar's pre-Lent ball and the area glowed for miles around. As the Vizir Ali Kashim alighted from the carriage with his entourage, Youssef accompanied him with a sense of unreality in this strange world, in this new position he had been placed. The cold was unbearable, and he felt uncomfortable dressed in this black tunic coat and the trousers so alien to him. He steadied the red fez on his head and looked around uneasily, tugging at his sleeve and secretly wishing the Queen Mother had never urged Mahmud to change the pantaloon-turban dress customary to Ottoman officials. Perhaps the

Janissaries were right in resenting these modernizations—perhaps the Sultan *had* gone too far. He pushed the thought from his mind, suddenly feeling guilty, afraid the old doubts would rise to haunt him again. What was done was done—on now, Youssef, he told himself. Still . . . he felt a strange misgiving. He shook the windswept snowflakes from his face as they climbed the wide stairs to the palace, silently vowing to serve his Sultan loyally, without question or complaint. A quick look at the Vizir noted his somber look, and Youssef realized that the older man, too, felt some misgivings. They both knew this was not an ordinary mission of peace—much depended on their performance here in Russia. They were on the brink of war, and if the Czar decided to strike, the Ottoman Empire would not only lose Greece, but have its very existence threatened.

They entered the brilliant foyer with other guests who had just arrived—the area outside had filled with carriages—and were ushered into the vast ballroom. It was breathtaking in its opulent splendor. Indeed, the magnificence of the Winter Palace was matched by no other in the world, not even Mahmud's, and though Youssef resented the thought, he could not help but agree. The doorman, resplendent in his gilded uniform, and a slightly effeminate young man, the Baron Malotov, ushered them to the royal family. Youssef watched his nervous mannerisms and the glint in the young Baron's eye with curious amusement. He seemed almost comical in his pompous efforts to hide his nervousness. What a strange society, thought the young Moslem, what manner of male is this? And he took careful note of the rich damask of the Baron's clothing, the silk shirt and heavy embellishments. It was indeed a strange land, this Russia, and an even stranger people.

Czar Nicholas I looked coldly at Kashim and his entourage, nodding his head as they bowed before him. He managed a reserved smile and, to the Moslems' annoyance, dismissed them by turning to the other guests. The Czarina, who was constantly perturbed by her husband's abruptness, extended her hand in warm greeting. Nothing she could say to the Czar effected his rigidity and his cold manner to others. But then the Czar was known to inspire fear and hatred, and to use these feelings as instruments of his power. Although the Empress had been brought up in the intrigue customary to politics, she resented it, perhaps because she realized Nicholas was not quite astute at playing the political game— he was never convincing . . . either he did not care to hide his feelings, or he was not able to. She wished, for the thousandth time, that Nicholas were more like his brother Alexander, the previous Czar. Though many considered Alexander complex and hypocritical, he at least knew the art of flattery and good manners. But then what can one expect, she thought. Alexander grew up in the atmosphere of the Enlightenment, while Nicholas was raised in the period of the wars against Napoleon.

Kashim and Youssef were introduced to various Russian government officials and were particularly impressed, though not favorably, with Count Alexander Benckendorff, the head of the Russian Secret Police, and his assistant Baron Kanilov—the two men said to be closest to the Czar. Youssef did not like them on sight, especially the Baron, whose greeting was less rigid than the Czar's but filled with antipathy and distrust. The young Moslem knew that it was the duty of the secret police to place foreign diplomats immediately under surveillance, yet it still gave him an uncomfortable feeling. All this was new to him—it was not only another world but another mode of behavior. He realized he must be alert at all times and cognizant of his responsibilities as a foreign officer of the Ottoman government. This new responsibility brought with it mystery, and excitement raced through him at the thought of whatever intrigue lay ahead.

Youssef turned to Kashim and noticed that the older man was scowling. So he, too, was annoyed. In reality Kashim was offended, but he smiled at Youssef in secret understanding and as a note of confidence. Yes, Kashim thought, Mahmud did well to select Youssef for the diplomatic service—they would work well together, at least they reacted similarly to this strange land.

Determined to ignore the cool atmosphere, the two men stood aside, watching the dancers, and as they admired the whirling figures, they began to plan, each in his own mind, ways of dissolving the Czar's antagonism, or at least skirting it, and accomplishing some good here. Engrossed as they were in their thoughts, they did not realize that they were the center of attention. They were handsome, imposing figures, their uneasiness in this foreign world well hidden, and stood calmly there, unaware of the other guests who watched them curiously. But within moments, the Czarina's lady-in-waiting appeared at the gracious Empress's request, to fill the embarrassing void and to make their guests more welcome. The Countess Crispini was a vivacious, charming woman and their small talk together set them at ease. Youssef made polite chatter with her while his eyes circled the ballroom. The music of the string orchestra had a magical effect in this opulent setting and he stood transfixed as the dancers twirled on the marble floor from one waltz to another, with mounting gaiety. Vodka and caviar drifted by on silver trays carried by somber-faced servants who weaved among the laughing, pompous counts and countesses, the barons and their ladies. The women prodded their daughters to smile, perhaps to entice the young Russian eligible males who stood by appraisingly. And though the young ladies cast admiring though forbidden glances at the handsome Moslem in the Vizir's entourage, Youssef found none of these ivory-skinned girls of the Russian aristocracy appealing. So the fact that he did not know ballroom dancing was of little matter to him—he had no intention of jumping around like a puppet on a string the way these foolish people did. In fact he found it strange that females should mix so openly with men . . . why, they were practically treated as equals. It was abominable the way the women carried on . . . and yet Youssef's eyes were riveted on these strange creatures of nobility. He felt the unfriendly glances upon him with little concern . . . they were stupid people. As for the Countess, he felt sorry for her as she tried desperately to warm the atmosphere and make it more cordial to the Turks. He smiled politely at her chatter as his eyes followed the dancers. Soon he was dizzy watching them speed past him, the women's huge voluminous gowns rustling to the strains of the music. The silks and satins, the diamonds and emeralds flashed in abundance before him as the dancing continued with a frenzy. And then he turned to the entrance foyer and saw her.

She wore a long, black cloak of fur with a hood over her head, and the sable glistened in the light from the thousands of candles that lit the ballroom. Her back was to him and he stared curiously, stunned as he recalled the cloaked figure of his dream. Youssef realized, at that moment, that this was the first time he recollected the dream without feeling turmoil. The fear and confusion that accompanied any thoughts of that nightmare did not surface now. Instead, he felt an anticipation—indeed, he felt very strange. When she turned, her eyes darted across the ballroom, encircling it at a glance, and rested in the spot where Youssef stood. No, she did not resemble Helena, now that he saw her face, but she was tall and regal, like her. He felt a tingling sensation in his spine as he stood immobile, trying to appear nonchalant, and met her gaze. Even at this distance he saw a face he would not forget. She was not beautiful in the sense of the word, but there was an air about her that made her stand out in the crowd. He was disappointed when a group of people gathering around her blocked her from his view, but soon she was gliding across the ballroom on the arm of her escort. She looked to be thirty—though he was to learn later that she was much older—and she diminished every young girl in her presence. All eyes followed her as she crossed the room to the royal couple. Youssef watched her curtsy before Nicholas, offer her hand to the dignitaries, and lean over to the Baron, who kissed her on the cheek. Youssef winced—the Baron seemed possessive of her. She lingered there, chatting in a friendly manner—she was obviously a member of their closed circle. As the ladies bent in closer conversation, Youssef saw her looking around—she seemed to miss nothing—nodding her head from time to time. Her eyes darted to Youssef and she smiled. Youssef's heart missed a beat, but he quickly concluded that she smiled at something the Czarina had said to her.

Kashim and a French diplomat were engrossed in conversation, and the Countess smiled as she followed Youssef's gaze.

"Oh, my dear," she volunteered anxiously, "you simply must meet our elegant Baron and Baroness Kanilov. He is involved in internal affairs—a somewhat unofficial Minister of State, you know . . . brilliant man. The Czar doesn't make a move without him."

"I did meet him."

So he was her husband. Yet she had arrived with another man. Was this permissible in Russian society?

"Oh, yes . . . of course," the Countess replied, and as though reading Youssef's mind, she added, "Then you must meet the Baroness, too. I suppose you wondered why she arrived with another man. My dear, it's simply draining of the Czar to insist the Baron be at his side every minute. Heaven knows the Baron adores his wife, but he gives most of his life to Nicholas, and the palace . . . and the poor Baroness, no one more faithful, you know. . . ."

Youssef listened with interest, trying to appear unassuming. The Countess watched him carefully . . . she was a clever woman in spite of her flippant attitude, and her instincts were alert.

"She *is* stunning, isn't she?" The Countess smiled, again reading Youssef's mind. "There isn't a man who can take his eyes off her . . . a lot of good it does them. . . . And you know, she's not exactly a young girl. . . ."

She said the last words with no intended malice.

"Yes, she is very attractive," Youssef replied cautiously.

An excitement raced through him and he felt the unwelcome atmosphere of the ballroom suddenly turn warm and inviting. He liked the feeling, although it puzzled him—the Baroness was not his age, nor beautifully alluring, as Selina. . . . In fact, at first she had reminded him of Helena, his mother. But that was perhaps because of her black cloak . . . and his dream. Now he felt, instinctively, that this woman would effect his life in some way. He wanted to meet her, but he did not want to appear too eager . . . he would wait awhile. As he turned to make idle chatter with the Countess—a thing he found extremely difficult, for after all, few Moslems conversed seriously with women—a buzz fell over the room and he paused. All eyes turned to the young man who entered the ballroom.

"Oh, my word, it's Pushkin," the Countess retorted, as though she'd seen a ghost. "He's here, Pushkin's here in St. Petersburg. How exciting!"

Then, turning to Kashim and Youssef, she added, "You have heard about Pushkin, your excellencies?"

Kashim smiled. "But of course, dear Countess."

And on seeing the blank look on Youssef's face, he added, "Who has not heard of Alexander Sergeyevich Pushkin, your famous poet?"

Youssef had not, but he was not about to reveal his ignorance. Instead, he assumed a knowledgeable pose and smiled in agreement. He had suddenly acquired a new self-assurance. Indeed, he had entered the world of diplomats and he would play the diplomatic game. The Countess looked at the men with new interest.

"We're quite proud of him, you know," she went on exuberantly, then lowered her voice in intrigue. "Just back from exile, my dears . . . returned to Moscow last fall."

"Yes, of course . . . the Czar finally realized Pushkin had no part in the Decembrist conspiracy," said Kashim. "I suppose because he was the only one of the conspirators who did not break down under the grilling. Quite a man, there, I say." Kashim was glad his information about Pushkin, gathered from hearsay, was serving him so well.

"I understand the Czar himself will be censoring Pushkin's work now."

The Countess was pleasantly surprised at the Turk's knowledge of someone from the Russian literati.

"But, your excellency," she replied, "that's much better than his being harassed by the censorship committee . . . I'm certain the Czar will be much more lenient."

Youssef listened to the conversation, unable to avoid casting furtive glances at the Baroness.

"Have you read any of his works, your excellency?" the Countess asked, realizing she was asking for too much. It was common knowledge that the Ottomans were illiterates . . . still, this Kashim did not quite fit into that category.

"Well . . . not really," Kashim replied, "but I have taken part in many discussions. His works have certainly stirred excitement and controversy. They say Pushkin was quite influenced by Lord Byron . . . is that so?"

"Yes ... I suppose so," she said, surprised again.

Kashim eyed her with amusement, searching his mind for some further anecdote on the poet. He was aware of the Russian opinion of his people's intelligence and found the chance to weaken it ... perhaps change it.

"It's interesting, dear Countess," he added with sudden enthusiasm, "that Pushkin's mother was the granddaughter of Abram Hannibal."

"Abram Hannibal?" She baited him.

"Yes," Kashim smiled and continued, "the Abyssinian princeling who was bought as a slave at Constantinople ... and later adopted by your Peter the Great."

He hoped the Countess would faint at his revelation and deliberately added, "Imagine ... a slave becoming comrade-in-arms to Peter."

"Of course, your excellency," she replied, "there isn't a Russian worth his vodka who doesn't know that. How romantic ... a black prince, the great-grandfather of Russian literature."

Her delight was genuine. How dare she, thought Kashim, look down on the chosen people of Allah, and yet acknowledge an African, a black, as a Russian's ancestor? But being a true diplomat, his anger lay buried in his best-mannered smile. Youssef stifled a laugh and quickly decided he must meet the Baroness.

"So people's backgrounds do not shock you, dear Countess?" He smiled, trying to appear casual. Before she could answer he added, "I, myself"—he hesitated just a moment—"am of Greek birth. . . ."

There, he said it ... he was surprised he had gotten it out at all. It was the first time he had admitted to this fact. The Countess looked at him for a moment, as though questioning his words, and then pleasure crossed her face.

"But of course, my dear," she said finally, and Youssef was surprised that she was not shocked. "It's common knowledge that the Empire's government officials are mostly of Christian origin...."

She really wanted to say that the Russians believed the Moslems lacked the intelligence and foresight to run not only their government affairs but all their businesses as well, and therefore Christians held key positions in every area of the Ottoman Empire. But she was too discreet to press this further. She knew her place here as a lady of nobility was to make the Czar's guests feel welcome. And so she simply smiled. He is very handsome, she thought, and very sweet . . . I should have known he is not a Turk. . . . I wish he could meet my niece in Moscow. But then she realized—it was impossible to even think such a thing. Origins or not, he was a former Janissary, a barbaric Moslem. . . . What a pity—oh, what a pity indeed, she thought, noting again his dark handsomeness, his composure, and obvious intelligence.

The general mood of the Russians was not conducive to the Turks of any position or rank. Both the peasants and the aristocracy of Russia had expressed sympathy with the Greek cause and they wished fervently that Nicholas would be more definite in his siding with the Greek revolution. At first the Czar tried to remain neutral, being, in principle, against all revolutions as were the other great powers. Indeed, revolution would upset the order of things and this did not sit well with empowered nations. But after two years on the throne, Nicholas leaned more and more toward the Greeks. He considered Russia, after all, the protectorate of all Eastern Orthodox religions, and possibly the leader of the Christian world. He believed that this year of 1827 would be the turning point, bringing the true path Russia would follow. It was that cursed England that was the thorn in the Czar's side. The English were pressuring him into taking a definite stand. Youssef knew all this and turned it over in his mind—having discussed it many times with Kashim—as he whirled the Countess around the ballroom.

"Your thoughts are far, far away," the Countess interrupted his thoughts.

"Please forgive me . . . my mind tends to drift at times. . . ." He bowed austerely.

"Business . . . or pleasure?" She laughed and the sound was pleasant.

It was difficult talking to this woman but once again Youssef decided to put aside all serious thoughts and try to enjoy the evening. He looked around the ballroom and paused as his eyes met the Baroness's. She watched him with an amused air and it was an effort for him to keep from stumbling.

When the music stopped, the Countess took both Kashim and Youssef by the arm and marched them to the Baroness Olga Kanilova. She was charming and slightly aloof in the aristocratic manner of nobility, but there was a spark of warmth in her eyes. She seemed faintly amused by Youssef, and when he bent to kiss the hand she offered him, his lips trembled. He looked down at her—though she was taller than most of the females there, he stood a good head above her—and into her eyes, noticing their deep gray color, their almond shape. Her face had a strange beauty—she reminded him of a tiger, yet he felt she was incapable of fierceness. Countess Crispini had said that the Baron and his wife were the envy of society, bound by love and loyalty to each other. Yet Youssef's first impression was that a deep sadness lay within this woman. She spoke with polite interest, but Youssef heard her voice as though from a foggy distance. He was intrigued by what lay inside her—a mystery he was certain existed. And when the Countess drew Kashim aside in conversation, Youssef found himself standing alone with the Baroness. To his pleasure he noticed that the tone of her voice changed . . . behind her aloof manner was the hint of an invitation . . . was it enticement or a challenge? Or could it be a cry of help . . . of despair? He felt foolish at these suppositions, and wondered if the romantic air of the palace had not stirred wild emotions in him, perhaps an allure for the unknown. He had had no experience with women of this breeding and sophistication and he decided, hesitantly, that it was merely his imagination playing games with him. He watched the Baroness closely as she talked . . . a light chatter, seemingly nonchalant. Was she trying to amuse herself with him? He did not understand the subleties of flirting and it began to disturb him. The hours passed quickly. They danced and talked and he noticed that from time to time she cast anxious glances at her husband, who was engrossed in conversation with one of the ministers. Oh, God, she thought, it's become an obsession with Andrey. His whole life is nothing more than a round of discussions and political meetings. She felt an emptiness inside, knowing that each day her husband grew further and further away from her . . . and now the loneliness was becoming unbearable. She finished the glass of vodka and called the servant for another.

It was midnight when the guests entered the banquet rooms. The Baroness had drunk a considerable amount of liquor, and though she handled it well, Youssef watched her with concern. All nobility drank in excess—why was he trying to make so much of this? And then an orgy of eating followed—the guests fell upon the feast before them as though they had not seen food for months. Several hours later the guests, stuffed with food and drink, dispersed to various rooms throughout the palace. Youssef and the Baroness took their apertifs in one of the studies. In the adjoining room, a crowd had gathered to smoke hashish, while the others drifted through the vast foyers and into the ballroom where the musicians still played. The elegance of the evening was complemented with an overabundance of everything—food, drink, hashish, merriment . . . paid for with the taxes of the serfs who toiled outside the majestic Winter Palace walls.

Across the room from the silken couch where Youssef and Baroness Olga sat, the Baron and Countess Crispini were engrossed in somber conversation. It's the first time this evening the Countess is not smiling and chattering, Youssef thought as he noted the worried expression on her face, the way she looked anxiously toward the door from time to time. The Czar had retired with several men of his cabinet and the Baron was to join them later. As the flames roared in the fireplace, Youssef watched their reflective glow on Olga's face. She was talking enthusiastically, asking him about his life, having learned of his Greek background. She wanted to know the details of his past, and Youssef was flattered at her interest. Ordinarily, he would have resented this prying into his life. Before he could speak, the Baron appeared at Olga's side.

"My dear, I think it's time you went home."

He lowered his voice, and in a half-whisper which Youssef could not help overhearing, he added harshly, "Don't you think you've had enough to drink?"

His tone was impatient, though trying to seem concerned. A pained expression crossed Olga's face but she covered it with a smile.

"What difference does it make, my love? We're going home together"—she looked at him anxiously—"aren't we?"

It had been a long time since Kanilov had gone home with his wife after a social event. It seemed he always had pressing matters to deal with. Why at night? She was puzzled at the late hours he was keeping. She sometimes wondered if it were another woman, but decided he was too ambitious for frivolities. Still, the thought disturbed her.

"I can't come home with you." There was slight annoyance in his voice as he caressed her hair. "An important matter came up, my dear, we must continue to discuss it with the Czar . . . he's waiting for me."

She did not believe him. Was he meeting the Countess Crispini? Was that why they had been so engrossed in each other? She rose now, and leaning over, whispered in his ear.

"Let me stay and wait for you . . . please."

She saw him stiffen, but persisted. "Please, Andrey, come home with me tonight."

He pulled her gently to the side, behind a tall statue where the others could not see them.

"Don't you understand? I cannot possibly leave now. Gorky will see you home."

His voice softened. "Bear with me, darling, it's only for a little while longer . . . for Russia . . . and the future."

"Is it Russia's future you're concerned with," she asked bitterly, "or the future of Baron Kanilov?"

Anger crossed his face and then a look of pain.

"That was unfair," he said, and he kissed her on the lips. He was not angry . . . how could she know what he was doing, what plans had been set?

She was sorry she had said the words and clung to him now.

"Forgive me, Andrey, oh, my dear, please forgive me."

Why did she act this way? She was remorseful and hated herself. But it had been months since they had had any physical contact . . . nearly two years since he had become so obsessed with his work. And she could not enjoy clandestine love affairs like the others. She loved Andrey—only Andrey—she had loved him since they were children. The thought that his once-passionate love for her had been devoured by his ambition tormented her now. She did not understand what was happening . . . it was all so mysterious. She wished he would confide in her, for whatever it was, it had obsessed him, taken his every waking moment . . . and it was taking him away from her. She had a premonition of danger.

"Something's happening, Andrey . . . I know it . . . something's happening to you . . . to us . . . I'm afraid."

The Baroness held on to her husband and closed her eyes to erase her uncertainties. She wanted to think only of his closeness.

WINDSWEPT

"Stop worrying, darling," he tried to comfort her, "nothing's going to happen to us . . . just be patient. Whatever I do, I do for our country . . . for us."

He kissed her again, deeply, with desire, like the old days. He did love her . . . the way he held her assured her . . . she must try to understand. . . .

When they returned to the fireside, Youssef saw the happy glow on her face—he means a great deal to her, he thought, and a deflated sensation went through him. On the way home he pondered the evening, assured that in spite of her love for Andrey, Olga was an unhappy woman. He tried to tell himself it was none of his affair, but something in him persisted. The carriage rolled along at a steady pace as the winds howled through the falling snow. Kashim turned to his aide and prodded him teasingly.

"Your thoughts are far away, Youssef, perhaps on a lovely lady?"

Youssef smiled but remained silent.

Kashim smiled and cleared his throat.

"The thing to do with women of society, my boy, is to keep away from the young ones. Now the older ones . . . that's another story. . . ."

"They're different here in Russia," Youssef observed. "The men here . . . they pay too much attention to their women, don't you think? Why, they engage in conversation as though they are equals."

"Indeed . . . this is another world, this Russia, my son . . . different peoples, different customs. I'm afraid the Russians may live to regret this freedom they allow their females. . . . Still, it's a custom we are forced to accept while we are here.

"And it's to your benefit," he added. "As a

103

young, virile male in the diplomatic service you might try reciprocating the advances of some of the . . . shall we say, mature ladies of this Russian nobility?"

So he noticed Olga and the attraction that crossed the room. Kashim is clever, Youssef thought, hedging as he is around the subject. But then, try as Youssef might have done to avoid it, his eyes inadvertently flashed to the spot where the Baroness stood . . . throughout the evening. Kashim was no fool.

"Mustn't offend these females," Kashim continued, in his all-wise manner, "and yet mustn't get too involved. The Sultan has something very good waiting for you back at the palace. Did you know? Why, half the palace will be yours one day."

Youssef looked at Kashim with surprise. He had completely forgotten the palace, the Sultan, Constantinople, everything during these exciting, strange hours at the Winter Palace.

"You didn't know?" Kashim asked at the puzzled look on Youssef's face. "Young man, Mahmud's going to marry you to one of his daughters—he will decide which one while you're away . . . he has quite a few of them tucked around the palace, you know." Kashim laughed aloud. "And, ah, what beauties . . ." He stared intently now. "Yes, I say if you must amuse yourself here, pick the older ones . . . the married ones"—he watched Youssef carefully with a glint in his eye—"that will guarantee no trouble on either side."

Aha, Kashim was referring to the Baroness. Youssef supposed his interest was obvious . . . and he had tried so hard to hide it.

"What about scandal? With a married woman?" Youssef asked matter-of-factly.

"My boy, adulterous love is the oldest game in the world ... particularly among diplomats and the nobility. ... The higher the class, the more rife it is ... and the more it is accepted. ... You must simply remember to be discreet, not to embarrass anyone publicly."

He laughed again. "Your hurried schooling in diplomacy did not cover this subject, but you will learn from experience ... I dare say." He dusted off a particle from Youssef's tunic. "Just remember that, done wisely and well, it might even help your diplomatic career."

"It might also destroy me...."

"Never ... keep in mind that you are also performing a welcome service: Wives of diplomats, of most government officials ... are bored and restless. You will be contributing to the peace and harmony of their household. A busy, happy wife is an asset to any home."

Youssef could not believe what Kashim was saying. The Koran strictly forbade coveting thy neighbor's wife. ...

Kashim smiled, guessing Youssef's thoughts.

"When in Rome, my boy, do as the Romans ..." He smiled.

And they call the Ottomans barbarians, thought Youssef bitterly. We may plunder and rape in battle, but we do not ever, in principle, take our friend or colleague's wife ... not if one is a man of honor. Here, in this civilized world, he was facing hypocrisy and deceit in practiced form. The irony of it ... He suddenly remembered the incident with Selina and shuddered at his unintended betrayal of Mahmud. He would never forgive himself.

He wished that night with Selina had not occurred. But what could he have done? What would any man have done in that situation? He would have withstood the temptation if he were a man of honor, he quickly scolded himself. But now he remembered the girl's seductive body against his, the silk sheets against their skin, and the passion of their night together. Selina was the most beautiful female he had ever seen, and more than any other woman she had stirred his animal instincts. Even now, his body ached at the thought of her. He had believed that this was the role of the female—to stir and tempt man, to be taken by him. At least he had believed it until tonight. Now he had met another type of woman. No, not another type, he told himself, another class. He was drawn to the Baroness in a way he could not readily explain. He was afraid to think further, afraid he might be harboring secret desires for this woman who was out of his reach. In spite of Kashim's words, he was certain the Baroness was not one to indulge in fleeting romances—it was written on her face as she stood at her husband's side. But why did Youssef concern himself with her? He wondered if she were to mean something in his life ... he felt strongly that she would.

That night Youssef tossed in his bed for hours, and when he finally fell asleep, the dream appeared. He watched Helena and Joanna melt in his arms, and as they looked up at him, their faces were those of Selina and the Baroness. But this time he did not wake up screaming. He sat down on the soft earth, staring at the pool of blood, and he wept ... softly ... in the wilderness. When he awoke the next morning, his uneasiness turned to fear, not for himself, but for the women. Was something about to happen to Helena? Or was it the Baroness? Were they both in danger? He poured a glass of wine before his morning meal, then another, and a third, and then decided to let time provide the answers. Of one thing he was certain—he would see the Baroness again.

CHAPTER 10

HER NOTE ARRIVED the next day. It was an invitation to take Sunday tea with her. On Saturday afternoon he went to the bird market to select a canary for her. He wandered among the hundreds of cages, listening to the chirping with great satisfaction—it was like a huge symphony orchestra playing in different keys. He stopped beside a cage of lovebirds, admiring their blue-tinted feathers, and for a moment was tempted to take them to her. But he thought better of it and settled for a small yellow and brown finch that was singing at the top of its voice. He thought of Helena—he would like to send her a finch too....

He arrived at Olga's villa on the outskirts of St. Petersburg and was surprised to find her gone. The servants assured him that she would be back shortly—she had gone out for her Sunday-afternoon ride. It sounded rather mysterious, since she had invited him at that time, and the servants seemed embarrassed. He was ushered into her salon and he sipped vodka as he watched the flames in the fireplace. He noticed the marble mantle with the ornate gold clock and the silver candelabra that adorned it ... and then his eye caught the gold-framed portrait. It was a little boy, a very handsome child with almond-shaped eyes and light brown hair; he looked seven or eight. He went up to it and stared, amazed at the resemblance to the Baroness.

"That is my Dimitri," her voice made him turn and his breath caught at sight of her.

She was flushed from the winter air and her gray dress, trimmed in fur of the same color, made her look almost ethereal. She had been crying. He went to her and kissed her hand. . . . She smiled and turned to the canary that had begun to sing.

"But how thoughtful of you . . ." She was beautiful when she smiled and the sadness in her eyes only made her more attractive.

They sat down, making idle chatter, while Youssef wondered what mystery lay in this house. And when the tea arrived, and she was warmed and relaxed, she told him of Dimitri.

"He died fifteen years ago . . . today. . . ." Her voice trailed off and her eyes were tortured. "So young, so pure . . . I do not understand the ways of God, Youssef. Despots live and triumph, lechers sponge off the fruit of society . . . and a little boy of eight dies. . . ."

So this was her Sunday ride . . . to the cemetery . . . why wasn't her husband with her? Youssef did not speak, overcome with the sight of her . . . the sadness of her. He wondered if it were proper for him to take her hand. . . . He decided to do nothing.

"I'm sorry, my dear, please forgive me." She was her old smiling self again. "It's rude of me to invite you here and talk of my misfortunes."

"Please . . ." He took her hand, and the look in his eyes told her he understood. "Would you like to tell me about it?"

"There are so many kinds of pain," she said, "so many losses a person feels. But nothing is as deep as the pain of a mother . . . a mother who has lost a child."

Her words struck a cord in Youssef. Helena's face suddenly appeared before him . . . and guilt, sadness swept over him. Why must he feel this way . . . he was furious with himself.

"Oh, I'm so sorry . . . I'm wandering again." She took his hand worriedly. "I did not mean to be so impolite."

He assured her it was all right, that he wanted her to talk, that he was flattered by it. He, too, wanted to tell her many thtings . . . about Helena . . . his life . . . he decided to wait until another time. The bird's song broke the awkward moment, filling the room with its melody. Their spirits rose as they sipped tea and ate warm biscuits, and soon they were talking as though they had been friends for years. Hours later, when it was time to leave, Youssef felt exhilarated in this new experience. And this was to be the first of many hours they would spend together—quiet afternoons and late evenings when she would gently coax Youssef to speak of his life. Before long he revealed emotions that lay hidden for many years.

The days passed, and Youssef learned a great deal from this woman. "Don't be afraid to feel emotion, my dear," she would tell him. "It's only human to love and hate, to fear and question, to wonder and to seek. We have to feel in order to be alive. Don't be afraid to be alive, Youssef. No one ever knows all the answers."

She was so wise, and yet she seemed, in all that she said to Youssef, to be trying to convince herself as well. He felt she was trying to open herself up, to tell him what lay inside, tormenting her. For he was certain it was more than the death of her son. She never spoke of her private life, or her husband, and he never asked, certain that the moment would come when she would tell him. He felt she was living a hapless life, bound by an insecure marriage. To all the world the Kanilovs may have seemed adoring lovers, but Youssef sensed that the Baron had strict control over his wife, that she feared him as much as she loved him, and that she was caught in a web she could not escape. He wished she would say something . . . but the weeks passed and their long discussions included other matters, fascinating subjects to the young Janissary who had been taught only what the Sultan's palace wanted him to know. They spoke of governments and nations, of the intrigue of politics, of religion—he, firm in his belief in Mohammedanism, arguing his point, and she, trying to explain Christianity and her own Eastern Orthodoxy that was linked to his mother's. He spoke of Helena then, and of the day they met again, after sixteen years of separation; and of how he had refused to accept her or her country as his own. It was then that slowly, with careful deliberation, she tried to give Youssef an insight on the Greek people and their struggle for freedom. He listened . . . it was the only subject in which she could not win him over. He would not hear anything against the Sultan or the Ottoman Empire and discreetly changed the subject at every opportunity. But he admired the Baroness's interest and knowledge in world affairs . . . and in all peoples. He knew that the aristocracy of countries was mostly involved with themselves— their well-being and comfort, their pleasures and luxuries. But here was a woman who cared for others. She seemed like a goddess to Youssef, and sometimes, when he was filled with vodka and his mind was just a little blurred—such quantities the two consumed—sitting there before her fireplace, he would have illusions of the two of them when she was younger. No matter how much Youssef drank he was in full control of his senses, but at one of those unguarded moments he said to her, "I wish I had known you when you were twenty."

She laughed and the sound of her voice filled the room . . . the canary joined in with its song, and the world was suddenly very beautiful to the young man.

"When I was twenty, my dear, you must have been . . . now let me see . . ." She knew his age, for she had asked him once . . . "you were every bit of . . . five. . . ." And then her voice trailed off. . . . "I had just given birth to Dimitri. . . ." Her eyes filled with tears and the magic moment was gone.

At another of their tête-à-têtes, he asked her why she did not have other children. A cloud went over her face and she bit her lip.

"Andrey refused to have any more children. . . ."

Youssef did not answer but he saw her look away in embarrassment and realized that she was not telling the truth. When she returned to him, she lowered her head.

"That's not true . . . I was ill, Youssef, quite ill. . . ." Her eyes darted to the door and a frightened expression came over her.

"Don't be afraid, Baroness, you have nothing to fear." Youssef tried to calm the tension that rose in her. "Whatever it is, it's over . . . I'm sorry, I shouldn't have brought it up."

He realized whatever it was, was not over. She was not telling him everything, but he did not prod. One day she would tell him everything. They talked on, as though the incident had not occurred, and he began to say what was on his own troubled mind—the massacre of Chios, the death of Jason, his twin brother, his short life with Joanna and the quiet love they had shared, but a love in which he felt he had been a substitute for Jason. All his frustrations came out those next weeks, and it was a catharsis—he was cleansing his soul to this gentle lady of nobility, this stranger who was now very close to his heart. And she listened to him, feeling his emotions, weeping, understanding . . . and as the months passed, they drew closer and closer together.

One Sunday afternoon she seemed particularly annoyed and was intent on discussing the falseness of their society, the shallowness of people. She told Youssef how sickened she had been when she first saw the wantonness that went on in the palace—she had tried to excuse herself, and insisted her husband take her home at such times. Then she touched on the subject of political intrigue, of how the Baron had steeped himself in projects that took all his time, that became obsessions with him.

"So you see, everyone has his own form of orgy," she said. "With Andrey it is the political orgies that excite him."

She wondered if she were not more jealous of his love for politics than she would have been of a mistress. For a moment she wanted to tell Youssef she had not slept with her husband for months, but she could not, at least not yet. Youssef knew that her husband's coldness to her was destroying her self-confidence, her security—after all this time, he could see this. And he wanted to help Olga, but he could only wait until she gave him the opportunity.

Eastern Orthodox Easter was nearing, and the Russians were preparing for this most festive and revered of Christian holidays. To the Orthodox Church, the Resurrection was more eminent, more reverent than the birth of the Christ Child, for it was the rebirth of the world, the casting out of sin, and the hope of an eternal life. And, as all Orthodox Christians, they prepared food and drink to follow the prayer in celebrating this holy occasion. The women baked their *kulich,* the raised sweet bread dotted with sugar, and the *pascha,* the pyramid-shaped bread containing the delicious homemade cheese. Both breads would be decorated with the letters *X.V.* for *Xristos Voskresse*. They dyed eggs bright colors and prepared various meat dishes with anticipation, after the long forty-day fast of the Lent season. And on midnight, when the priest would proclaim the holy words, *Xristos Voskresse*, all thoughts of poverty would leave the serfs, all worries of politics would desert the diplomats, and rich and poor would join in the worldwide proclamation of all Orthodox Christians, *"Xristos Voskresse*—Christ has risen!" And the reply would ring out, *Christos Voistinu!* "—Indeed He is Risen!" Christ would rise from the dead, and the congregations would hurry home after the liturgy service, in the morning hours after midnight's Resurrection, to partake of the feasts their womenfolk had prepared. In the palace, the Czar would receive his staff and government personnel. He would accept the customary congratulations for the great day, and pass out the dyed eggs to his staff, while his soldiers and government officials would be handed porcelain eggs as remembrances of the holiday. Kashim considered it blasphemous both to Allah and to the Russians' God to join in such celebrations, but Youssef could not resist the temptation to watch the festivities which were so similar to those he had witnessed with Joanna and Helena those few years on Chios.

News from Greece told of the Greek rebels' progress, despite some reversals on the mainland. They had lost several small areas to the Turks but were hoping to recover them. Most important of all, Greek-born Ioannis Kapodistrias, the Russian Foreign Minister who had returned to his homeland to fight for its liberation, had been proclaimed President of the new nation of Greece—the small area of liberated territory which would hopefully grow to include other regions who waited for the day of freedom from foreign yokes. It was April, spring, and the new state held high its hopes for the future, trying to squelch the internal strife and bitterness that had set in among the various groups within it. Fighting between Turks and Greeks continued in the surrounding areas, for there were many Greek villages waiting to be returned to their people. The Russians were pleased at the good news of their Christian brothers and vodka flowed like water. And, in turn, Kashim felt the attitudes not only of the government officials, but of all the Russian people, growing more antagonistic toward the Ottoman Sultan. He began to wonder how long Kashim and his entourage would be welcome here. There was little they could do to sway the stubborn Czar, whose advisers had vehemently refused all attempts for a closer alliance with the Ottomans. Youssef did his work diligently, but he knew that all of their attempts to change the Russian attitude were hopeless. And still they held on, trying to do the impossible.

"The only good thing that came of all this, my boy," Kashim said to Youssef one day after a discouraging meeting, "is that you have matured this past year."

Youssef looked at him in surprise.

"Yes, the environment here has done you good. Your character has been enriched and you have acquired wisdom beyond your years . . . there is no doubt of this."

"You have been an excellent teacher," Youssef replied.

But he knew, as Kashim, too, realized, that his mental growth was due to the stimulation of the learned, cultured friend he had made—the Baroness. In these few months he had found a new perspective, perhaps not the answers to all that troubled him, but an awareness of what was around him, an understanding of others, a better conception of himself.

Youssef's friendship with the Baroness had become an important thing in his life. He looked forward to his visits to her home, not so much the formal dinner parties she gave in their lavish mansion that was, he learned, a part of her wedding dowry, but the quiet Sunday afternoons or late evenings that had become a ritual with them. In the months that followed he saw the Baron only at the palace—the Baroness was alone no matter what hour Youssef arrived or what time he left. She had told her husband of her friendship with the young diplomat, and he was pleased that she had something to occupy her time.

CHAPTER 11

THE BARON WATCHED the last of the guests leave, and turning to his wife, kissed her good night.

"Run along to bed now, dear . . . we're going to carry on our discussion, the few that remained. . . ."

He was anxious to get back to the other men who waited in the study. The door was half open, smoke from the water pipes drifted into the foyer and the sound of the bubbling water mixed with the murmur of voices. It had been a pleasant evening—the dinner was superb, the company stimulating. But then, Pushkin's appearance anywhere was the highlight of the event. Olga had been surprised that Andrey would invite the controversial poet . . . but then perhaps it was his way of showing his democratic leanings. To have a confidant of Czar Nicholas entertaining a former political prisoner was excellent for government relations . . . the people would rejoice. And yet, something was amiss . . . Olga had a feeling there was more to Pushkin's presence than met the eye.

"Darling, you're getting more mysterious every day." She looked at her husband anxiously. "What *is* going on?"

He frowned. "Don't question me, Olga . . . and not now!"

"Andrey, I'm your wife . . . I want to know . . . I care."

"You'll know when the time comes."

He checked his anger as he put his arms around her and led her to the stairway.

"I promise to come to you tonight," he whispered, "I'll be in your room, later," and he kissed her. "No matter what time we're through . . . would that please you?"

She looked blankly at him—she would not beg for his bed.

"As you wish . . ."

"I do wish." He paused, smiling. "And I promise I'll do my best to get away early."

He kissed her again, tenderly, holding her for a moment, and she felt the old yearning, the old sense of security of the past, when Andrey loved her and made her aware of it. He watched her as she climbed the stairs to her room. When she shut her door, he crossed the foyer to the huge velvet-draped window. From behind the folds, the Countess Crispini slipped out.

"My dear, I feel like a thief hiding like this."

She had been at the dinner party and to all appearances had left with the other guests. Together with Andrey she quickly entered the study where the four others waited. They huddled around the small table near the fireplace, pouring from a bottle of vodka as one of them shuffled a batch of papers. The Countess brought forth a velvet pouch, smiled at everyone proudly, and emptied it on the table. The men stared at the diamond-and-sapphire necklace, the pearl choker, and the emerald brooch that lay there. They looked at each other, nodding in satisfaction.

"But this is more than we expected...."

"*You* are the gem, Countess...."

"Ha, but you can't use me to buy ammunition, can you?" She laughed and they joined her.

"Priceless..."

The Baron was silent. He knew the Countess was doing this more for him than for her country, but he would accept no personal responsibility. He had never encouraged any relationship but the friendship he and Olga had shared with her through the years.

"Are you certain you want to do this?" Andrey asked, looking somberly at the Countess. He really did not care if she were certain or not, but he wanted to make his position clear ... and yet leave a thread of possibility dangling.

"Yes," she replied. "I do this for my country ... and for you, Andrey."

She looked into the Baron's eyes, trying to convey a message he chose to ignore. The others busied themselves looking at the stones, but they smiled inwardly. Ah, the power of desire, they thought.

"Will this help?" she asked Andrey, insisting on looking into his eyes for some message.

The Baron smiled and kissed her on the forehead.

"But of course it will help ... we are very grateful to you, Countess." He looked toward the door and frowned. "Money is never enough ... we have men to pay, supplies to purchase ... indeed, we owe you a debt of gratitude." And then he looked deep into her eyes; after all, he owed her something. "I will never forget you for this." And he pressed her hand.

She was elated ... it was worth giving up her

jewels, at least these pieces. Andrey was warming to her . . . her heart skipped a beat. But, she added to herself, it is for Russia too, for Mother Russia. They sat down together staring at the jewelry which the men fondled in appraisal.

"I would like to terminate our meeting as soon as possible, gentlemen . . . and dear Countess."

Her heart skipped . . . so soon? Would he ask to see her afterward?

"I must speak with my wife . . . now." An idea had struck him. "I may persuade her to add to this collection."

They hastened the discussion, presenting the various reports that were in order, counting tax monies from the serfs which had found their way from the palace to this room.

"After all," remarked one of the men, smiling, "these rubles will probably buy the serfs their freedom . . . so it's really not wrong to take them."

They were all of the same opinion . . . the end justified the means. They were not happy about having to steal from treasury funds . . . it was dangerous. But the present Czar was dangerous . . . Nicholas was a tragic mistake, a mistake that could destroy Russia. It was Constantine who belonged on the throne—the country would never breathe free as long as the tyrant Nicholas ruled her. He was a despot in the full sense of the word and his regime was one of despotism and autocracy. The Decembrist rebellion at the beginning of his reign had made him mistrust the gentry and all independence and initiative on the part of his subjects. Indeed, Nicholas had a mania for direct order, absolute obedience, and precision—he wanted machines, not humans, beside him. But all the discipline and smooth functioning of government in which he prided himself was nothing more than a facade that covered corruption and confusion. And it was almost comical the way he ran his government on committees—one after another was formed and the Emperor often took an active part in them. But most of these committees failed to perform their tasks—then he would dissolve them and form new ones. The problem of serfdom had already gone through four committees with no end in sight, and no worthwhile results.

"I am certain, dear Baron"—it was Count Bronsky who spoke—"that between the four of us we can manage a few more pieces. . . ." He turned to the others. "Am I correct, gentlemen?"

They all nodded in agreement, thinking of their wives' jewelry caches. The Baron sorted the papers and brought out a diagram which he placed on the center of the table. Another list of names was passed around for the men's perusal and they sat down to the business at hand.

It was a little past two o'clock when the Baron slipped into Olga's bedroom. She lay half asleep, almost in a stupor—and he bent over her, whispering as he took her in his arms and kissed her. She responded faintly.

"Darling, I'm here. . . ." He shook her gently.

"Oh . . . I didn't think you'd come . . . you hardly do, you know. . . ." She smiled drowsily. "I'm sorry, darling."

She turned her head the other way, and exasperated, he laid her back on the bed, standing there to stare at the whiteness of her face.

"My poor Olga," he whispered, and sighed. The sleeping powder was working well.

Everything happens for the best, he told himself as he went to her jewelry box and removed several pieces. He wrapped them in a handkerchief and tiptoed out of the room.

The next morning, he did not leave as usual before breakfast. Instead, he waited for her to come down. She was surprised, and they sipped coffee together, an awkward pause between them.

"I'm sorry, darling," she finally said, "I didn't believe you when you said you'd come last night...."

"I must say I was disappointed."

"Perhaps another night ... soon...." she looked into his eyes for the answer.

"Of course ... but things have reached a peak, my dear ... it's going to be more difficult from now on...."

He hesitated a moment.

"By the way," he said cautiously, taking out some legal papers, "we're going to have some taxation problems on the property in Moscow. I know it was part of your dowry ... as you know, my dear, I refused to have it placed in my name at the time." He leaned over and kissed her. "I didn't care about your dowry ... it was only you I wanted."

She smiled, remembering the days of their courtship and the happiness of those early years.

"But you care about it now ... Andrey?"

"It would merely simplify matters if the land were in my name...." He handed her the papers. "Would you mind, darling?"

"Why should I?" she said, wondering why he should come to such a decision suddenly.

He could not sell anything that was a part of her dowry, even if it were in his name. She did not know that the law had been circled in many instances—the result of the Baron's own pressure on Nicholas, backed up by the committee for the treasury which was headed by Count Bronsky.

Everything I have is his, Olga thought, and he knows it. No matter, I will sign it and he can do as he likes . . . what does it matter? There was more land, and the house. She smiled, remembering how Andrey had insisted her father keep everything in Olga's name, and how impressed with this they had all been. How gallant of him . . . but then he came from a wealthy family himself, he had no need of her money. She signed the papers now and walked him to the door.

"I'll be home for dinner tonight . . . you can count on that." He kissed her again, tenderly, and a tinge of guilt went through him.

She was delighted. Perhaps things would work out for them after all. She hoped those persistent headaches would not catch up with her today . . . she wanted to look her best for Andrey tonight.

Andrey did not arrive for dinner that evening . . . or the next. He was involved in his committee meetings . . . and when she realized that she would be alone a third evening, she notified Youssef and they sat together in another of their interesting nights of talk and warm brandy by the fireplace. When she was with this young man, somehow the pain of Olga's own life eased, and she relaxed, listening to his stories. He was warm and sweet, reserved and yet groping for the hand of someone to understand him, to look into his soul. There was so much pent up in him, so much he wanted to say. And now, in Olga, he had found the right person to hear him.

It was nearly midnight and Youssef had talked about his first battle in which he had taken part as a Janissary—the battle of Chios, his mother's island home. He described that final moment when his twin brother—his enemy—died in his arms, on the earth that the Turks had laid bare and wasted. He spoke sadly, with a calm voice that tried to hide the guilt and pain, the emptiness and remorse inside him. And when he looked at Olga, he saw that she felt his pain too, that her heart was out to him. This must be the ultimate union wise men speak about, he thought, the spiritual union . . . something I believed men incapable of sharing with women.

He was silent now, deep in thought, and she watched him. Smiling sadly, she leaned over and stroked his hair. Her fingers moved over his face . . . and it was like an electric shock. He stared at her, not certain of how he should react, wanting to touch her, too, grateful for the compassion she offered. He realized at that moment that he needed— that he wanted—something more than this platonic love they shared. And then he saw a tear roll down her cheek, and his fingers touched it gently, and wiped it away. Her skin was smooth, like silk, and he remembered wiping Helena's tears that last day he said good-bye to his mother. Her skin was smooth, too, though hers was dark, olive. Olga's was white and pink. Why did he think of Helena at this moment? It was only for a moment, however, for when he looked at the Baroness again, into her deep gray eyes, it was not his mother he saw, but a sexually desirable woman, mature in mind and body,

WINDSWEPT

beautiful in face and spirit. He wanted to take her in his arms. What matter that she was older? Who cares, he thought.

Suddenly, Olga stood up and walked over to the window ... and the spell was broken.

CHAPTER 12

SPRING CAME AND though the snows remained, the sun shone brightly, making the white mounds glisten in the light. Youssef was becoming used to the cold weather; even the blizzards became a part of his daily life. He rather enjoyed them those late evenings when they sat beside the fireplace, watching the flames as the snowflakes tumbled to earth outside the windows. There was something clean and pure about the snow . . . it uplifted Youssef's spirit. The cold, fresh air was refreshing and he realized that he had hardly missed the climate of Constantinople. The news from the Ottoman palace was grim. It did not look as though the Empire would survive the Greek onslaught that had begun seven years ago.

It was nearing midnight. Kashim had discussed the latest developments with Youssef as they smoked their water pipes in the parlor. They were too tired to play cards, their favorite pastime, for they were exhausted from their long meeting with the Russians that day. What exhausted them even more was that they were no further ahead at the end of the day than when they had begun early that morning. Kashim had asked point-blank what Russia demanded to stay out of Greece. There had been a moment of stony silence, and then the Czar himself played his double-handed game.

"Turkey must guarantee us that England will gain absolutely no influence on the Greek peninsula," he replied.

It was a preposterous request, one the Czar knew could never be met. Why, England had fought alongside the Greek rebels since the beginning of the revolution.

"Your excellency"—Kashim was aghast, trying to keep his composure—"you know we cannot possibly guarantee such a thing."

He saw the look of scorn on the Czar's face and hastily added, "But I assure you, your excellency, I shall immediately write Sultan Mahmud of your request. Perhaps he may think of some other solution."

The Czar nodded coldly and Kashim looked furtively at Youssef and Mavrozoumis, the Third Secretary of the Ottoman mission. Mavrozoumis half smiled and nodded, knowing full well they had been backed up against the wall. He knew that all this was merely evading or rather postponing the final decision of the Russians. But the Turks were determined to stall, too, hoping to gain time before the moment they dreaded came upon them.

Now all except Kashim and Youssef had retired for the night. The blizzard raged outside . . . was there no end to these damned blizzards, Youssef wondered. He thought of the winds of Chios, fierce but warm, flagging but refreshing in the summer heat . . . nostalgia came over him. How different the winds were there—even in Constantinople there was nothing so cold and cruel as the knifelike strokes of these Russian blasts. The glow of the fire and its warmth were enticing, and he suddenly wished someone other than Kashim could be enjoying it with him tonight.

Suddenly a knock came from the outside door, and a servant entered with a message for Youssef. It was an urgent plea from the Baroness . . . she must see him at once . . . her carriage waited outside.

Kashim smiled knowingly.

"You've had a hard day . . . go out awhile," he said, "our problems will still be here when you return."

Kashim wondered if Youssef were taking his friendship or affair or whatever it was with the Baroness too seriously. He noticed that his young aide seemed preoccupied lately, forgetful, skeptical. He hoped Youssef had not gotten himself into a difficult situation.

The Baroness was standing at the fireplace when Youssef entered the salon, her head resting on the mantel. When she turned, he was shocked at her appearance. She was pale, dead-white, and her eyes were glazed. He took the goblet from her hand and led her to the sofa. As he kissed her hand, he felt her tremble, and when she refused to sit down, he stood looking at her, wondering what to do. She was not able to talk but looked up at him instead, with eyes pleading . . . he saw tears brimming there. She leaned on his shoulder and he put his arms around her . . . and they stood there together, as she began to weep uncontrollably. He led her to the sofa and with his handkerchief gently wiped her face. It is so beautiful, he thought, even in its tear-streaked whiteness. His efforts to question her failed and she began to cry again, softly. She was living her own tragedy now, he knew that—the rejection of the person she loved, the only family she had, in a world gone mad with turmoil and rebellion. He waited, feeling helpless as she slipped to the floor by the fire and leaned her head against a small armchair. He sat on the floor beside her, waiting patiently for her to speak, and he stared into the fire, glancing at her from time to time with worried concern. Until finally the tears ended . . . and she looked at him and sighed. He kissed her hand and went to get brandy for them both.

"Thank God I have someone to turn to. . . ." She smiled sadly, with gratitude, as she took the goblet from his hand.

She sipped the liquid and felt its warmth inside her. Then she pressed against him, nestling her head on his chest. He braced himself, while hammers pounded inside his temples, and she felt him stiffen, his heartbeats coming fast against her ear. She looked up, startled, and she was like a surprised child. Then she smiled and he knew she was pleased . . . food to a starving man. What a fool the Baron is, he thought, what a fool! And then a look of such longing came over her that Youssef wondered if she were pretending her husband was beside her. Could it be for him? Was it a look of enticement or a plea . . . was it desire? He held her against him, not caring what it was as long as she needed him.

"Where are the servants?" he whispered.

"They're asleep . . . the other side of the house."

She put her arms around his neck and a sob escaped her. He held her for a few moments, his mind churning with indecision. Then together, their bodies still entwined, they slid down on the thick carpet beside the fireplace. The flaming logs crackled and the snow beat against the windows as the Baroness Kanilova gave herself to the young Moslem, hungrily, desperately, without hesitation or regret. It was what she needed at this moment, what she had needed these past lonely months—to feel like a woman again, desired, loved. And in this giving and taking, Youssef felt himself being fulfilled as a man . . . no longer a young soldier, a boy . . . a man with a mature woman in his arms. Never before had he felt the passion of the flesh so entwined with spiritual passion. He was almost afraid, but she urged him on in her silence, in the closeness of her agony. They pressed against each other almost desperately, each fulfilling his own need—and the Baroness forgot, for a moment, the sorrows that ate away her days, and Youssef found a rare union he had never dreamed could exist.

He kissed her over and over and his shyness left as the passion in him burst into her. And as their two bodies joined, and the moment of their ecstasy arrived, everything unpleasant and ugly was blocked out. Oh, the joy of it . . . they satiated their thirst for life together, their hunger for happiness, for peace, if only for this night. The hours passed without their knowing . . . or caring . . . they made love through the night, as the fire turned to embers and dawn appeared.

Youssef looked at the smoldering ashes in the fireplace and turned to the woman in his arms. He did not want to leave, but he was concerned about the Baron's return.

"He won't be back tonight," she whispered.

And suddenly she panicked.

"Don't leave me, Youssef, please . . . don't leave me. . . ."

He held her silently for a few moments. She looked at him hesitantly....

"I have so much to tell you."

He stayed . . . he would stay as long as she wanted him, to hold her, to protect her. He rose and went to the kitchen where he fumbled to prepare some coffee before the servants woke . . . thick black Turkish coffee to sober them. And she waited, quietly fortified in his love and concern, prepared to face this unbelievable development in her marriage . . . and the fate of Russia.

He would not let her talk until she had drunk the warm brew; it soon stimulated them both. She did not know how to begin.

"I should not drag you into all this . . . it's messy, my dear. . . ." Her eyes avoided his. "You will turn from me."

"Turn from you?"

He took her hands and kissed them, and she saw such love in his eyes that her own filled with tears. It was the love she once had seen in Andrey's eyes, the love she so desperately needed now . . . that her husband was denying her. But this young Moslem opened his heart to her and she knew, in that moment, that he would do anything for her.

As though reading her thoughts, he smiled reassuredly.

"There is nothing I wouldn't do for you, Olga . . . nothing . . . just ask me. . . ."

He had never felt like this before. He would have forsaken the Empire, the Sultan, everything, for this woman. For he believed she was worthy of any sacrifice . . . she was a spirit that he never dreamed existed in the female form.

"I have been ill, Youssef . . . very ill . . . ," she said and looked away.

He kissed her again, patiently, and urged her on.

"So . . . you were very ill. . . ."

"After the boy died, I collapsed . . . they took me away . . . it was a long, difficult road back to sanity."

He could see how difficult this was for her.

"Andrey . . . Andrey came to see me very often then . . . at first. I went home . . . and I was all right for a while . . . but soon I was ill again . . . and I went back. It went on for several years . . . until the last time. . . . Andrey . . . Andrey did not come to see me very often . . . his work had begun to take all his time. I suspected then that I would lose him . . . but not like this."

She sighed and paused, and though Youssef was confused, he did not show it. . . . She gathered strength from his look.

"It was all very strange, this love for the Empire, his sudden devotion to Nicholas, even his work with the Third Department—the Secret Police, you know. It did not seem right, somehow . . . his late-night meetings were not with the people of those departments. I had begun to suspect something even then. And then . . . then, I came across the papers . . . and I discovered that some of my jewels were missing. Last week he asked me to sign over a piece of property from my dowry. . . . Oh, Youssef, I don't care about property or jewelry . . . I care about what's happening to him . . . what he's doing to us . . . and to the Czar, our friend, our Emperor. Yes, and the Russian people . . . Russia must have some stability. . . .

"Do you think he's working against the Czar?"

"Of course . . . I have proof. He's working with people from the Decembrist movement."

"But they were all executed . . . or sent to Siberia, weren't they?"

"Yes . . . but there are others, sympathizers, who have picked up the cause."

She rose and paced the floor, and her anguish made her even more desirable to Youssef. For he saw how different she was from the women he had known—the passive females meant only for the bedchamber.

"I'm not saying that Nicholas is the savior of Russia," she tried to rationalize, "he has a long way to go. But he's been here so short a time . . . they haven't given him a chance to do anything. . . ."

Youssef was confused . . . what did all this matter to her? But she continued, frantic, unable to stop.

"He's very much against serfdom you know, Youssef," she said and her eyes sparkled, her face flushed, "and he will abolish it, I know. . . . What can they expect in a little over two years? I'm afraid Andrey's taking matters into his own hands . . . and it's not the proper way to save Russia."

"And you're afraid he'll be caught?" It hurt Youssef that she still loved her husband. As for the serfs, he thought it ridiculous to make it a subject of concern or upheaval. After all, what country did not have inferiors doing their menial work—be they serfs, slaves, subjects, or *giaours,* whatever the title. All he cared about was Olga. And he could see that she was afraid for her husband.

"You love him very much, don't you." It was more a statement than a question.

Olga looked away, embarrassed.

"Youssef, he's my husband. . . ." She went to him now and took his hand. "My feelings for you are no less, my dear . . . believe me."

She turned away again and began to pace the floor. Then she paused a few moments at the window and stared out. She turned slowly and faced Youssef. She decided to tell him everything.

"There's more . . . I suppose the end justifies the means to them . . . but they're embezzling from the treasury. Embezzling, Youssef! And they're blackmailing loyal officials. . . ." She sighed and smiled bitterly. "And Andrey knows I know. He's not certain I'll say anything, but he's going to stop me . . . just in case."

"He wouldn't harm you," Youssef insisted, but his words rang hollow.

She hesitated, not wanting to continue, but she was determined.

"Ever since my illness—my last one, three years ago—I've had to take a drug . . . every day . . . and once a week they administer another medicine with a needle. . . . Someone could easily increase the dosage, and I would never know."

"They would kill you?" Féar ran through Youssef. "What drug are you taking?"

"Please don't ask me details, Youssef . . . I don't know what to do. I don't know if I should have told you all I did . . . but I have no one to turn to. The Countess Crispini, our best friend, is, I'm afraid, a part of Andrey's little group. For all I know they may be having an affair besides . . . but I am certain they are working together to overthrow Nicholas . . . perhaps to assassinate him. They wanted Constantine from the beginning. . . . I never dreamed they would go this far."

"How does your husband know that you know?" Youssef asked. "Did you confront him?"

"Yes, I told him what I had discovered . . . I asked him to explain what was happening. At first he said I was imagining things, that it was the drug. But I persisted, and finally he admitted it. He said it was for the Russian people, that all he was doing and would ever do was to save the Russian people from this despot who was destroying them. When I begged him to stay away from such a plot, to work with Nicholas instead of against him, to give him a chance, he scoffed. And when I threatened to go to the Czar, he laughed. He said no one would believe the ravings of a mad woman."

She grabbed Youssef's arm.

"I'm not mad, Youssef . . . I'm saner than all of them. And I've got to stop them."

"Have you told anyone?" Youssef could see that Olga had gone above her head, that she was now involved and that her life might indeed be in danger. He watched her carefully, wondering about her words.

"A few days ago I notified Minister Trosky through an aide. I asked him to see me on an urgent matter. He sent word back that he was leaving the city and would return in ten days."

There was a frantic look in her eyes.

"You think your husband reached him first?"

"I'm sure of it." She was desperate. "Then I saw the wife of the Secretary. I told her I had a serious matter to discuss with her husband. She promised she would urge him to see me. Again . . . nothing. It's hopeless."

"How do you know that these people you've contacted are not in on the plot?"

"That's just it . . . I don't know. . . ."

Youssef was in a quandary at these revelations. Although his main concern was Olga, he realized that he had an obligation, to reveal these new developments . . . after all, it was important to their mission here. The Sultan should know of this plot—it might possibly work to their advantage. But Olga . . . could Youssef risk Olga's life? Youssef's mind whirled with doubt and confusion, twisting and intertwining his sense of duty to the Empire with his own love for the woman who had changed his life. He wracked his brain . . . Kashim was wise and trustworthy, he must turn to him. Perhaps the older man could think of some way to help Olga before the news was leaked out. Yet Kashim would never keep such a secret from Mahmud, of that Youssef was certain.

"Allah," Youssef cried silently, "help me Allah, help me!"

The sound of Olga's voice brought him back to reality.

"Poor Russia," she was saying, and Youssef was astonished that her love for her country could make her forget her own danger. "Poor Russia, she will never raise her head . . . they will never allow her, not with all this strife and conflict going on. If these people would only wait, be patient . . . learn to work together."

Fear for Olga's life was Youssef's only concern . . . Russia could go to hell, for all he cared. As for Kashim, he decided he would take a chance and go to him.

"That drug you're taking . . . where is it? And when did you take it last?"

He looked around the room suspiciously as a

thought dawned. If the Baron knew Olga had discovered him, why would he leave her alone, free to see and speak with anyone? Could he possibly want her to do just that? Was he counting on her seeing someone, perhaps Youssef? But why? For a moment he wondered if perhaps Olga might indeed be imagining all this, but he looked at her face and knew she was speaking reality.

She took a small container from a drawer and showed him the white powder inside.

"This is what I take every night before going to bed . . . in a glass of milk."

"Who prepares the milk?"

"Andrey used to bring it to me, usually before going out to his meetings . . . but lately Marushka, the servant, brings it in."

"Where is the box kept?"

"In the medicine cabinet . . . and it's locked . . . I have to put it back before Marushka finds out her key is missing."

"And Andrey replenishes the contents?"

"Yes."

"Have you noticed any changes lately?"

"But of course . . . why am I so distraught? Look at me. My vision is becoming blurred. I've had violent headaches this week. At first I thought it was from the shock of my discovery . . . from my confrontation with Andrey . . . but now, I'm afraid it's more than that. . . ."

"What about your doctor? Has he seen you lately?" Then with apprehension he added, "Can he be trusted?"

Who knows what lengths this conspiracy has taken, Youssef was thinking.

"I called him several days ago but he seemed to

be humoring me. He took the powder and brought me a new supply . . . to alleviate my fears, he said. He found nothing wrong."

"Did you tell him anything about Andrey?"

"Yes . . . Dr. Levin's been in the family for years . . . I know I can trust him."

Youssef was silent; he was not certain she was right. In such circumstances, no one is completely trustworthy. Youssef was well aware of this from his own experiences.

"And you've been taking this?" Youssef took the powder in his fingertips and put some to his lips. It was bitter but he could not define the taste. Still, he was concerned about arsenic.

"What happens if you don't take the drug?"

"I . . . I don't know. I've never been without it . . . since I came from the sanitorium . . . over a year ago . . . It makes me sleep . . . relaxes me."

Youssef took some of the powder, put it in his handkerchief, and placed it in his pocket.

"I'm going to try to find out about this. Don't take any more until I get back to you."

He put his arms around her and kissed her gently. She clung to him, the tears drying on her cheeks, afraid to let go. Youssef stroked her hair as he wracked his mind for answers.

"Would the Czar believe you if you went to him? Those papers you saw . . . did you take any of them?"

"He would not believe me, and no, I did not take any papers." She realized it was hopeless. "It would be my word against Andrey's, and Nicholas swears by the Baron—he would stake his life on my husband's loyalty. . . . Oh, God, there's nowhere to turn."

Youssef tried to find some outlet but it seemed to get worse with everything Olga said. At any rate, his main concern was Olga's well-being . . . he had to find some way to help her. He paced the floor and stopped by the fireplace where he stared, hypnotized, into the fire. Olga sat forlornly on the sofa. She looked so helpless—and yet Youssef found such grandeur in her despair. Again he wondered if all this could possibly be her imagination—a result of her illness, the brooding over her son's loss, the months of confinement, her husband's neglect. He thought of every possible reason she might be in this state. But no, no, she was telling the truth. She had not imagined the incriminating papers, the missing jewels. . . . But the drug . . . what if the doctor were in this conspiracy, too? She was murmuring something about Russia again, shaking her head . . . it annoyed Youssef, this lack of concern for herself.

"Stop it, Olga." He pulled her up from the sofa. "Forget Russia and the Czar and your precious Russian people . . . let them fight their own battles . . . you've got to think of yourself."

"Oh, my darling, you don't understand," she replied, "this is the one thing about me you cannot see. . . ."

"I do see . . . I see that you're a woman and you have no business involving yourself in government affairs . . . at least, not when it means your life."

"Oh, Youssef, what is life, after all . . . ?"

He was stunned at her reply. She had indicated such fear for what was happening to her . . . now she made little sense. Then her fears were not for herself, but for Russia. Damned Russia, he thought. But as he damned her country, pride in her choked him inside ... and at that moment he thought of Helena. It was just what his mother would have said—how she would have reacted—placing honor above herself. And the feeling that was growing in him these past months for his mother rose to new heights. Olga had done this to him. She had opened up new worlds, new emotions ... and now he might lose her. The thought made him shudder.

"I love you," he said simply, quietly, and took her face in his hands. "Whatever it is ... whatever you are facing ... I'll help you ... I'll face it with you."

And in spite of his fear for her safety, his heart was singing, silently, within him. ... I love her, I love her, it sang. He was never more positive of anything in his life.

The dawn fought its way through the blizzard, the fierce winds sweeping the snowflakes in whirling masses that finally settled to the ground as the storm turned to a light snowfall. Olga walked Youssef to the door, and stood there in his arms again, hesitating to let him go until he promised her he would be back as soon as he could. From upstairs came the sound of the servants awakening.

"Try to put this out of your mind ... don't ask your husband any more questions ... please, promise me. Let him think you've forgotten the matter."

Youssef kissed her again and hurried out into the morning where her carriage and the faithful Grisha waited to drive him back. From the window she watched them disappear, and glancing across the street she saw a man standing at the curb, looking in the direction of the carriage. Frightened, she checked her door to make sure it was bolted and went up to her room. Thoughts of her surrender to Youssef filled her now, and she was surprised that she did not feel guilty. She had thought she could only love Andrey . . . and yet these months with the young Moslem brought her a peace, a comforting, silent love that warmed her heart. Because of this she had gone to him last night. The trust she felt in Youssef awakened a passion in her that had lain dormant since her husband's aloofness separated them. She wondered if she really loved Youssef . . . were there many types of love? What a blessed feeling it was . . . she had never thought this possible.

All the way back Youssef thought of Olga. He was surprised that a woman of such strength and dignity should be so vulnerable, yet he realized this made him love her more. So there was really no one in the world who could stand alone . . . or was there? Everyone seemed to need, at one time or other, another human to touch, to hold on to. Thoughts inside him whirled—it was confusing, yet clear; sad, yet joyous. Even in sadness, in desperate moments, there can be sweetness and discovery, he thought. He looked out the window as the carriage slowed down—they had arrived.

Kashim, who stood anxiously at the window, hurried to open the door, and the moment Youssef saw his face he knew something was wrong—very wrong.

"I'm sorry I took so long . . . I . . . please, I'd like to talk to you." Youssef wanted to explain his absence, to ask Kashim's advice.

"You listen, my boy. . . ." Kashim was pale and

tense as he led Youssef into the parlor and closed the doors behind him.

"We are to leave immediately," he said gravely, "Russia is declaring war on the Empire."

Youssef looked at Kashim in stunned silence. War between Russia and the Ottomans? They both had known this was coming, yet they did not believe it would come so soon. Not now, thought Youssef, oh, not now . . . Olga was uppermost in his mind.

"We're to leave . . . immediately, you say?"

"Yes . . . I received the word an hour ago . . . I was very disturbed at your absence." He paused a moment, studying Youssef with disapproval. "My boy, this is no time for personal crises . . . I hope you have not involved yourself too deeply."

Youssef did not reply, thinking it best to wait until later.

"My problem can wait, there are more important things to do now, your excellency. . . ." His problem could not wait, but he did not want to add to Kashim's distress. "Please tell me . . . what happened?"

I cannot leave Russia now, he thought, by Allah, not now. . . . why is Fate working so cruelly against us all?

"A great deal has happened, my boy," said Kashim. "Vizir Mehmet arrived from the palace with news. You know of the disastrous loss at Navarino. It was worse than we heard. They destroyed the whole Egyptian fleet Mahmud had summoned there . . . and our own as well."

Kashim knew that Russia had joined forces with England and France to help Greece at Navarino. The palace, through Neguib, had sent orders to Ibrahim at Navarino harbor to continue the war against the Greeks on land only, and to refrain from endangering the fleet . . . they were to avoid any naval confrontation.

"Neguib's letter was intercepted by the British. And Ibrahim, who was always impatient, fired against the allied powers who had sailed into the bay with no intention of doing battle." Kashim shook his head. "It was madness . . . he touched off the fiercest naval battle we've ever fought. There were eighty-nine Turkish and Egyptian vessels of war in the harbor. After the battle only twenty-nine remained afloat, and those were all crippled."

"Then that was the beginning of the end. . . ."

"Yes, I'm afraid it was," Kashim said. "The allies had merely anchored in the harbor, they had no intention of attacking. That fool Neguib . . . what a twist of Fate."

Youssef's whole world was crumbling.

"But the battle at Navarino was months ago . . . why this, now?" he asked.

"It was working up to this, my boy. We always knew that Russian sympathy was with the Greeks . . . well, I suppose that's that. . . ."

"And now Nicholas wants us to leave?"

"What else? He's broken off relations with the palace."

Kashim was calm . . . he had great composure, although his insides churned madly.

"If only they had resolved the Balkan conflict . . . I know the great powers would not have turned against us then."

Before he left Constantinople, Kashim had tried in vain to reason with Mahmud. He warned him that Russia would side with England and France if the Sultan did not bend. Now it had come to pass

. . . just as he had predicted. Kashim stared at Youssef and they both thought the same thing—what a blow this would be to their Sultan.

"What's done is done," Kashim snapped, rallying quickly. "Let's get our things in order, Youssef, we're to be on the ship sailing tomorrow morning."

"Tomorrow?" And, as though to himself, he mumbled, "Olga, I must notify Olga. . . ."

"What is it, my boy?"

Youssef wanted, at that moment, to tell Kashim everything. But something held him back—was it shame, guilt? Had he the right to think of his own feelings during a political crisis? He looked at Kashim, desperate to find a sign of encouragement.

"Are you in trouble, Youssef?"

Hesitantly, he told him a little of what had transpired, careful not to mention his decision to take Olga back with him. Yes, he would take her to Constantinople, he would not think of leaving her behind now.

"You love her then," the wise Kashim said as Youssef expressed fear for Olga's safety.

Youssef looked at the older man, embarrassed, and nodded his head.

"Diplomats are meant to smooth out complications, not create them, my boy," Kashim finally said.

And then he smiled, and there was understanding in his eyes. Praise Allah, thought Youssef, praise Allah for this, at least.

"I must see her," Youssef said, not daring to speak what was really on his mind. He could not risk being refused passage for her.

"See her if you must, my boy, but be careful . . .

this is dangerous business. You should not have gotten involved so deeply."

He watched the younger man solemnly.

"Youssef, I can understand how you feel. You are young, vibrant, full of life . . . but please, my boy, don't do anything you'll regret later. Think of the Empire, my son, think of your duty—they must come first."

They have always come first, Youssef thought, always. I wonder now, if that is so right. Why should one's life be deprived of personal fulfillment? Isn't it better for a country to have happy, contented citizens? Now he was being childish, and he knew it. But his thoughts turned so quickly in his mind. . . . Ah, Youssef, happy, contented citizens do not fight battles and spread empires . . . or bring glory, the little voice he had almost forgotten, said inside him. And of course, it was right. All these thoughts whirled in Youssef's mind as Kashim watched him with concern.

"I cannot help you solve your problem now, my boy," he said, "there is too much at stake in our positions here. You will have to make your own decision . . . but think carefully, Youssef."

And with that, he turned and left the room. Youssef hurriedly dispatched a message to Olga with his trusted servant, one of their entourage . . . he must see her.

They met that afternoon in the bird market, and Youssef felt new hope. She looked much better in the light, and in this pleasant setting of singing birds—hundreds of them—who chirped a symphony of joy, she was calm, almost rested. She must have slept a few hours; perhaps she had resolved matters in her mind, her heart. Was that why there was a certain peace about her? Or had she given up? He was uneasy but did not show his feelings. He sighed as he looked around them . . . the sun was shining while the birds sang, and he wondered how such beauty could survive the pain of life. What a strange combination, he thought—pain and beauty.

He went to her and hastily laid out his plans, urging her to follow them carefully. She must go home and pack—bare essentials only—and he would pick her up early the next morning, at dawn. The carriage would take them to the ship. She shook her head, smiling sadly.

"I cannot leave Russia, Youssef . . . I will not! This is my home."

Tears filled her eyes and she turned toward the birds which were now chirping in symphonic clashes. She thought of the little finch in her salon, the one Youssef had brought her that first day he visited her. It was in her bedroom now, where she could hear its song on awakening. Each morning, the maid would pull the drapes, uncover the cage, and the finch would greet her with its warm melody.

"I won't leave without you. . . ." Youssef was frantic. He had not wanted to frighten Olga, but now he had to tell her. "Listen to me . . . you *must* listen. That powder is mixed with arsenic—I had it analyzed this morning. There's no time to lose. . . ."

She was not surprised . . . she looked at Youssef calmly, as though she had expected it. Andrey, her beloved Andrey was poisoning her . . . her heart turned over with pain. She would have died gladly for him . . . willingly, but not this way. Oh, Andrey . . . She held on to Youssef to steady herself.

"Go to the Czar if it will make you feel better. . . . He'll see you, you're his friend." Youssef knew he made no sense but he was desperate, trying to convince her to leave with him. "Try . . . try, if you must. But if you can't see him, then you will come with me . . . without qualms. You tried to do your part for your Emperor, and for your Russia. Forget them all . . . think of yourself, Olga . . . and of us!"

"No . . . no. My dear, dear Youssef . . ." She smiled sadly. "It would be useless. I realize now that even if I spoke to the Czar he would never believe me. What proof do I have? My illness, Youssef—remember that once my mind had gone completely. And now, the drugs . . . Oh, Andrey, has taken good care to cover his tracks."

Youssef knew, now, that this was the reason Andrey had not kept Olga under surveillance. Who would listen to a woman from a sanatorium, under the influence of drugs? He was angry that she refused to save herself, to take the only way out.

"Olga, listen to me . . ." he pleaded. "What is a country, a home, without someone to love, to trust? It's all meaningless!"

She's a fool, he thought, and I won't let her throw her life away. Youssef persisted now, pleading, trying to reason with Olga, and when she still would not bend, he threatened to desert his post and remain with her in Russia.

"We'll take the consequences together," he said, hoping she would not allow this, that she would go away with him. And yet he was determined to stay with her if she refused.

Tears filled her eyes. What had she done to this man? In her selfishness she was taking him down with her. Andrey would never let Youssef live, should he remain in Russia. She looked at him now, with such love—or was it gratitude—that he wanted to take her in his arms there in the crowd and crush her against him. He loved her more this moment than ever before.

"I can't fight you any longer, Youssef, not when you're ready to give up everything for me," she suddenly conceded.

"We can live and be happy together, Olga . . . live without fear . . . away from all this."

She felt old at that moment, as though she had lived a hundred years. She was tired—tired of fighting loneliness, despair, anxiety. Was Andrey and their life together worth it, after all? She forgot Russia for the moment.

"I'll be at your home at dawn." He broke her reverie.

"Please . . . don't come near the house. Andrey may be there . . . and the servants. . . . I'll meet you at the ship." She looked away.

"Oh no you won't, my lady," he challenged, wanting to scold her, but instead he feigned amusement.

"I promise you, Youssef . . . my word of honor."

"I can't risk it," he replied. "At least meet me down the road from your house. I'll have the carriage around the corner."

Once again Youssef began to feel uneasy. She saw fear in his eyes and smiled to reassure him.

"I'll be there, my dear." She removed a gold chain from around her neck with a small cross, the Russian Orthodox cross with the double bar, and pressed it into his hand.

"This is to seal our bond . . . my baptismal cross

..." she said. "I have worn this since my christening... it's my most treasured possession."

He did not speak . . . he could not . . . he pulled her behind several tall cages away from the browsers in the marketplace.

"Someday you will wear it around your neck... for me." She pressed her fingers over his fist and kissed it gently.

He would wear that piece of gold because it was hers—in spite of its being a cross—he would wear irons for her. He grabbed her and kissed her long, passionately, holding her as though he would never let go.

"I'll see you, my love," she said as she broke away, "at five o'clock tomorrow morning . . . good-bye for now."

"If you're not there, I'll give you ten minutes," he threatened, smiling, "and I'll come storming into your house after you . . . and no one can stop me." He was serious now. "Remember that, Olga . . . and remember that I'm a Janissary, and I can swing a saber like none of your countrymen."

She shuddered but he kissed her again, gently this time, and hoping to calm her fears he whispered in her ear, "You'll forget all this, Olga, I promise you. I'll take you to Chios to meet Helena."

As he looked at Olga, the vision of his mother came before him.

"You'll like her, Olga," he said somberly, "you'll like her very much."

He tried to imagine Helena's joy in seeing him again, and with Olga, a woman of her own faith. He could not wait for the day to come. They parted and Olga hurried off, planning the next morning's move, like a child planning a trip of fantasy, for that was all it was. Andrey would be asleep in his own room, if he were home at all. The servants, too, would not be up that early. She would slip off quietly before five. She smiled to herself. My dear Olga, she told herself, you are beginning to believe your own little games of pretense.

Youssef watched her disappear into the crowd with a sigh of relief. He waited until he saw her carriage in the distance, then leaped on his horse and sped away, trying to throw off the morbid feeling that began to grow inside him. Would Olga do as she promised? Did she give in too readily? But I tormented her, he thought, I threatened my future for her. She had to say yes, she would never let me desert my post, my country. But what country, he added, what country would I be giving up? I don't even know which country is mine anymore. He was surprised and relieved that he had no qualms or guilt feelings about this. And yet, he did not want to desert the Sultan . . . deep inside he would not have wanted to do this. No matter, Olga was coming with him. And he would take her to Helena—the thought excited him—she would love Olga, she would be so proud of them both.

Still, his uneasiness did not leave. The cold wind beat against his face as his horse sped onward. It was April and although the unbearable cold had somewhat subsided, it was still colder than it had ever been in Constantinople. Youssef felt the chill penetrate his bones . . . his very soul. It was a frightening chill. He had the strange feeling that the end of the world was coming . . . it would freeze away. But he was going home—his heart sang—and Olga was coming with him. He tried to reassure himself, saying the words over and over again, but the doubt inside him persisted. He could not wait for tomorrow to come.

Their papers were in order, all protocol had been cleared, their bags packed and ready, and all that the Ottoman mission needed was for morning to arrive. With heavy hearts the men went from room to room, making certain all their belongings had been taken . . . and then, at midnight, they went to bed. Youssef tossed for hours and finally dozed off, but only in sporadic sleep. By three in the morning, he was up and dressed, and at four the two carriages arrived. Youssef, one of the aides, and all the baggage would leave first. Kashim would go an hour later with the others.

Youssef had confessed his plan to Kashim, unable to keep the secret any longer. The older man warned him against his decision to take Olga with them. Youssef knew that Kashim had the power to refuse them passage, for the Sultan's wrath might be great, and Kashim would pay dearly. But the older man could not find it in his heart to forbid Youssef from doing what he chose, in his heart, to do. I'm an old man after all, thought Kashim, I've lived my life. What can Mahmud do but speed my entrance to Paradise? The two men shook hands and Youssef saw the older man's eyes tear.

"Good luck, my boy . . . Allah be with you." He turned away quickly. "We'll meet as planned on the ship."

Youssef's heart filled with emotion, with gratitude to this man—he ran outside.

There was no newfallen snow—even nature had stopped in Youssef's anxiety—the old had settled and gathered dust. The winds were fierce and the driver whipped the horses to hasten them on. It was ten minutes of five when he arrived. Then five o'clock. Five minutes passed, and Olga was nowhere in sight. Ten minutes past five . . . fifteen . . . and he ordered the carriage to drive to her front door. He stood before it, his heart beating wildly, paused a moment, then gently turned the knob. It was unlocked . . . she must have left it open for him. He entered stealthily and waited a moment. Olga was not in the foyer. He crossed the room and looked inside the library, then the salon . . . on to the other rooms. There was no one anywhere. He waited again, listening, then turned quietly and climbed the stairs to the second floor.

CHAPTER 13

IT WAS LONG past midnight when Olga, pretending sleep at the sound of Andrey's footsteps, opened her eyes to see her husband standing at her bedside, staring solemnly down at her. He smiled and bent to kiss her. She was startled when he began to undress ... she fumbled to her feet.

"Isn't this rather sudden, Andrey?" she asked, and her tone was chilled.

He had never seen her look at him like this before. So the young Turkish upstart influenced her after all, he thought.

"I've just decided I should spend more time with my wife ..." he said and began to unbutton his shirt.

She took his arm. "You're a little late, Andrey, don't you think?"

Aha, so our Janissary friend has really taken over, he thought. He was about to say it aloud but decided it was not the wise thing to do ... there were other ways to deal with Olga. He smiled at her, and her resentment faded when she saw a look from the past. For a moment it was the Andrey she once knew and loved so deeply ... and trusted.

"Not tonight, Andrey," she begged and sat down

on the loveseat in the corner. "Let's talk a while, shall we?"

"Whatever you say, my dear," He sat down beside her.

He was still as handsome as when they were married, dashing though cold in his manner. But tonight ... tonight she wanted to see him as he was when his love for her was the most important thing in his life.

"Andrey ... what happened to us?"

He seemed uncomfortable.

"Nothing, my darling, it's all in your mind."

She wanted to scream ... he was going to start on her mind again ... everything was in her mind, to Andrey. She suddenly felt crushed, defeated ... there was not even the strength to fight with him. He seemed impervious to her turmoil, and put his arm around her shoulder.

"I know I've neglected you ... but I promise it will soon be over. And when it is, my dear, we'll have the life we knew once before." He took her hand in his. "Trust me, Olga."

He did not seem like a man who was poisoning his wife. . . . She was confused, but the thought of the Czar and his welfare made her go on.

"Andrey, how can you? Nicholas is our friend ... we have eaten with him, laughed with him, cried with him and the Empress. They love us, trust us."

She tried to make him see.

"Oh, Andrey, if you go through with this, it can never be the same for us. I cannot be a part of someone who betrays his own people." She was pleading now. "Darling, give Nicholas a chance ... don't destroy whatever good has been done. Russia will never grow, never come out of her darkness if this keeps up."

His face was blank . . . he listened politely to her words.

"The Czar trusts you with his life, Andrey. . . ."

Andrey smiled. "Yes, he does."

"And you're plotting to kill him. . . ."

He rose, angered but composed.

"You're raving again, Olga . . . if this keeps up, my dear, I'm afraid I'll be forced to have you committed again. . . ."

He was sorry he said it the minute the words were out. The look of a wounded animal crossed her face and he went to her with remorse, wishing he did not have to resort to all this. His sudden show of concern confused her again, made her wonder if perhaps all this were not really in her mind after all. Perhaps Andrey was not really the conspirator she had grown to fear and even hate, but her own Andrey, the boy she had played with as a child, the man she had loved and married. But the moment passed, and she knew he was a dangerous man who would disregard everything to reach his goal.

"I'm sorry, my darling, I didn't mean that." He put his arms around her and kissed her forehead.

She wanted to believe him. Why? Am I really insane, she wondered. One moment she feared him, the next she was ready to place her life in his hands. Her head rested on his shoulder, and although that intense feeling came over her again, a desire to believe him, to love him, she knew she would never have the old Andrey back—the obsession of his new power had consumed him. He would love her for a moment . . . he would whisk in and out between his conspiracies and plots . . . and she would watch loyalty and duty being crushed, and have to be a part of it. Or die . . . for she was certain he would never stand for any opposition from her. She let him hold her now . . . she would pretend one more time that it was ten years ago.

She let him take her to her bed and make love to her. This is a freak moment, she thought, it will never come again. She stayed in his arms, lying beside him, and when he kissed her lips and fondled her body, she felt, just a little, that old, sweet passion of their early years together. And as they lay side by side together, on their nuptial bed, he wondered if perhaps he could pacify her and keep her on his side after all—without having to resort to violence. He would stop the arsenic . . . he did not want to lose her . . . not unless it was absolutely necessary, the last alternative. They slept a few hours . . . at least Andrey slept heavily. Olga lay still, thinking of Youssef and of her broken promise. She knew she could not go to him, but the fantasy of that thought was beautiful, a comforting dream. Just before dawn Andrey rose, put on his dressing gown, and left the room. He returned carrying a silver tray.

"We will breakfast on champagne and caviar," he said smiling as she watched him from her bed, "as we did on our honeymoon."

She smiled sadly and watched him bending over the tray, pouring the champagne into silver goblets. Her heart almost stopped beating. Why was he taking so long? What was he doing? He turned to her suddenly and saw the fear on her face.

"Darling, what's the matter? You look as if you'd seen a ghost!"

He went up to her and kissed her on the lips.

And he laughed when he saw her staring, dazed, at the goblets.

"Ah, but of course, you're afraid I'm poisoning you ... darling, come now, take any cup you like."

He knew of her fears and her confession to the young Turk—his spies had done their work well. But he avoided any such confrontation with her. He had his own methods with Olga.

"Andrey, please don't joke about such a thing."

He took one of the glasses and handed it to her. Then together, he toasted their happiness. But before they could drink there was a noise downstairs. Voices drifted up to them—one of the servants was talking with someone. . . . Andrey hurried out to see what was going on. It was one of Countess Crispini's men with a message from her. Annoyed at the interruption, he grabbed the note and read it quickly.

"Tell her I already know about this. . . . The fool," he hissed, "of all times . . ."

He hurried upstairs. Olga had grasped this opportunity . . . she hurriedly took the small container from the bedside table and emptied the white powder into both goblets. She sighed with pleasure, and relief . . . she had found the solution for them both. The Baroness could not live away from Russia, even if the thought of Youssef's love was the greatest comfort she had known in years. Nicholas's death was too high a price to pay for her peace of mind . . . she would find it elsewhere . . . with Andrey, who would not harm the Czar or Russia ever again. And they would be together for always. She thought of her son, Dimitri, and tears filled her eyes. Yes, soon they would all be together.

Andrey returned. "War . . . the Czar's declaring

war on the Ottomans tomorrow . . . that fool Crispini . . . I knew it this morning, but she had to disrupt my household at this hour."

He held out his arms to her. "Come here, my dear."

She went to him and took the goblet he handed her.

"To us, Andrey, and to Russia."

She drank it slowly and he watched her with little expression on his face. Then she walked to her bed and lay down, gently, pulling the silken covers to her waist. She turned to Andrey and smiled at him.

"Aren't you going to drink to my toast?"

"But of course."

He raised his cup as the door burst open and Youssef stood there staring wildly. Andrey put the goblet back down on the tray.

"How dare you, sir? What is the meaning of this?"

Youssef ignored him . . . he turned to the Baroness.

"Olga!" It was a cry of pain.

She was gasping and her arm stretched out, calling him. Andrey did not move, a sad half-smile on his face.

"She's calling you . . . go to your lover," he said calmly.

As Youssef reached Olga's side, she was choking. He was shocked, watching her writhe on the bed, not knowing what to do. She looked at him, tried to speak, and he took her in his arms. He looked into her pained, tormented eyes, and before he could say a word, she was gone. Andrey had not expected her to go so fast—he had put just enough in the goblet to put her to sleep. He thought it strange but dismissed it, keeping his composure, guiltless in the belief that what he had done was for Russia, for something Olga, too, believed in, in her heart, in her own way. A moment of sadness flashed through him, remembering how he had loved this woman, but power is all-engulfing, all-sacrificing. He steeled himself—he must not weaken.

Youssef stood frozen over Olga's body. His face was ashen white and his insides churned until he thought they would burst. The nerves in his temple beat wildly and he opened and closed his eyes, unwilling to believe what he had seen. She was dead . . . Olga was dead. He turned, a wild look in his eyes. Andrey was standing near the table, calm and composed, the goblet in his hand. He shook his head sadly and raised his cup.

"She died for her beloved Russia . . . so it will be saved." He watched Youssef who stood frozen to the spot. "Nothing and no one comes before one's country, my friend . . . as well you should know." He smiled. "Youssef, the Janissary of the Sultan of the Ottoman Empire. Now go home where you belong and let us take care of our own affairs."

The drink was halfway down his throat when Youssef's knife pierced his belly. Over and over he struck, all his fury and hate in every thrust. Andrey's face grimaced with pain, his tongue hung out, and his eyes rolled . . . he was a fearsome, pitiful sight, this Russian of noble birth. The drug had hardly begun its work when the knife found its mark. Blood splattered on the table and the champagne tray, and seeped into the thick carpet. In the confusion, the birdcage toppled over and the little finch began to call frantically for help. Youssef stood transfixed over the body of Andrey, who gasped for breath and looked from him to Olga. The shrieking of the bird caught his attention and he went to it, picked it up, mechanical in his movements, and stared at the small bit of life. It had contained his love for Olga and he closed his fingers over it protectively, consolingly. But his fury controlled his strength and unknowingly he crushed the little finch. It trembled spastically for a moment and finally lay still in his hand. Youssef looked at the lifeless body and shook his head sadly, remorsefully.

"I didn't mean to do that," he whispered, and the pain in his heart was unbearable.

He walked over to the bed and laid the bird beside Olga's head. She had loved it so, in life. He kissed her lips and caressed her hair . . . and the pain beat within him, tearing his insides. He wanted to scream, to yell at the top of his lungs, to let it all out. He had lost another precious thing he had found in his life . . . perhaps the most precious of all. Once again, another part of him was torn away, gone. . . . He turned, dazed, and walked out of the room, past the frightened servants who huddled fearfully in the corner. The driver of his carriage saw him, blood-spattered and staggering, and helped him into the cab, rushing him back to the mission just as Kashim was about to leave. The servants quickly washed the blood away and changed Youssef's clothing; and within the half hour, both carriages were on their way to the ship that waited in the harbor. Youssef sat in stunned silence, barely knowing what was happening around him. They boarded the ship and Kashim silently praised Allah for allowing matters to take this course. Youssef was free to return to the palace now, free of personal ties and complications. His heart went out to the young man, and he vowed to help him find his way again. This was all a part of life, a part of Youssef's initiation into the world of civilized adults, of politics. Time will heal whatever must be healed, he thought, and tried to comfort him. But Youssef knew it would never heal—it was too deep, too long in coming.

The sailors on board the vessel buzzed with the latest developments in the Winter Palace. The conspiracy against Nicholas had been uncovered . . . the traitors were caught and Nicholas was safe. Kashim heard all this and was comforted that Youssef, too, was safe. Even if the murder could be linked to him, the Czar was well rid of an enemy he had considered his closest friend. A pall of sadness would fall over the Russian palace; the Czar, understandably, would be crushed at his friend's betrayal, but time would pass and it would all be set aside, if not forgotten, as all plots and conspiracies must be . . . until new ones are uncovered.

They sailed in the fog, and it was a journey from death, a journey of sadness, loneliness. Youssef felt as though he were in a vast wilderness, alone, without a soul in the world. And as he sat near the masthead, in the night, holding the gold cross in his hand, the only tangible thing he had of Olga, he remembered his dream. And he realized that its prophecy had come to pass. The wilderness in his nightmare was the vast emptiness in Youssef's heart, in his life. And the pool of blood . . . it, too, had come to be. Helena had become Olga in his dream and had died, melting out of his arms. The thought of Helena was the only comforting thing now. It was a bittersweet thought—a ray of light, hope in the blackness of his life. He had a sudden desire to see her, to talk to her, to feel the comfort of her arms around him. As for the other girl in his dream—Selina—he did not care whether she lived or died. He would return to the palace, but first he would stop in Chios to see his mother.

Part III

CHAPTER 14

Chios ... 1828

HELENA STEPPED OUT into the small terrace of her home and took a deep breath of the clean, spring air. She looked down at the valley below, sparsely dotted with pine and the newly blossomed almond trees. How she loved the almond blossoms—they reminded her of bridal bouquets. Every spring Chios was rich with the scented flowers of almond and orange and lemon trees. The heavenly fragrance drifted for miles, and ships that passed that part of the Aegean needed no compass to tell them it was Chios, the island of winds and scented blossoms. Helena stood there basking in the beauty around her. She never wanted to leave this place—no matter how many years passed, each spring brought new anticipation, and the changing seasons brought joy and excitement in the offerings of her island home.

This year the springtime had a special meaning for Helena. It was, she felt, the beginning of contentment in the autumn of her life. She sighed as she stood there, remembering the past and those years of heartbreak. Was it really thirty years ago when that girl of eighteen met and fell in love with the handsome sea captain who peddled romantic dreams to foolish virgins? So much had happened since then . . . yet somehow she had managed to pick up the pieces of a shattered life and fit them together again, year after year. Helena was a survivor, she refused to be broken.

The song of the finch drifting from her kitchen broke her thoughts. She smiled with pleasure and her heart filled with joy . . . and longing for Joseph. She had thought her son had forgotten her these past two years. And then a ship docked at the harbor, bringing wheat from Russia, and a sailor brought her the little bird in its wooden cage . . . all the way from St. Petersburg. Oh, the joy of it. Youssef, the fierce Janissary, had remembered his mother. The little finch was his way of saying what he could never say to her before, when he tried, in vain, to replace Jason. He does think of me, her heart sang now . . . he is not completely lost. She believed, how she wanted to believe, that soon she would hear more of Joseph, that he would come back to the land and the people who had born him.

The winds blew softly and their soft caress made her exuberant. Today was her wedding day—after twenty-seven years she would be whole again . . . a woman. Her secret longings and desires, so firmly checked to guard her honor, would reveal themselves in all their passion. She stepped inside and went to her mirror, staring curiously, and pleased, into her reflection. She removed her robe and stood in her white embroidered petticoat. Her black hair cascaded loosely over her shoulders—not a gray hair in the thick mane. She touched her neck and smiled—there were no wrinkles. Her olive skin was smooth and shiny . . . the years of struggle had taken no toll of her beauty. She smiled again, sadly this time, and shook her head. Oh, yes, God was generous in this case. Remember the scales, Helena, she told herself . . . somehow, some way, they always balance. He takes and He gives. He has deprived you of womanhood, of your sons, these many years, but now He brings you another fulfillment. And she knew that one cannot truly feel joy without knowing sadness . . . or ecstasy without despair. She was still young in the flesh and in spirit . . . time had stood still for Helena. The other village women looked old at thirty-five, yet Helena was vibrant and beautiful at forty-eight. My God, she gasped, I'm a grandmother of forty-eight . . . and today I feel like a bride. She was ashamed, and turned quickly away from the mirror as though some eyes might see and ridicule her.

The song of the finch suddenly filled the air and Helena went to the cage to tease the little bird by sticking her finger between the bars. Little Jason was being cared for by his cousins today, since it was highly improper for him to witness Helena's marriage to his grandfather. How ironic is Fate, she thought. Petros lost his daughter, and I lost a son . . . and now the two of us, together, will join to become the substitute parents for our own grandson. She went to her closet and took out the dress she would wear for the ceremony, while the water boiled on the stove for her morning tea. Cousin Anna would arrive soon to help her with the preparations . . . but she really wanted to be alone this morning, this glorious morning of her new life. Excitement raced through her and she whirled around the room in a moment of giddiness.

Big Ears hobbled along the path to the church carrying the precious package Xenophon had entrusted to him. It was an honor to carry the *stephana,* the traditional wreaths for the ceremony, and the two large candles, and the sugared almonds that would complete the ritual of the Greek Orthodox wedding. How glad I am, he thought, at last *Kyra* Helena will have someone to take care of her, to keep her from being lonely. Big Ears knew what loneliness was since his mother's death. He had known Helena all his life and had felt her joys and sorrows. And he loved her, as he had loved Jason, for they were the only ones in the village who treated him like an equal, who never teased or taunted him. When he was with Helena or Jason he forgot his ugly appearance and the hurt of being laughed at. *Kyra* Helena always gave him a drachma or two when he carried her packages from market. Then he would hurry to buy *raki* with the precious coins. He sighed now, thinking of Jason, remembering the horrible massacre a few years ago and how he had wept beside Jason's body sprawled on the ground in a pool of blood. What good was it all, he decided now, in the ironic wisdom of idiocy . . . what good was all that secret planning for the revolution that Jason had been so excited about? Chios was back where she was before, still under the Turks, and worse off. Most of the beauty was marred by the ashes and burned stumps that were still visible. And so many of the villagers were gone. But at least Xenophon was still here, and the good merchant of Thymiana kept Big Ears on in his employ so that he could eke out his living. His mother was gone, too, and though he once had thought he would be glad to be rid of her nagging, and the constant mania she had about his washing his feet, there was emptiness, "butterflies" in the pit of his stomach when he arrived at his barren room each night.

He sighed again as he trudged on with his load, trying suddenly to wiggle his ears because they itched and his hands were not free to scratch them. But again, for a moment, he forgot that those damned Turks had lopped off his one ear, and the remaining one now wiggled gently, protruding from the side of his head like a banner. He took very good care of this ear, washing it almost every week, caressing it as he gently dried it with the towel, patting it frequently as though to make certain it was still there. How sorry he was that he had resented those ears of his—not now, never. At least the villagers still called him Big Ears, seeming not to notice his loss.

He reached the church and set his thoughts aside when he looked up at Saint Efstratios, which stood on a slope outside the fortress walls of Thymiana in all its glory. This church had been built by the villagers and sustained by them with great pride. Here they were baptized as infants, married as adults, and finally buried. It was a pillar of faith and strength and hope for the people in both sorrowed and happy days. In reality, it was the only consistent thing in the villagers' lives.

Helena would have preferred being married in the chapel of her favorite saint, the Prophet Elias, where she went to pray and meditate all the years of her life. But the memory of that tragic night with Yusbasi Hassan outside that other chapel of the Prophet on the Greek mainland would not allow her to be married here now. For she could never erase that scene . . . Hassan's touch on her cringing flesh, his lips on her neck, and the dagger she had plunged into his belly. And then, running in the night, leaping over bushes, down ravines, clutching little Jason, holding Costa's loving arm that guided them to the hidden bay and to freedom. And as they sailed away in the blackness of that night, her heart, a part of her remained behind with Joseph, her lost son, and with Costa who lay on the shore bleeding from the Turkish sentry's dagger.

She smiled through her tears now, shaking the memories away as she walked down the aisle of Saint Efstratios to where Petros waited with Xenophon. She felt the steady arm of her Cousin Anna who smiled encouragement. It is all in the past, she told herself; put it aside Helena, and rejoice in whatever happiness God is granting you now. The son she had saved that night of terror was gone now, the son she had left behind was alive . . . and he had remembered his mother. She was wearing his gift to her—the white silk kerchief embroidered with silk flowers of many shades and colors . . . it lay gently over her black hair and she held it at her neck with trembling fingers. Joseph had sent this lovely token of his thoughts from Russia. And to little Jason he had sent a velvet coat and suit from the finest tailors of St. Petersburg. Perhaps one day God would see fit to grant her Joseph's return, too. Now she had a new life awaiting her with Petros. She smiled through tears of joy and looked at him—his love for her lay unmasked in his eyes—and at Xenophon, her dear, loving cousin Xenophon beside Petros, waiting to exchange the wreaths as the *koumbaro*, their best man. Oh, he is indeed a best man, she thought, the kindest, wisest, most understanding cousin a woman could have—he was actually her uncle, but he was so near her age that she could not think of him as such. He had stood beside her through all the bitter, difficult years. No brother would have meant more to Helena. . . . She nodded to him now, trying to show her gratitude in her look. Xenophon nodded back and smiled. He understood . . . he could always read the thoughts of those he loved. He turned his head abruptly so she could not see the glint of tears in his eyes. He was remembering many things, too—her son Jason and their long talks . . . his wife Alexandra, and their life together before the massacre. He sighed and shook his head, as though reassuring himself that life was for the living, that life must go on. Father Constantine raised his hand and began the marriage ceremony.

"The servant of God Petros is betrothed to the servant of God Helena, in the name of the Father, and the Son, and the Holy Spirit. . . . The servant of God Helena is betrothed to the servant of God Petros, in the name of the Father, and the Son, and Holy Spirit."

Big Ears stood at the side and watched the ceremony in awe. Helena looked so beautiful, so peaceful and content. In fact everyone looked beautiful to Big Ears today . . . it was one of the special days of his life. Besides seeing his beloved *Kyra* Helena finally settled in marriage, he knew he would be offered good *raki* and perhaps wine too, with the many appetizers they would serve at Cousin Anna's house, later. The families, what was left of them, would gather for the couple's well-wishes, and those delicious little meatballs would be served, and stuffed grapevine leaves, and roe salad . . . ah, Big Ears's mouth was watering . . . he wished the priest would hurry with his chanting. Why did these church ceremonies take so long? He shifted his feet and patted his ear, hoping it would all be over soon . . . he was getting hungrier by the minute. He wondered, suddenly, why he had not considered marriage, and he squinted as he stared at the iconostas, trying to find an answer. It was not a bad idea . . . but who would have the village idiot? What girl would even consider such a union? And then, as the priest brought the cup of wine and offered it to the couple for the customary sip, Big Ears had a unique idea . . . why hadn't he thought of it before? There must be a girl somewhere in the neighboring villages like him . . . well, not quite like him . . . certainly not with one ear . . . but one who was not as bright as the others, who could understand his ways. Perhaps they could have a life together. He could not wait to talk about it to someone, and looked around anxiously. Talk . . . to whom? Who else but his employer, the good Master Xenophon. The words of the priest interrupted his thoughts.

"Go, my children, with my blessings and the blessings of our church . . . be happy, you both deserve it."

The family friends gathered to shake hands and kiss the couple, and when it was Big Ears's turn, he offered his wishes and sidled near Xenophon.

"Please, Master Xenophon, I have something important to tell you . . . can I see you, later?"

"Yes, yes of course, Yorgo," the man replied absent-mindedly.

"When?" Big Ears asked quickly. "It's important."

"Later, later, Yorgo." He tried not to show his impatience. "It's Helena's wedding day."

Big Ears had not even noticed that Xenophon called him by his Christian name, which was indeed an honor befitting the occasion. He was hurt, and Xenophon regretted his abruptness.

"All right, Big Ears," he added, smiling, "we can talk at the house. Come to the reception for a little wine."

Big Ears nodded gleefully and followed the small group that left the church on their way to Cousin Anna's home where the others waited.

Helena had wanted a small, simple wedding, as befitting her status. How she wished this were her first marriage . . . that Petros was her first love. But never mind, her silent voice told her, this is stronger, more real, more sustaining, Helena. This is mature love, binding love, forever and ever. . . . She looked up at Petros who watched her silently, enigmatically, wondering what she was thinking. The look in her eyes set his mind at ease. She did love him, he was satisfied. He could not wait to take her in his arms and make her a part of himself. He had waited six years for this—a lifetime.

The moon was at its peak, and all the stars in the heavens came out for the occasion. Helena and Petros stood on her small terrace and watched the magnificence of nature. She had witnessed many star-kissed nights before, so breathtaking in their splendor, but it was always with a sad heart, with a lonely one. She remembered wondering how so much beauty could exist amidst such unhappiness and tragedy—the tragedy of her life and those around her. But now, more than ever, the scales were balanced. She was admiring the wonders of God with peace in her heart, for this man at her side, this strong, loving man had pledged to love and protect her always. She knew he was a man of his word, that she would finally have love and companionship and understanding. She looked up at him now, her heart beating fast, and he drew in his breath. He had waited so long. Here, in this house where she was born, where she knew the joys of her childhood, the house once fallen and rebuilt again, she would be a part of the holy union she would cherish. Later, they would go to live in Petros's estate in Kambos, the valley of the wealthier Chiotes and Turks . . . but tonight would be spent in her ancestral home. He stroked her hair and touched her cheek, caressing it gently. Then he pulled her to him and kissed her with all the passion of his lost youth . . . his loneliness. They walked into the house together, their arms about each other, and to the bed that was dressed in its bridal splendor. Petros did not care that the sheets were gleaming white, starched and waiting, with the intricate embroidery on the edges. He only cared that Helena would finally belong to him. They stood together near the bed, and Petros watched her, half smiling, as she hesitated.

"Forgive me," she said somberly. She wanted to add . . . it's been twenty years . . . so long . . . but she was ashamed.

He understood, and though his blood pulsed and he wanted to grab her and fall with her onto those starched sheets, he would be patient.

"I love you," he said and watched her intently.

"Helena, I love you . . . you are my wife . . . it's all right now."

She had fought her emotions, her sense of honor, for so many years . . . because they were both married. Each of their mates had gone his own way, but the laws of the Church were laws Helena refused to break. Only after both Maria and Stratis were gone, dead, would she consider this union with Petros. It was a battle that tore her insides, that made her body ache, and her mind flare with frustration. But she had won the battle . . . all of it, and she was proud. She was going to Petros with an open, free heart. Her conscience would never let her do otherwise. And she was glad, for it made her victory all the more rewarding, all the more triumphant. A human being is nothing, she had always said, without dignity. And that was what had sustained her.

She took the cup of wine Petros offered her from the decanter on the small table. God bless Cousin Anna, Petros thought, for remembering this. They toasted their marriage, and the warmth of the liquor soothed Helena and gave her courage. She put the cup down and untied her robe. Underneath was the ivory gown she had embroidered so carefully. Petros came to her and gently unbuttoned the front. When he reached the waist, he slipped it off her shoulders and it fell to the floor. She stood there in her nakedness, embarrassed but pleased at the look on his face. Her body was more than he had expected—the body of a young woman beautifully encased in maturity. He held his breath, unable to take his eyes off it. She bit her lip and felt, suddenly, like a virgin bride, waiting for her loved one's touch. And then she stepped forward, careful not to break the spell, and went to him.

They did not sleep all night . . . it was as though they had only this moment, these hours, to make up for the years of waiting. And when he entered her, it was like entering a virgin . . . he moaned at the unexpected surprise . . . and she was glad of her years of abstinence. She wanted him to be pleased . . . and she knew it was more than he had anticipated. The two were locked together in an ecstasy far beyond their dreams. At first she was tense, but by the time the moon had set, she had flung all her inhibitions aside, and exploded in a climax made up of sunbursts and rainbows, waterfalls and flowing brooks. She laughed to herself at such adolescent responses . . . but were they adolescent? No, this was all the stages of life put together, all senses touched, all feelings alerted—it was the ultimate of unions. And after each period of lovemaking, he held her as they lay together, exhausted and joyous, with her head on his chest. It was the happiest, most wonderful night of her life, far surpassing the innocent passion and excitement of her first love, her ill-fated love for Stratis. This was a feeling that had grown through friendship, and time, and understanding. Her love for Stratis was a romantic girl's dream that became momentarily real in the presence of the handsome stranger. How different love can be, she thought. . . . Thank you, God, oh thank you. . . . It's true, then, that the end honors the beginning. It's not how one begins but how one ends—and that is what really matters. By the time the first rooster crowed, they were both asleep, tired and happy, content and grateful.

CHAPTER 15

THE WEEK PASSED quickly, and Helena felt a new sense of contentment and peace—one she never dreamed could be hers. Petros, too, was revitalized in this blessed union, and he set about to renovate his large home in Kambos, anxious to bring his bride there. He had known no marital happiness inside these walls, but it had brought him a sense of returning to his roots when he came to it after Constantinople. Even his cool relationship with Maria could not mar the fact that he had come back to the home of his father and the past glories his family had known on the island. Now his happiness would be complete—he would be bringing the woman he loved to his ancestral home. The workers set about their tasks and Petros supervised the work with the excitement of any newlywed.

May passed and June came, bringing with it the first hints of summer heat. The blossoms that adorned the nearly bare island began to wither . . . before June was gone, they too, would disappear to make room for the luscious fruit that would follow. Whatever thoughts Petros might have had about relocating to Constantinople were dimmed now. The latest uprising on the island had created further bitter feelings between the Ottomans and the Chiotes, and he did not believe he would be welcome in the Ottoman capital again.

It seemed that Fate was against the freedom of this island. Their third rebellion last October had resulted in another failure. Petros now realized they probably would not see Chios free in their lifetime. And so, he accepted what he could not change and decided to let matters take their course. He would turn to his own needs and desires. Chios would always be in his heart but he would accept the yoke that was around them . . . until Fate, or God, or perhaps the devil, saw fit to liberate this island of the winds and mastic. Yes, he would make the most of what years were left—devote himself to Helena and the child. And perhaps one day, the child of his grandson would rise to free their island.

It was late afternoon when Petros left his orchards in Kambos and headed for Thymiana, where he stopped at Xenophon's to exchange the latest news. The village merchant was still the first to learn of the latest happenings, for he continued to represent the town, to act as its liaison, to receive and transmit various messages, and, when requested, to give advice and opinions. The people of Thymiana depended on Xenophon, and he continued always to be a wise friend and a capable leader. More importantly, he gave them some stability in this most unstable time of their lives.

Xenophon opened a bottle of wine and brought some bread and olives to accompany it. It was good, at the end of the day, to have a drink and a chat with a friend. The matter of current interest was the peaked conflict between Russia and Turkey—war between the two was a good sign for the Greeks. Now their greatest concern was Joseph, and they waited anxiously for news of his return. Helena was greatly troubled, though Petros and Xenophon assured her the Turkish diplomats would be allowed escort and safe passage through enemy waters. Because of this development, Petros did not pressure Helena into moving to Kambos and he stalled the workmen to give her more time.

"Helena doesn't really want to move to Kambos, you know," Petros said. "Do you think I'm wrong to ask her to live in the house Maria and I shared?"

Xenophon was silent a moment, weighing the question. He had noticed the change in Helena's mood and thought it strange, for she had loved Petros's estate.

"A woman's place is with her husband," Xenophon finally replied. "His home is hers and his family her own . . . and Helena is the kind of woman who would abide by that."

"I know . . . I know," Petros said, "she would never refuse. But I've watched her . . . she seems relieved with every delay that arises."

"Helena loved Maria . . . she spoke often of the good days she spent in your house."

Xenophon suspected there were many bad days as well, although Helena had never indicated such a thing. But his keen insight had told him all was not well between Petros and Maria, and that Helena was carrying more than her own burden those dark days of the first rebellion.

Big Ears stumbled into the room gasping for breath.

"Master Joseph . . . Master Joseph . . . the ship

... ugh ... here ..." He could never make sense when he was excited.

"All right now, Big Ears, calm down and start over." Xenophon poured Big Ears a cup of wine and waited while he gulped it down.

Big Ears smacked his lips, wiped them with his sleeve and sat down.

"A Russian ship landed. . . ." He spoke slowly, carefully, realizing the importance of his message. "The Turks let it pass through ... it's carrying the Sultan's ... ugh ..." Oh, he almost had it. Groping for more words he stuttered and stopped. "The di ... di ... diplomats."

"Well, Big Ears," Xenophon said, smiling, "you're becoming almost literate ... bravo ... come on now, you're making sense ... good boy."

He slapped Big Ears on the back.

"What else? Go on, Yorgo," Petros said, pressing him on, "what else?"

"The messenger came ashore ... and told them ... I asked the guard, you see."

Big Ears was so proud of himself he could barely get the words out.

"And the guard said, they'd be coming ashore soon ... might even be there now ... I hurried to tell you."

There, it was all out and he was out of breath and happy.

"Good work, man." Petros slapped him happily. "Joseph will be on the ship." He turned to Xenophon. "I'll go and tell Helena ... we can meet him in Chora."

As he hurried out he called behind him, "Oh, by the way, Xenophon, we'll be moving to Kambos next week." Petros felt the timing was perfect. "Can we have Big Ears to help us a few hours?"

He knew Big Ears would consider this a great compliment, and Helena, too, would feel some security in having the familiar Big Ears help her about the new house. Yes, he was a small link to her days with Jason. He hurried up the slope to the Andreadis home.

Within minutes their carriage was on the road to the harbor. Helena's heart pounded while little Jason sat quietly in his seat. Helena had often spoken of Joseph, trying to keep his image alive. But young Jason had shown little interest. Now she looked at him and smiled, and the child wished Joseph had left them alone . . . why did he come to disturb their happy family? He would only leave again. Jason shrugged, telling himself he did not care what Joseph did . . . or where he went. But he turned away so Helena could not see the angry tears that filled his eyes.

CHAPTER 16

JOSEPH WAS WAITING at the dock . . . thinner, a little paler, with dark lines under his eyes . . . and that sadness more deeply etched on his face. Helena's breath caught at sight of him. What had happened? He had aged . . . could two years have made such an impression on so young a man? She wanted to throw her arms around him but hesitated, waiting for his first move.

A half-smile crossed his face as he came forward to greet them. In a quick glance he took in Helena, Petros, the child, but his eyes came back to rest on his mother. She has not changed at all, he thought . . . by Allah, she is the same as the first time I saw her. He offered his hand and Helena took it in both of hers. She wanted to stroke his face, to kiss him, but she bit her lip and ordered herself into control. Wait . . . wait until later, she said silently.

They ate quietly, Joseph avoiding discussions of any detail. Petros did not insist or prod. They talked of matter-of-fact things, of his life in Russia, the war that had broken out with Turkey.

"Russia has been trying to start the rumble for a long time . . ." Joseph said. "Well, she finally succeeded."

"Did you enjoy life in Russia?" his mother asked, trying to sound nonchalant.

"Very opulent . . . very extravagant . . ."

"Like the palace of the Sultan?" Helena could not help asking.

Joseph smiled. "Yes, but even more so. I thought Mahmud's palace was the richest in the world, but the Russians have exceeded it. . . ." He paused a moment. "So much wealth . . . the rich are so wealthy, and the common people starve. And they dare to criticize the Ottomans . . . I wager there are more starving Russians than all the Ottoman Empire put together."

"Well, it could be a tie," Petros said in jest, but having sailed to Russia many times, he knew it to be the truth.

Helena was overjoyed . . . Joseph was talking . . . anything, she thought, let him say anything, just so he opens up to us.

"At least we don't pretend to be noblemen," Joseph continued. "Do you know"—he spoke with more enthusiasm now—"once, at a state dinner, the Russian host knocked down a servant because he served the wrong dish . . . in front of thirty guests . . . and they call *us* barbarians!"

Helena wanted to say that the Ottomans were not far behind. At least, the Russians had some sophistication. But she kept still, afraid of offending Joseph. All she could think of was the possibility of his staying awhile longer with them.

"They say that we believe the Sultan is God's Vice-Regent. . . . Well, the Russians believe the Czar goes to heaven once a week and holds conferences with God." And with that, Joseph began to laugh—beautiful music to Helena. It was infectious and they were all laughing now. The air filled with the happy sound . . . it was a warm, happy moment for the small family.

"How was your social life?" Petros asked when they had quieted down. "The women—did you find them interesting?"

Joseph's face turned white and Petros was sorry he mentioned it. Helena began to clear the table.

"How long will you be staying with us?" She wanted to talk with him alone . . . there was so much she wanted to hear.

"A day or two . . . until the other ship arrives." He watched her carefully. "Perhaps three days."

The Russian ship had escorted them as far as Chios. One of the Sultan's vessels would be arriving soon to take them to Constantinople.

One day . . . three, she thought, only moments. But it was better than nothing. If she only could have him a little while. Her heart ached so . . . she had missed so many years of Joseph . . . so many years.

They sipped the thick, rich coffee in their small salon and Petros brought Joseph up to date on life in Chios, and their planned move to Kambos. Her son was pleased that Helena had finally married Petros. He was a good man . . . Joseph was fond of him. He thought suddenly of Stratis. Helena would never have married unless he were dead. Joseph was surprised that his father should come to mind . . . in all his years, he had never cared or questioned his existence. It did not matter now, either, except that his mother was free to begin a new life. He wished he could sit down and talk with her, just the two of them . . . to tell her about Olga and the many things he understood now. . . . But it was too fresh

... the pain of Olga's loss was still new, and he could not bring himself to speak of her.

Little Jason sat quietly throughout the meal, avoiding Joseph's gaze, pretending this intrusion did not concern him. He took the package Joseph handed him and ran to put it in his room. He would not let his father see his secret excitement ... as he did not show his pleasure when the velvet coat and suit had arrived from Russia. Jason was pleased that Joseph remembered him, but he would not allow the others to know it. Actually, he tried to hide it even from himself ... afraid to admit he cared for this man who would be leaving again. And he was glad when it was time for bed. He shook hands with the visitor, kissed his grandmother, and lay down to ponder his secret excitement. Perhaps his father might stay, this time. He wondered if it would do any good to talk to him. After tossing for an hour or so he decided to try in the morning.

The sun began its rise and the Sofronis household was up early. Helena could be heard puttering in the kitchen while Joseph went down to gather eggs and pay his respects to the chickens in the storage room. It felt good to see chickens in their roost again ... although the ones he left two years ago had long ago graced his mother's stewpot. He thought of Helena's delicious chicken soup, with the egg, lemon, and rice ... perhaps he would ask her to make some. There was a warm feeling here in this house, one he had not felt before. He did not seem a stranger. How odd, he felt a part of it ... like a loved relative come to visit. It was good to be back after all ... even for a few days. As he ran upstairs with the eggs, he wondered what Helena would say if he asked them to come and spend some time in Constantinople . . . perhaps a month or so. He would be so proud to introduce them to Mahmud. He wanted very much for his mother to see the position of trust and honor he held in the palace . . . and in the Sultan's heart. He decided to talk to them about it.

The four sat in embarrassed silence as they took their morning meal . . . the thick, black coffee, fresh boiled eggs, cheese, black olives, and Helena's warm, fresh bread. Little Jason ate quietly, looking at Joseph anxiously from time to time. He had spoken to his grandmother with all the seriousness he could muster, about his plan. Yes, he had decided he would ask Joseph to stay with them. Helena's heart went out to the boy . . . she dreaded the disappointment ahead of him. But she would not stop him from trying—it might be good for both of them, perhaps strengthen the bond. But she knew it would take a miracle to bring Joseph back to his family.

"I'm going to help Petros with the carriage, it has a broken wheel," Helena said and followed Petros out the door, leaving Joseph and the boy alone.

Joseph wanted to stop her, to say, no, don't leave me alone with him . . . what will I do? He was uncomfortable, embarrassed . . . and the serious look on the boy's face frightened him. He looked at the child and waited.

They were both silent—the two generations who sat staring at each other across the table. Why is he eyeing me so curiously, so seriously, Joseph thought. He felt like a prisoner set for interrogation. He looked around him helplessly, wondering what to say. . . groping for words.

"Do . . . do you remember me?" Joseph was sorry the moment he asked the foolish question.

"Yes, sir, I do," the boy answered politely, "you're my father."

Youssef managed a half-smile. By Allah, facing this child was worse than facing an adversary. He wished Helena had not left them alone.

"Are you really my father?"

The question jolted Youssef. He looked at the boy with a startled expression. "Of course . . . of course I'm your father. Why do you ask such a thing?"

"Well, if you're really my father, why did you go away and leave me?"

The child's words jolted Youssef—his uncomfortable feeling turned to near-panic. How foolish I am, he thought, letting a child disturb me. All I have to do is give him a simple answer . . . tell him the truth. But he said nothing. In the name of Allah speak up, he scolded himself, what kind of a man are you? Tell him you're not his father . . . it's time he knew.

"Well . . . I . . . you see, I was a soldier . . . a Janissary . . . of Sultan Mahmud . . ." he plodded on. "And I had to go back . . . it was my duty. . . ."

"Don't you like me?" The little voice was almost pleading. "I'm really not a bad child. . . ."

Youssef did not answer and little Jason looked around the room, hesitated a moment, then went on.

"I guess you heard about the time I threw the nails down the magazine stairs. . . ." He bowed his head, moving his hands nervously.

"It wasn't a nice thing to do . . . especially since

I knew Aunt Anna was going down to feed the chickens for grandmother. . . ."

Youssef smothered a laugh and eyed the child sternly.

"Oh, you do things like that, do you?"

Little Jason panicked . . . so his father didn't find out . . . he had given himself away.

"But, sir, that was a long time ago . . . I was only four then. I'm six, you know . . . six going on seven."

And he still remembered it . . . after two years . . . thought Joseph.

The child stood up from his chair and approached Youssef slowly. He stopped midway, waiting for Youssef's response.

"Aunt Anna was very fat then . . . it was an awful thing to do . . . she could have killed herself down those steps . . . I'm truly sorry. . . ." He smiled suddenly. "She's thinner now . . . very much thinner, you'll see when you meet her."

As though it mattered to Joseph. He put out his hand to the child.

"Come here, Jason . . . come sit on my lap." Now why on earth did I say a stupid thing like that, he wondered. On my lap indeed.

Little Jason smiled and ran to him.

"On second thought, you're a little too big to sit on my lap, don't you think? Why don't we sit together on the sofa?"

He took the child's hand and led him to the small couch against the wall. It was the same as he remembered, with the soft tapestry and the crocheted pieces on the arms. They sat down and looked at each other in silence.

"Look, son . . ."

The child waited anxiously.

Joseph paused a moment—he was about to tell the boy he was not his father . . . it was time he knew the truth . . . but he was not prepared for this sudden show of interest. He had hardly thought of little Jason—at least not more than a few times—in the past two years. Guilt swept over him now—after all, he was the man who had first held the baby in his arms. He had taken his brother Jason's place . . . he had loved the boy in spite of his inability to show it . . . in spite of his own frustrations. He tried to convince himself the child should know the truth. Perhaps then Joseph would not feel so guilty at his desertion, or neglect, or whatever anyone wanted to call it. Perhaps then little Jason would not feel unloved or unwanted. It hurt Joseph, now, to see that in spite of all the love Helena and her relatives had showered on little Jason, it was his father's absence he missed, his father's presence he longed for. I never had a father, he thought suddenly, and I survived. But how, Youssef, that voice inside him answered, how *did* you survive? Do you want the child, your own nephew, to suffer the emptiness of your own life?

"What's the matter, Father? Did I say something to upset you?" Little Jason was remorseful. "I'm sorry, please forgive me."

Joseph looked into the child's eyes and cursed himself softly. He shook his head . . . no, he could not crush little Jason's faith. Be damned . . . *he,* Youssef, was the father . . . by Allah, he had nurtured the infant, heard his first word, watched him take his first step. No matter that he left it . . . his responsibility would never leave. He pulled the child to him and smiled.

"I am your father, Jason." He put his arms around the small shoulders and held him . . . but only for a moment lest he show signs of unmanliness. He released him and smiled, offering his hand.

"We're going to shake hands like men, and I'm going to explain to you why I had to leave. But I want you to know that I always think of you . . . and always will."

The child's eyes lit up and Joseph thought he saw tears, but the boy turned his head away quickly. Helena has done a remarkable job on him, he thought. He is not a whining sissy or a clinging little monster like some of the other children in the village. Joseph was very proud.

"Grandmother explained about your work . . . and about how you must travel. . . ."

"Well, then, why should you think I'm not your father?" A thought crossed Joseph's mind. "And furthermore, don't your little friends have fathers who sail ships? What about them? They leave home . . . don't they?"

Little Jason thought awhile. It was true, most of the Chiotes were merchant seamen, leaving their families behind while they earned their livelihood. Joseph waited for the child's answer. Little Jason paused . . . it was true, other fathers left, too . . . but that was different. Why did he sense it was not the same? He looked at Joseph in a puzzzled manner.

Joseph wondered if the villagers' gossip had reached the child's ears. Joanna was only two months into her pregnancy when Jason was killed in the massacre. He married her quickly . . . barely a week later . . . for he was to return to Constantinople. Besides, Helena was terrified about Joanna's condition and her reputation . . . in all the holocaust, the bloodshed, people might still begin to count the months, to wonder what went wrong with the gentle, well-mannered Joanna. Joseph was not sorry he married this girl so quickly, for he wanted her the first moment he glimpsed her in the prisoners' quarters.

The child coughed politely and Joseph woke from his reverie.

"It's not easy having a father who goes off to other places. . . . I can't understand this thing about Constantinople, honestly I can't. I know Chios belongs to the Turks, but do you have to help them?"

So Helena had begun her own indoctrination. Somehow Joseph did not mind too much. . . . It looked like little Jason was a full-blooded Greek . . . like his father.

"It's a long story, son," Joseph said, relishing the word "son," and feeling it more than he had ever felt it before. "When you're older you'll understand. In the meantime, when this is over, and it soon will be, how would you like to sail with me to Constantinople and visit the palace?"

At this the child jumped in delight and clapped his hands. Joseph rumpled his hair and felt the urge to swing him into the air. But he was embarrassed at such a display of emotion and held himself back. He put his hand on the boy's shoulder and the two walked out into the terrace where Helena had set the table for their noon meal. The sun shone brightly and the winds blew, bending the trees in the horizon. The smell of the blossoms still persisted although the flowers had begun to fall. Summer was in the air—a summer of contentment. Helena, who had come in holding fish she had just bought from the peddler, looked at her two loved ones and held her breath with happiness. Even if Joseph were to leave, the ice had broken . . . Joseph was slowly coming back to them . . . she sensed it somehow. Soon . . . soon, dear God, she told herself. And so, in a day or two she would watch him go with new hope in her heart. She leaned to the side of the terrace to see if Petros were nearby, and went in to prepare her fish dinner.

The village women stood in the doorways of their homes and watched the strange trio walking down the slope. Three men—three generations, each with his arm around the other's shoulder, smiling as they hurried to the main street of the village where they would browse around and see old friends. Captain Petros, his son-in-law Joseph, and his grandchild, little Jason, were indeed a sight to behold. Their joy was evident as they waved to everyone along the way. The whole village was in a joyous mood—the stone quarries were working full-time again, building was on the rise—there was always a new home or a shop going up. The news from the Greek mainland was good—the war with the Turks was nearing its end, the new Greek government was bearing up well in spite of frequent rumbles among its own members, and hopefully, all Greece would be completely free soon. The Chiotes knew, however, that their island would not be free for a while—it would be years before they would be able to rise again. In the meantime, their businesses flourished and the merchant ships went about carrying precious cargo everywhere. They had had enough bloodshed, they could stand no more. Let the generations to come free Chios from the loose yoke of the Turks. What they wanted was to build up the island again to what it once was—the center of business and education.

The three arrived at Karanikolas's coffeehouse and Joseph turned to little Jason, guessing the child's thoughts.

"Unless I'm mistaken, you would like a piece of . . . say, *pasteli*." Joseph watched the boy break into a wide grin. He had loved the honeyed sesame-seed bar since he was able to chew.

Joseph ordered it from Karanikolas's son—the poor old man was no longer able to work, a quivering mass since the massacre. Little Jason bit into the candy and chewed with glee. They boarded the carriage with another of Karanikolas's sons at the reins and set off for the harbor. Petros would be checking on his own ship, while Joseph spoke to the people on the dock for news of the Moslem vessel due there.

When they arrived they found the harbor in a turmoil. The Sultan's ship had arrived to pick up the diplomats, but there had been an accident . . . they would have to stay over until the mast was repaired. Joseph was secretly pleased and began to turn over the thought of taking his family back with him for a visit.

By sunset, Captain Petros had completed his own work and met Joseph and the boy at Vounaki, the town square, sitting at the small tables under the oak trees. Little Jason knew that this particular oak beside them had served to hang the Chiotes hostages taken by the Turkish governor some years ago. His grandmother had told him the story . . . he wanted to mention it to Joseph but thought better of it. He was puzzled as to why his own father would still be with the enemies of the Greeks. Little Jason did not really hate the Turks . . . in fact he often played with some of the children from the Turkish neighborhood near Thymiana. They were pleasant to be with . . . friendly and easy to get along with. He sighed, doubting he would ever understand the ways of grown-ups.

Petros ordered a cup of Turkish coffee, sweet . . . he emphasized two teaspoons of sugar . . . and turned to Joseph.

"I'm getting the ship ready for possible sailing in a week or two. I was thinking . . . perhaps I would go to Constantinople and see about resuming trade with them again."

"Oh, Grandfather, how wonderful," cried the child. "Can I go too? Please, Grandfather . . . my father said that he'd like us to visit the palace . . . didn't you, Father?"

Captain Petros looked at them, startled. Joseph smiled.

"It seems we've all been reading each other's minds."

Excitement raced through Joseph and he looked at Petros anxiously.

"I would be very proud for the Sultan to meet you . . . and *Kyra* Helena . . . and the boy. . . ."

The idea seemed more appealing to Petros by the minute. How happy Helena would be . . . the thought of pleasing her was uppermost in his mind, for she had brought him the strongest, most sustaining love a human being can feel—he loved Helena with the passion of a twenty-year-old but with the soul and maturity of all his forty-eight years. She had made him feel like an adolescent, giving herself to him with complete abandonment. But most of all, she had made him feel like a man, sharing with him her thoughts and her innermost hopes . . . what few couples share in these turbulent times.

"Let's talk about it tonight with your mother," he said, and got up.

Perhaps it would not be too difficult for him, after all. The rebellion was over and past, and shipping would go on as usual. God knows when we'll see Joseph again, anyway, he thought . . . why not kill two birds with one stone. The more he thought of it, the more the idea appealed to him, and the more anxious he was to go home and surprise Helena.

"Come, men," he ordered again, "let's be off with the good news."

They boarded the carriage and hurried off to Thymiana.

CHAPTER 17

Constantinople

BESMA SMILED AS she pressed the three sesame seeds into the baby's navel. She looked at the tiny face that bobbed from left to right and could not help smiling at this tiny bit of life she had watched come into the world. Remembering her own sons and the joy she had felt when they placed them in her arms, she hugged it tenderly. Selina's baby was dark, like its father . . . it would have been nice to have a little blond one, thought Besma—all the children in the harem are so dark. What a shame that the baby had nothing of Selina's. Besma turned to the exhausted mother who had been bathed and was now being wrapped in the customary rich shawls with the blue beads, the onion and garlic, and the Koran to guard her against the evil eye. She was crying softly. Indeed, mused Besma, she is being accorded the honors of a Sultana, and she dares to cry. The ordeal must have been too much for her . . . it was not an easy time, this birth, but Selina has done well for herself. I suppose she deserves these honors—she has rejuvenated Mahmud. Besma could not help feeling tiny pangs of jealousy, and even envy, when she thought of Mahmud with Selina. For Selina, though quite unknowingly, had awakened Mahmud only to herself. He was still impotent with the woman he loved. . . . Besma trembled with disappointment and frustration at the thought. On the occasions when she lay in the Sultan's bed, their lovemaking consisted merely of caresses and fond words which culminated in nothing more than an embrace, a good-night kiss, and sleep. Besma often wondered, during such moments, if Selina's potion had not also contained a hex against other women in the Sultan's bed. But there was little she could do except pray that the Sultan did not fall in love with Selina. After all, the Serbian slave girl had not only a great sexual power over Mahmud . . . now she had born him a son. The thought gnawed at Besma's insides and she tried to brush it aside by rationalizing—so many beautiful girls had come to the Sultan's bed and given him fiery pleasure, yet he had never wavered in his love for Besma. Why should she worry now? Had he not reduced the number of his concubines after Besma came to him? She would always be the favored one, the only woman Mahmud would ever love.

"Ah, my Sultana," Mahmud often said to Besma's expressed fears, "the physical union may be beautiful, but we have much more. You and I have had many years together . . . I have fathered you six sons. Let these aging years of mine have their fill of winter's carnal passion."

He spoke to her patiently, and kissed her hands, and she was comforted.

"Selina is a beautiful child I take to my bed," he added. "But you, Besma . . . you are the woman I take to my heart."

What could Besma say? She would smile gratefully and leave, content and self-assured in this knowledge, remembering their conjugal bed of old with bittersweet memories.

Mahmud ordered new quarters for Selina and the new child, with the accompanying servants. Motherhood agreed with the Serbian beauty; she was more lovely than ever. Her skin was like dew, her body had taken on a new voluptuousness and the Sultan looked at her with lust, with a greater desire than he had ever felt these autumnal years of his life. He saw the infant briefly, for he was a busy man —all his children saw little of him. His main personal concern was the return of Selina to his bed. The stimulation of their erotic union had worked wonders in his daily life. His body and mind had recaptured a certain peace and satisfaction so long absent. He felt young again, confident, relaxed, better able to cope with the daily problems of his position. He decided to reduce his concubines once again, for now he had no desire to take anyone else to his bed. He trembled with anticipation when he thought of Selina and counted the days until she could come to him.

The months passed—the baby grew handsome and cherubic—a joy to its mother who spent all her time with it. At night she performed her duties with the usual aplomb, but Mahmud noticed that her carefree abandonment, the old gleeful enthusiasm had somehow tempered. True, she was as spirited and capable as always, and even more desirable in motherhood's beauty . . . he never ceased to marvel at the ecstasy she brought his tired body. Yes, he was grateful to Selina, and would do anything to please her. When it came time to name her son, she asked him hesitantly if she could give him her father's name, allowing naturally, the Moslem equivalent. She would call him Saki, which was her contraction of Youssefaki or Joseph. She did not dare speak the name Youssef, for fear her voice would give her away. For the nights she had lain in her bed, large with child, thinking of the handsome Janissary, were tortuous ones. She had never known young love before—the tender passion, the strange outpouring of emotion Youssef had shown her. He was with her always, and she fell asleep with his name on her lips. From the moment of the baby's arrival, her body had ached for Youssef's touch. At first she was not certain the baby was his . . . but now there was no doubt in her mind. The boy was six months old and she could not miss the dark, sad eyes, the features of the man she loved so deeply, a man who was not for her. And yet, was the resemblance only in her eyes? No one seemed to notice. Perhaps it was because Youssef's color and facial structure faintly resembled the Sultan's. She prayed her secret would remain hers, for she knew the alternative meant death for all three of them.

It was the Sultan's first night with Selina after childbirth. She had cried herself to sleep the night before and she looked pale the next morning, her eyes still red. Not wanting to disappoint Mahmud, who nearly went mad those forty days of her required abstinence, she took an aphrodisiac which he delighted in feeding her, and tried to concentrate on their lovemaking. The moments passed and as the Sultan lay over her and gasped his climactic sigh of ecstasy, she tried to stifle a cry. A muffled sob escaped and the Sultan was surprised to see tears stream down her face.

"What is the matter, my little one?" he asked with deep concern. "Is something wrong? Tell me ... whatever it is, I will make it right."

She smiled and held him tightly.

"No, no ... it's just ..." She struggled for an excuse. "Sometimes ... sometimes ..." She groped for words. "... my home ... I think of my family in Serbia."

"Indeed? At such an odd time?" he tried not to show his annoyance. "You think of them, my pet, here in my bed?"

She began to weep uncontrollably and his annoyance turned to compassion. The great, powerful Sultan, the feared ruler of an empire, was moved. . . . He took the weeping girl in his arms and let her cry. Perhaps it is a release, he thought. He knew women felt moments of depression after giving birth, just as they experienced them during monthly periods. Not that he had ever put up with such tantrums before, or expected to ever do so. He would sooner have the girl beheaded than prove such a nuisance. But now he rose from the bed and walked to one of the small tables at the end of the room. From a jewel-encrusted box he removed a large ruby and returned with it to the bed.

"Here"—he smiled—"this is for you ... don't cry."

He tucked the brilliant red stone inside her navel and gently patted her belly. Moved by his gesture, she smiled through her tears and pulled him down to her.

"I'm crying because I'm happy ... and grateful, too, my *effendi*."

Oh, Selina, Sophia, whoever you are, she thought as she kissed him passionately on the lips, how well you play your part. The tears began to flow again, streaming over her naked skin, trickling down to where the ruby gleamed. Mahmud wiped them away, as a sudden thought came to him. Perhaps she had some relatives, someone from Serbia still alive—he might send for them, bring them here to comfort her. Anything, to make her happy again. He promised to look into this matter as he fondled her naked body—by Allah, she was a delight no matter what mood she was in. And later, as Mahmud dozed off with Selina curled up at his side, he scolded himself. Ah, Mahmud, you are concerning yourself too much over a female. This young slave is merely your bedmate. . . . Besma is your true love . . . you must not forget it. Yet, in spite of himself, Mahmud felt the strong attachment to Selina grow even stronger with each day that passed.

CHAPTER 18

"THE PIGS . . . THE dirty, Russian pigs."

Mahmud raged as he paced up and down the room, beating a path in the Oriental rug beneath his pompomed feet. He twisted his beard, raised his fists in the air, fumed and sputtered in a temper that sent the servants scurrying and left his aides frozen in their places. When the Sultan was angry, truly angry, it was best to be silent, for heads rolled at the slightest whim of the Emperor.

"So he finally did it," Mahmud went on, stopping in front of Vizir Al Kashim who had arrived early this morning with his entourage from Russia. Even the presence of his beloved Youssef could not pacify the enraged Sultan who felt cornered by Russia's shocking declaration of war. The forces that kept pounding in Greece had crushed his plans for Greek submission—he was certain that, unless a miracle occurred the last minute, Greece would be lost to the Empire. And now Russia, and that accursed Czar Nicholas, who had played his game of neutrality to blind Mahmud, had finally shown his treacherous colors.

"It was the Greeks," Mahmud screamed at the Vizir, "it was those cursed infidel dogs that brought on this war with Russia . . . Nicholas would not have done this if not for the Greek question."

"Great Sultan, please let me speak," Kashim tried to appease him. "It was inevitable. We all know that the Greek matter has cast the allied powers against us. But know, great and powerful Sultan, that in truth their main concern is not the Greeks, but their own selfish gains."

"What do I care about the reason, Kashim? I only know that the Russians are attacking us, now at this crucial moment when we are embroiled with the Greeks—and one of our battlefields will suffer."

Kashim did not reply. He knew that the Greek war of independence was nearing its end, and that the Ottoman Empire would be the loser. It was decreed so—all world opinion was against the Ottomans. That cursed massacre of Chios had turned the great powers against them and nothing could save the situation. If Mahmud had only listened to Kashim then. But it was too late now. . . . there was a new front and Mahmud must turn his attention to the Russians, for they were the new and greater danger. Still he doubted that Britain would sit back and allow Constantinople to fall into Russian hands. It was a game of personal winnings for each of the great powers. What would be the next move? Only Fate would decree.

"You do not speak, Kashim . . ." Mahmud said, impatient with his Foreign Minister. "You have been in Russia nearly two years. . . . What have you to say?"

"What can I say, your excellency? I have told you everything."

And indeed, he had spent the whole morning and most of the afternoon going over every detail of his stay in St. Petersburg.

"You are getting old, Kashim . . . old and

feeble." Mahmud was merciless when he wanted to be. "I want no excuses, no ideologies. . . . So, the great powers do not care about the Greeks? Bah! The great powers seek their own benefits! Now you have shown me the light."

He turned and threw his hands in the air as he began to pace the floor again.

"Fool . . . of course they seek their own benefit . . . who does not seek his own benefit. . . . I'm confronted with a bunch of idiots, imbeciles, senile diplomats!"

His eye caught Youssef's and he paused, embarrassed. The young man stood at the side, watching Mahmud grimly, wanting to speak but deciding against it. Mahmud saw recrimination in his eyes and it disturbed him . . . he did not want to demean himself before Youssef. But curse it all, he had reason to be enraged.

"Youssef, my boy . . . look at the catastrophe around us. . . . I sent your mission to Russia to save the situation, not bring it to this state of affairs."

Youssef was shocked at Mahmud's unreasoning. How could he possibly blame them for Nicholas's declaration of war?

"Speak up, son . . . speak up," Mahmud prodded.

Youssef could not understand the scene before him. It was only a few hours since their lengthy meeting where they had detailed their stay in Russia, step by step, to the Sultan. Mahmud seemed, then, to have accepted whatever occurred. He listened again to the reason Czar Nicholas had cited for his declaration of war—the protocol of April 4, 1826, which stated that in the event that Mahmud did not act as provided in the protocol with regard to Greece, the great powers were free to intervene either separately or as a group. And since the other powers had made no move, Russia had decided to act on her own. Calculating but true. True and reasonable . . . Mahmud had accepted it calmly. But now, two hours later, Mahmud was raving like a maniac. What his diplomats did not know was that the Sultan had suddenly felt all sides caving in on him. The Greeks on one side, the Russians on the other, and finally Selina, pale and listless, who refused, for the first time, to cater to him. He had left his meeting this past afternoon and hurried to his bedchamber, where he sent for her to help him over this moment of distress. For now he was able to release his frustrations and angers in the act of lovemaking. Praise Allah, it was his salvation, his therapy, his survival. When Selina arrived, it was all she could do to lie down beside him. She was unsmiling, and a strange look crossed her face when she gazed at Mahmud's naked body on the bed. He was infuriated, and would have had her beheaded that very moment. But he thought better of it and sent her away, calling for Besma instead, who calmed his fears momentarily and soothed his wounded ego. She begged him to overlook the whim of a sickly girl.

"She has not been herself since the birth," Besma said to him. "Please, Master, overlook it . . . you have so many important things on your mind . . . do not trouble yourself with such minor things. Her sexual pleasure will return soon . . . wait and see."

"Wait? It's almost a year, woman, and she only goes from bad to worse. Besides, it is her duty to perform for her Sultan, and curse her pleasure."

Besma managed to soothe him, at least to the

point where he erased the thought of beheading her. As he returned to his meeting with Kashim his anger was transferred to the emissary, and to the cursed Russians.

"I have come to a decision," Mahmud said, turning to Youssef. "I am sending a ship to the mainland with more supplies. You will be on it, Youssef . . . you will head a mission there, my boy. You will go to Morea, where the fighting is segregated. This is the area with concentrated troops and the greatest danger. You will meet with our Ahmet Bey, and see about a possible meeting with the Greek rebel leaders . . . perhaps you can work out a solution. Offer them position, power, win them over to our side. . . . there must be *some* leader who can be bought."

He looked grimly at Youssef and touched his shoulder. "This is very important, my son . . . the boundaries are being drawn up by the new Greek government. At least, if we lose, we must try to make them as narrow as possible. But first, kill the *giaours* . . . and meet with their leaders later."

The words rang in Youssef's head—"Kill the *giaours* . . ." Morea . . . so he would be going to the Greek mainland . . . and to Morea, the region of his birthplace. Helena had told him the village of Zagora was located in Thessaly which was the area north of Morea. How strange that Fate should send him there now. The winds had swept him to Chios and Russia, and now he would be going where he least expected . . . the circle was nearing its completion. A chill went through him and he gripped his hands behind him. And then excitement raced through his blood. He would see the place of his childhood . . . but he must help destroy the people there. Frustration . . . confusion . . . could it be guilt . . . set in. He thought of Captain Petros and Helena and realized he must send word to them immediately. There was no point in their coming to Constantinople . . . not when Youssef would be gone . . . not when the Greek situation was so inflamed. They would surely be in danger. . . . He would get word to them immediately.

Youssef excused himself early, soon after the evening meal. And Mahmud, too, in his present state, was more than willing to retire early. His pleasure in seeing Youssef had dimmed only by his turmoil at the state of events, but he made it clear that his personal feelings toward the young man were in no way affected. And Youssef understood, for he knew Mahmud had many problems, many perplexing decisions to make.

Youssef went to his bedchamber before the gong sounded ten. The flames from the lanterns cast eerie shadows on the walls and as he poured himself a cup of *raki* his eyes wandered around the room. He thought of Olga and a stab of pain went through him. He had forced himself not to think of her, to fill his thoughts only with Helena and Chios during his trip back. But now he was home. Home? What a strange-sounding word it seemed now . . . somehow it had lost its meaning. Why, he wondered? Where *is* my home? Home was once Joanna . . . home was Olga . . . he smiled sadly, bitterly. He would never have believed that a woman, a female, would dictate the meaning of home to his heart. What had happened to the fierce Janissary, the loner who needed no one, who wanted nothing except to serve his master, the Sultan Mahmud? He would give anything to have Olga beside him now—to hold her in his arms. To sit on the sofa and talk with her . . . to listen endlessly to her words, her thoughts, her ideas on life and the world. His heart beat fast and his head began to throb. He poured another cup of *raki* and sat down on the bed, his head in his hands. What was the matter with him? A cold sweat covered his brow and he shook his head to clear it. As he lifted his face, his gaze fell to the corner of the room where the huge palms stood. The lanterns' glow cast shadows of the leaves against the wall. For a moment he thought he saw a face behind it— Olga? Was he seeing Olga's face, in his longing, his yearning for her? And then the face moved, and a figure stepped from behind the shrub. She held a child in her arms . . . she looked frightened and pale . . . she was the most beautiful female he had ever seen.

"Selina!" He gasped, and anger overtook him. She was the last person he wanted to see. The child whimpered and he looked at it with curiosity . . . it looked familiar.

"I had to come . . . I had to, Youssef. . . ." She began to cry and he hurried to her lest the servants hear. "I wanted you to see your son."

Youssef's breath stopped for a moment, and his heart beat fast. His first reaction was anger, but when he looked at the child again, into his deep black eyes, the half-closed lids, the nose, the mouth. . . .

"My son?" he said, half question, half answer, for he knew, almost immediately, that the child was his.

He approached them, and touched the boy's

head, the dark hair, his olive skin. A half-smile crossed his face—a son . . . he had a son. And yet he could never claim him.

"I'm leaving for the Greek mainland. . . ." was all he could say.

"I haven't been able to sleep or eat . . . or do anything since the baby came." Her eyes pleaded with Youssef, and her love for him filled her countenance. "I love you, Youssef, you are the only man I will ever love."

"I feel . . . I can't find words to say how I feel, Selina . . . this should have never happened. It's my fault . . . I should have made you leave that night."

He suddenly became angry and turned on her.

"You little bitch . . . I told you to stay away from me. . . . Look what you've caused . . . it's not enough that we'll get ourselves beheaded"—as though it mattered to him now—"but this child . . . why should this child pay for our mistakes?" If Mahmud found out, the child would surely be put to death.

"Don't you understand?" she pleaded, ignoring his anger as the tears rolled down her cheeks. "You are everything to me . . . the only man I ever loved."

"You will forget me . . . you *have* to. . . ." His anger slowly dissolved and his head spun in confusion. "It was a mistake . . . such a thing is impossible. . . ." He tried to reason with her . . . the very idea of continuing their relationship was maddening.

"It's not impossible . . . please . . . don't you see."

"You have Mahmud . . . and your son . . ." he said firmly.

"I have Mahmud . . . and *your* son," she shouted back, barely able to see him through her tears.

He stood there, not moving, not speaking . . . trying to absorb her words. . . . His son . . . his son! Guilt and pleasure intertwined, squeezing each other as though to crush it, so that each could rise, the conqueror.

"My son?" he said finally, "by Allah, I am caught in a labyrinth, in a web that will crush us all."

Youssef looked at the little boy again, more carefully this time, scrutinizing him. Was she lying? Could she be using this ploy to be with him again? Well, it wouldn't work—child or no child, she would never be in his bed again. His thoughts were interrupted by the appearance of a servant girl, one of Selina's who took the child away, as though on cue. Selina waited and when Youssef made no move toward her, she moved quietly about the room, finally pausing to pour herself some *raki*. Youssef stood there watching her, her every movement fascinating him in spite of his anger. He had no desire for a woman tonight, not that way . . . all desire had left him since Olga's death.

"You're wasting your time, Selina . . . go away before you get your head lopped off."

He did not want to be unkind, but he was suddenly very tired. Tired of the palace, of his life, of everything. He turned his back and stared out the window at the half moon in the sky. There were no stars, and the empty blackness brought him a dark foreboding. He wished he were alone with his thoughts. He would drink more *raki* and go straight to bed . . . it had been a tiring day.

He turned around and faced Selina in her nakedness . . . she had removed her clothing and stood there somberly, a sheer piece of silk in her hand. She was a vision, a goddess in the night, and Youssef could not help admiring the perfection of her. He shook his head vehemently, grabbed her clothing from the floor and handed it to her.

"Go . . ." he said gently. "I have too many things on my mind tonight."

He did not have the strength or the desire to fight with her . . . even to reprimand her any longer. And she sensed this, for without an argument, she took her clothing and walked away. His eyes followed her to the door, watching her small buttocks swaying like small waves in the ocean, the whiteness of her thighs, her dainty ankles. And her hair . . . he looked up at the head of pure gold that cascaded over her back. He reached her as she touched the door. Without a word he picked her up in his arms and took her to his bed. Then, drawing the silk drapes around the cushions, he lay down beside her, his passion overcoming his reason. He loved Olga, he missed her, longed for her . . . but he was young and virile, and this beautiful creature was more than he could bear. He moved inside her and her legs held him tightly, as though she would never let go. She moaned and shrieked and whispered her love for him. And he held her all night, moving over her, letting her lay over him in all her shamelessness. They dozed on and off through the night, waking to make love, sleeping again, and just before the dawn broke, Youssef had the dream again. He was watching the two women slip from his arms, and as he looked on Olga's pleading face, dissolving at his feet, he turned to the younger girl, to Selina, who was melting into a pool of blood. She woke, frightened, staring at the strange look of Youssef.

Then, gently trying to calm him, she helped him lie back on the bed.

"Olga . . ." he whispered. "Olga . . . the blood . . . the omen." He stared at Selina, "And now, Selina . . ."

He turned his face away so the girl would not see the horror there. He did not want to frighten Selina, and tried to explain that it was merely a bad dream, probably from too much liquor. And just before she left, he tried to tell her they must not see each other again. But his words fell empty . . . she had no intention of listening to him . . . and he knew it.

"You will be leaving soon . . . I know. . . ."

"As soon as the ship is loaded. . . ."

"Will you be gone long?"

"I don't know. . . ." But his heart said, I don't care. No place seemed to hold him. He wondered how he would find his village, the people who were his enemies . . . and his bloodline. What a strange combination, he thought. Yet he wanted to go, he was curious to see these Greeks of the mainland who had caused such turmoil in the world. This would be his first contact with them . . . he felt there was much to be learned.

He felt guilty about Selina—he did not want to betray Mahmud in this way. And yet, he would be gone in a week or so . . . would it be so bad to take whatever pleasure he could, when he could? He had the feeling that he would not be seeing slave girls like this again . . . or riches and palaces . . . or, for that matter, Constantinople. He was beginning to feel that in betraying Mahmud he was giving up his rights as an Ottoman. He cursed himself, not knowing what he sensed . . . or how he really felt. He seemed to be dangling on strings.

I have never been my own man, he thought . . . but then, who is? Yes, who really is? He knew that when Mahmud learned of his betrayal—if he did—Youssef's life would not be worth the clothes he wore. And so, he rationalized, he would let Selina in his bed . . . he would drink of her sweetness, for with Selina the pain disappeared for a little while, clothed as it was in her love and fiery passion.

But when the sun was at its peak and his mind had cleared in the daylight, remorse swept over him again. How could he betray his Sultan, the only father he ever knew? And he swore he would not touch Selina again.

Several days passed . . . Selina came to Youssef at every chance. She brought the child and he played with him, holding his chubby fingers in his hands, watching him giggle as his mother tickled him. He was walking now and he tottered around, falling from time to time, getting up and dusting himself off, watching Youssef with his deep, serious eyes. Youssef thought of Helena at these moments . . . he wished she could see little Saki . . . and yet guilt swept over him, and shame, too. What would she think, Helena of all people. . . . At such moments he wished he, Youssef, had never been born. And then he quickly dispatched a letter to the Sofronis household telling Petros and Helena of the change in his plans—there was no point in her coming with little Jason. Even Petros's arrival was not a sound judgment, in view of the Greek situation. The Greeks of Constantinople, who had always been accepted as part of the Ottoman community, were looked upon unfavorably now. He knew Helena would worry about his departure for the Greek mainland, and assured her he would be serving only in a diplomatic capacity, that he would not be involved in fighting with the Greeks. . . . Poor Helena, another blow for her to bear, wondering if her son would be off to slaughter his own people. Somehow the taste for blood Youssef once knew was gone—he had little desire to cut down Christians, much less the Greeks. He longed to find peace somewhere, to find his own soul, his niche in life. He hoped it was not too late. Soon this would be over, the bloodshed and the fighting . . . and then, then perhaps he would find where he belonged, make a new life. He was afraid to wish for too much.

The nights were easier now, with Selina at his side. She came to him at stolen moments, whatever hours she could spare when Mahmud did not need her. And Youssef poured his pain and his anxieties into her body, finding relief in her arms, in the smoothness of her white, silken skin, the sweetness of her lips, the ecstasy of their physical union. But this liaison with Selina was little more than a physical one—he felt pity for her, knowing how she suffered, how much more she would suffer after he was gone, but his heart was buried with Olga . . . it could never belong to another woman.

The Ottoman ship sailed in clear weather, and after a few days one of Mahmud's trusted servants asked for a private audience with the Sultan. It was a matter of grave importance . . . he had uncovered a startling secret, and hoping for a rich reward, he revealed the betrayal of Selina and Youssef, and the child of their union. Mahmud listened to the man in disbelief.

"And how did you learn this startling bit of information?"

"My wife, great Sultan"—the servant smiled with self-confidence—"my wife is Selina's personal maid."

"Indeed," Mahmud replied, watching the informer carefully, smiling as he nodded. "You should be very pleased with yourself."

Then turning to a servant, he ordered the immediate presence of the man's wife. When the trembling girl hesitated before the Sultan, the informer whispered in her ear, prodding her to speak, reminding her of the rich rewards that awaited them. She reaffirmed her husband's revelation and stood silently watching the color creep up in the Sultan's face . . . he looked as though he were about to burst his blood vessels. The informer waited for some word from Mahmud and upon hearing nothing, spoke again.

"We have rendered you a valuable service, *effendi*, we know you are pleased with our loyalty."

"Indeed I am," Mahmud finally replied, barely able to speak, as something choked him.

"Yes, I am pleased . . . and grateful . . . and you deserve a rich reward."

He motioned to a servant who left the room and returned with one of the palace guards.

The reward must be so valuable, the Sultan is furnishing me a guard, the informer thought with glee and winked at his wife who stood pale and trembling beside him. Mahmud looked at the guard and pointed to the informers. The cries were stifled in their throats as the saber came down on them—the man's head rolled on the floor and the girl lay bleeding on the Persian rug. Mahmud stormed out of the room raging, and Besma, who was hiding behind the thick draperies rushed off to warn Selina.

Selina's quarters were in an uproar as Besma shouted her warnings.

"The child," she cried, "give me the child, Selina ... and go hide.... I will try to fend him off."

But Selina had no intention of leaving. She would pacify Mahmud ... she was confident of her power ... and if perhaps she failed, what did it matter? Youssef had gone, she would probably never see him again. But the law of self-preservation overruled her heart's passion and she set about to create the mood for her meeting with the Master.

Besma took the child to one of her trusted servants—but how trusted can she be, she wondered, in view of what happened to Selina—and instructed her to hide him. She ordered a guard to follow her and make certain all was well before reporting back to her. Then she rushed off to Mahmud, hoping to prevent further retaliation.

Mahmud burst through Selina's door and walked into her salon. She was lying on pillows drinking wine, and when she saw him she jumped to her feet. She was wearing very little and he saw the outline of her body through the silk cloth.

"Such a beautiful body ..." He smiled sardonically. "... and I thought it was only for me."

"But it was, *effendi*, it is. ..." She smiled and her eyes twinkled as they had in the past. "It will always be yours."

"My little Slavic beauty," he said, grinning wryly, "my little actress ..."

He spied the pearl necklace around her neck.

"I see you wear the pearls I gave you at our first meeting."

"Yes, Sire, do you remember that night?"

"You lied even then," he said and he signaled to the guard who had entered the room. "Come here, my little blonde wench."

She came and pressed against him and he kissed her lips harshly, then her neck. She felt him fire up with passion, but he suddenly tensed and straightened up, holding her a few feet away from him. He expected her to plead and beg ... for she knew why he was here. Oh, the clever, treacherous female knew very well why he was here. But Selina made no effort ... it did not matter to her.

The guard came closer and Mahmud raised his hand. The pearls broke and scattered in different directions, bouncing on the marble floor, leaving trailing dots of red in their path. The blood splattered everywhere, and Selina's body crumpled at Mahmud's feet, the throat slashed, the large ruby stone remaining firm inside her navel. Selina felt little pain, for the head was practically severed—it had been a quick death. Mahmud was sorry it was over so quickly—he had wanted to see her squirm with pain, shriek in horror. He looked down at her, infuriated to see a half-smile on her face. She had won the last word after all. He turned away, sick in his heart and body, in his mind. He hated Selina ... but most of all he hated that infidel pig, Youssef. . . .

"Those cursed Greeks . . . they're never to be trusted. I should have killed him off with the other Janissaries ... he will hound me forever."

He was crushed ... his most trusted servant, the soldier who guarded him, who worshiped him, whom he had trusted with his very life ... Youssef had betrayed him more than anyone else.

A scream of rage and passion, of heartbreak and disillusionment, shattered the air. Mahmud looked up at the ceiling, crying to Allah for revenge.

"Send word immediately," the Sultan shouted, "send word to the Greek mainland . . . the traitor must die . . . death to the cursed Youssef."

A ship was ordered to prepare for sailing. The kindly, loving Sultan wanted Youssef's head, too . . . wanted it shipped to the palace as proof of his death. He would not rest until the blood of that cursed Greek flowed on that cursed soil of his people. He paced in his room like a caged animal.

"The child," he screamed, suddenly remembering the offspring of the traitors, "find the child and behead him."

The guards set out to search the harems and the children's quarters. But Besma had done her work well. The child had gone from hand to hand—from the palace, outside to the city, where it was taken to Greeks who would eventually place it on a ship leaving Constantinople. The ship would be making a stop in Syros, an island not too far from Chios in the Aegean Sea, on its way south to Egypt. It would be safe there, and perhaps one day it would find its way to Chios, to its grandmother. Besma had researched her work well—she was a mother and she knew the pain, she felt the compassion. As she pondered the final moves of her workings, she received a message from Mahmud. He had locked himself in his quarters for days—now he wanted Besma, and only Besma, to come to him, to hold him and comfort him. She is my woman, he thought, my own kind, my true love. And he waited with anxiety to fall in her arms and let his emotions bare.

Part IV

CHAPTER 19

At Sea . . . 1828

THE SKIES DARKENED and storm clouds moved swiftly across the horizon. From the deck of the *Sultan II*, sailors scurried around the sails that billowed in the ever-increasing velocity of the winds. Youssef leaned on the railing and looked down on the frothing waves. Yes, a storm was brewing, and it was like the turmoil inside his soul. The closer they came to Greek territory, the more tense, the more apprehensive he became. He was not in the mood for facing Greeks . . . he was not in the mood for facing anyone. All he wanted was to be left alone in his misery and confusion. The thought of the little boy he had left behind brought a strange, bitter joy to this man who could not decide who he really was, or where he really belonged. Now, more than ever, he felt a stranger among all men. Perhaps if he would concentrate on the work before him, he might forget his own frustrations. He stared at the black waters, but even here he saw the face of the child—his child—and a new pain crowded in with the old. It was not until a huge wave struck the ship, almost knocking him to the deck that he realized where he was. As the men shouted danger he rushed to help the others who had come on deck.

It was more than a summer storm—there, sighted in the distance, were swirling black clouds coming their way. The ship was in the center of the storm and the helmsman turned pale as confusion overtook the ship. The captain began to shout orders, hoping to avoid the panic that seemed inevitable, cursing his men for it. The winds howled and the ship began to reel sideways, up and down, tossing about helplessly in the darkness that engulfed them.

"Change course . . ." shouted the captain to his man at the wheel, hoping to avoid the brunt of the storm. "Six degrees starboard . . . hurry!"

He turned to the crew and shouted against the wind.

"Man the sails! We're switching course!"

They would lead to the land in the distance, westward. The men scurried about like frightened animals, hurrying to carry out the commands, as huge waves beat against the ship and washed over the deck. The men held on tightly for dear life as the water swept over them, and it seemed to Youssef that Allah had joined all the foreign gods in the heavens to prevent this ship from reaching its destination.

They had now made the turn and the ship rolled over the waves, up and down, like a toy in the waters, as it headed west. The winds seemed to be pushing the ship, prodding it stubbornly toward the islands in the distance. For a while the storm seemed to subside and a steady rain fell ominously, but the winds began to rage again and it went on for a day and a night, and finally, when the men were too exhausted even to care about the danger, the winds subsided and the ship began to sail on calm seas. The men fell to their knees and praised Allah, and while the captain charted the new course, they went about their work cleaning up the debris and setting about to repair a hole near the stern where a mast had fallen. Several members of the crew were missing, and the others realized, after careful search, that they had been washed overboard. It was a bad omen, and the men cursed the Greek infidels who were the reason for this voyage.

Youssef was in the stateroom with Vizir Kayam, the elder statesman who would represent Mahmud at the council in Morea. And as they sipped *raki* from golden cups, they pondered the route of this voyage, wondering where they were, and where Fate would take them. For they knew they were considerably off course, and that these were dangerous waters. The Greek Revolution was approaching its end and patience on all sides was exhausted. The once-friendly feelings between many Greeks and Turks who had coexisted for many years had been cut by the seven long years of bloodshed and poverty—the costly price of freedom. But the *giaours* wanted freedom, so let them pay.

"To the Greeks"—Kayam raised his cup and smiled bitterly—"may they never breathe the air of freedom."

Youssef remained silent, eyeing Kayam without expression.

"And yet it seems they will be breathing it, *effendi*," Youssef finally said.

"They are dogs," Kayam bellowed. "So they win independence . . . they won't be breathing free air . . . not for long. No, my friend, they are bickering and fighting among themselves already. Ha!" He gulped his drink and poured another. "The Greeks don't have to worry about us . . . they'll annihilate each other if we just leave them alone."

Youssef felt uneasy at Kayam's words. But what did he care what happened to the Greeks? He pondered awhile . . . so that was it, they were fighting among themselves! He suddenly wished their ship had not pulled through the storm . . . he had no desire to reach any destination, be it Ottoman or Greek.

A cry from the deck made them start.

"A ship! A ship with the Russian flag!" the watch shouted in the calm of the aftermath.

Youssef and Kayam ran up on deck and saw the small vessel in the distance. The watch at the top of the mast was looking through his glass. He called down to them again.

"It's a Russian flag."

"Must be a Greek ship," Kayam said, "the Greeks use the Russian flag."

The Greeks had once run up the flag of their own design—white, with an icon of the Holy Virgin in the center, which assured safety against attack by Christian corsairs, but since the Treaty of Kuchuk-Kainarji in 1774, they had been flying the Russian flag.

The watch looked again, and shouted to those below.

"I beg forgiveness, *effendis*, my error . . . it is our flag . . . an Ottoman ship." He breathed a sigh of relief.

Yet he could have sworn the first look showed a Russian flag.

"The fool," muttered Kayam and looked more closely at the approaching ship.

As it came nearer, they could see the red Ottoman banner with its horizontal blue stripe across the center. The ship approached and both crews gathered on deck as Youssef watched curiously from the other side. Then he turned abruptly and ran to the captain. Before he could reach him the cannonball ripped the air, hitting the ship's mast. It cracked and slowly fell to the deck. Youssef shouted a warning to Kayam but it was too late. The mast fell on the unfortunate Vizir crushing him instantly, as the flying debris sent Youssef sprawling on the deck. Another cannonball split the ship in half, throwing him into the water with the others. In minutes the *Sultan II* was at the bottom of the Aegean, strewn pieces of its remnants bobbing up and down in the water with a few survivors clinging to them. The Greek ship continued its course . . . en route for Morea with supplies and ammunition. Hopefully, this would be the last voyage of the *Seagull* in warring conditions. Soon it would be sailing as part of the new Greek merchant navy. Praise be to God, the sailors shouted with joy as their ship headed for their destination.

Youssef clutched the piece of wood and drifted with the waves as he watched the island in the horizon. If he could reach shore, all was well. But the thought had no sooner lodged in his mind than the storm brewed again, beginning with a light rain that seemed to pierce his head. The winds increased and tossed him west, away from the island. He looked anxiously for the others, but there were only pieces of flotsam here and there. He was being swept away toward the mainland on the other side. And though he did not know his direction, he was floating toward the small peninsula where the tiny village of

Zagora nested. Fate plays strange games in man's life . . . a chessboard where he is moved front and back, where he is crowned or abolished. And the Fates had decided that Youssef was to return to his birthplace . . . and so the winds cooperated, and swept him along, tossing him finally onto the shores of Thessaly.

He lay on the pebbled sands exhausted, breathing deeply of the clear, fresh air. The sun was out, as though to welcome the long-lost voyager. He looked around him wondering where he was and tried to chart in his mind the route he had taken. They were near Skyros when the typhoon appeared, and since they headed west he gathered the island he had passed was Skiathos . . . or was it Skopelos? He was not certain. He knew however, that he was on the Greek mainland, and if the island were indeed Skiathos, he was not too far away from his village. How strange, he thought, that I should refer to Zagora as my village . . . it is not my village at all. It was the home of *Kyra* Helena and Jason . . . not of Youssef, the Janissary. He smiled in spite of himself. How ironic that he should refer to himself still as the Janissary, when the Janissaries were no more. Ah, Youssef, he said to himself, actually you are nothing. . . you are no one . . . and he lay back on the sands, letting the hot sun warm his skin.

He fell into a deep, exhausted sleep, and when he woke, the sun was almost setting. He jumped to his feet and ran up the slope, losing himself in the thick foliage. He would have to find something to eat, and then . . . then what? He would not think further. Whatever would be, would be. It was August and wild berries were ripened on the bushes. He ate them hungrily, and hurried on, hoping to find water somewhere. By nightfall, he was very thirsty and when he reached the first village he waited until midnight when all was quiet, to steal to the well where he drank his fill. He then filled a goatskin that lay nearby, helped himself to several tomatoes hanging outside to dry, and went on his way. For two days he hid, coming out only at night to steal food.

On the second evening, he reached the outskirts of Zagora . . . unbeknown to him, Fate had planned his destination. A strange feeling came over him, and somehow he knew he was on sacred ground . . . the twisting of his insides told him, and the flutter of his heart . . . and he felt ashamed . . . ashamed to be acting in what was an unmanly manner. He reached a small incline and hid in the thick bushes to watch a group of men sitting around a fire. There were over twenty of them and he noticed muskets at their feet and the pistols in their belts. There were daggers too—jewel-encrusted daggers stashed in their waistbands—and Youssef wondered from what Turks they had taken them. One of the men was engrossed in the whittling of a piece of wood and Youssef watched the flames glow against his face as he leaned over the fire to catch the light for his work. An old man, wrinkled and bent, sat between two younger men who were younger images of him. They looked at him from time to time and smiled as he smoked his long, two-foot pipe. Youssef could not help noticing the Ottoman custom so happily espoused. How similar these people are, he thought. Actually they could be Turks sitting around that fire, with their black mustaches and sunburned skins. Youssef listened as one of the men spoke.

"It's almost over," he said, and Youssef wondered if he were the leader of the group.

"My men are ready to leave anytime," said another.

"Mine, too . . ."

"When do we start out?"

They were a group of leaders from the various bands in the area. Anthos, the man who stood up, was the oldest in experience and most respected by the others.

"We know that Russia sent over a million and a half rubles . . . and France sent five hundred thousand francs, for a start. . . ."

The men's eyes lit up.

"That means there's enough money to finish the fight."

"Yes . . . and to help in setting up our new nation . . ." Anthos replied solemnly. "It's going to be a difficult, long road. . . ."

"But we've got to finish off the fighting in Morea . . . there're just a few ends to tie up, they say, and we can all sit and breathe free again."

One of the men hesitated. "Anthos . . . tell me," he said finally, "is it true that the leaders in Morea are fighting among themselves?"

"Who told you such a thing?"

"The crew from the *Seagull* was talking about it. . . ."

The men from that Chian ship had been transporting supplies and ammunition to Morea since the onset of the rebellion, and had maintained contact with the fighters there. They carried back the news of this bickering that had started—gossip the Greeks could ill afford to have spread.

"Forget it," Anthos quickly retorted. "So the

leaders had some misunderstandings . . . it's only natural."

The chief was uncomfortable, unconvinced by his own words . . . for he did not believe them.

"Remember, men, that we Greeks are human . . . and seven years of hunger and struggle and despair can bring about many emotions. . . . Our aim is to unite now, to smash the enemy these final days of our great war of independence."

A wild rabbit scurried in the bushes in front of Youssef and he fell abruptly to the ground. The group of men stopped, a hushed silence filling the night air. From afar, the song of a nightingale drifted in the wind, and for a moment all God's world was stilled, listening to the music.

"Who's there?" Andriko's voice broke the stillness.

Several of the others leaped up with rifles in hand. Youssef held his breath; then, without thinking, or hesitating, he parted the bushes and stepped forward. He walked slowly to the fire as one of the men aimed his rifle.

"Stop!" Anthos shouted to his man seeing that Youssef was unarmed. "Don't shoot."

All eyes stared at the ragged Ottoman clothes.

"A Turk . . . a filthy Turkish pig . . ." Andriko jumped up from his whittling and leaped at Youssef with his knife.

"Wait, Andriko . . . wait, I say!" Anthos blocked him with his huge, peasant body.

"Let me rip his heart out, Captain, the way they ripped out the hearts of our women. . . ."

"You've done your share of ripping hearts, I'm sure," Youssef said quietly, unafraid before this enemy who waited to tear him apart.

And then Anthos spoke. He looked at Youssef intently, curiously, with a question in his mind . . . but there was no question in his words.

"Yes, my Ottoman enemy," Anthos said slowly, "yes, perhaps we, too, have ripped out many hearts. War is cruel, and unjust. But we ripped those hearts out to gain our freedom, and to avenge the thousands that fell under your Sultan's sword. But you . . . you killed so that we remain your slaves."

Youssef looked at Anthos, unaffected by his words. The Greek took a deep breath and continued.

"Know this, Turk . . . a Greek kills for two reasons and two reasons only . . . one is freedom, that evasive bird that flies above us these four hundred years . . . and the other—the other is honor. Remember that!"

No one spoke. Youssef stood rooted to the ground, the words of Anthos penetrating his brain, piercing it, burning him. These were the infidels, the dogs that needed cutting down, that required subjugation. He felt a flutter of wings near him, and turned abruptly, looking for the bird. Was it in his mind? And then he felt a presence beside him . . . it was Jason . . . he could swear that he felt his brother beside him . . . and Jason was smiling, as though at last he was able to communicate to Youssef what he meant about being a Greek. Youssef shook his head, terrified that he was losing his mind, and finally looked up at the men who watched him with suspicion and amusement.

"He looks mad . . ." said Yorgos.

"Let's shoot him and be done with it."

"Wait." It was Anthos again. "Who are you, and how did you get here?"

He pulled him closer to the fire and looked at his face carefully.

"What are you waiting for, Anthos?" shouted his second in command. "Why do you waste time? Kill him and let's be off . . . we have more important things to do."

Anthos ignored the words and signaled for his men to be seated again. He motioned for them to give Youssef a piece of the meat from the spit, and poured him a cup of wine, ignoring the angry looks of the others.

Youssef ate hungrily, grateful for the generosity of Anthos. When he had finished and drank his second cup of wine he wiped his mouth and sat back, watching the angry fighters whose eyes pierced him. And then he told them of his sea voyage, the wreckage and his mission to Morea with the Vizir.

"So the Sultan finally accepted Fates' decree—that Greece will be free at last."

Anthos found this man strange. "Where did you learn to speak Greek so well?" he asked, knowing that many Ottomans spoke the Greek language, just as Greeks spoke fluent Turkish. Yet he had a suspicion there was more to the language than met the eye.

"I lived in Chios for several years . . . I was married to a Greek girl. . . ." He changed the subject quickly, "I was to sit in on the drawing of the boundaries of the new nation. I had the proper credentials . . . but everything was lost in the storm."

"Kill him, Anthos . . . you'll be sorry if you don't," the men persisted.

"He's of no use to us . . . get rid of him."

"Were you of Christian birth?" a voice asked softly, and they all turned to the figure of a man with one arm. He was about fifty, darker in skin than the others, with lines on his face and his muscled body bulging through his clothes.

"I am an Ottoman in the diplomatic service of the Sultan Mahmud," he said proudly, "and I was once the Sultan's favorite Janissary."

"Janissary!" The one-armed man leaped from the ground and ran to Youssef. He pulled him closer to the fire and looked at him, scrutinizing his face.

"I knew it! I knew it was you . . . Joseph! . . . the moment I looked at you I knew!" Tears filled the man's eyes and he embraced Youssef, who drew back warily. The men sat numb in their places, startled at this strange scene.

"Joseph, I'm Costas . . . Costas . . . try to remember," the man said. "Think back . . . I used to take you fishing . . . fishing and hunting too. . . ." He laughed aloud, slapping his thigh and turning to the others. "This boy's a Greek—a Greek from Zagora. I knew his mother, the family . . . I practically raised him and his twin brother. . . . My God." He looked at Youssef, unable to believe his eyes. "It's twenty-three years ago, and I recognized you." He laughed nervously, embarrassed that tears had filled his eyes again. "God and all saints in heaven . . . you're back, Joseph."

"I am not your Joseph . . . I am Youssef, the Ottoman Janissary."

Costas chose to ignore the remark. He patted the stump of his missing left arm.

"So I didn't lose the arm for nothing . . . *halali, halali* to the arm."

And Costas quickly told his comrades of the night Helena had escaped with Jason after killing Yusbasi Hassan, the abductor of her other son, Joseph.

Costas had fought off Turkish sentries who had caught them as they rowed to the escape ship that waited in the harbor, bound for Chios with refugees from the Turkish sword.

Anthos was confused by it all. Whatever the story, legally this was a Turkish prisoner . . . by the law of the hills he should be shot on sight. Yet, looking at Costas, he knew he could not issue the order. He sent Youssef off with two men while he conducted a hasty meeting.

"Look, Anthos," Costas pleaded, "you have nothing to gain by killing him. He could prove helpful to us. Believe me, he won't harm us . . . or betray us, I'll stake my life on that. Let's take him with us to Morea. If we run into the Turks, he can be of considerable help . . . and if we're with the Greeks, well, we can use him as an interpreter or liaison . . . or whatever. . . ." He grabbed Anthos's arm and held it. "Don't shoot him, Anthos, I beg of you."

"We leave in a few days," Anthos finally said. "All right, Costas, you will get your way. You have been a brave fighter and served your country better than most two-armed men. . . ." He smiled and slapped him on the back. "But you will be responsible for him . . . are you willing to come along?"

"Come along? Why, you couldn't hold me back." He let out a cry of joy and slapped his knee.

"That one arm of yours certainly gets a lot of use," Anthos said laughing as he slapped Costas, too, and whistled for the men to return. They doused the fire, picked up the remnants of the meat which they wrapped in cloth, and headed back to the village. Youssef went with Costas quietly, with fear and apprehension of what he was to discover, but he asked no questions, showed no emotion. Costas talked incessantly, trying to put the young man at ease.

"My wife will prepare hot water for you . . . a nice bath, then change your clothing and have a good night's sleep." Costa talked to him patiently now, as though humoring him, and Youssef tried not to show his annoyance.

The next morning as he sat with the couple at the table he felt rested and more optimistic about himself. He drank his warm milk quietly, watching Costas and his wife dunk their bread with gusto and eat it with brown olives . . . Chian olives. The three of them ate without talking, and the silence was embarrassing. Finally Costas spoke.

"As soon as we've finished, I'll take you around so you can see the village . . . you were born here, Joseph, I'm sure you'll remember many things."

Youssef looked at him without replying, and Costas somehow understood. It was a long time, lifetimes ago . . . what can one expect from a child torn from its mother's arms at such an early age?

They spent the day walking through the hills, looking at the streams, following the paths down the mountain to the sea where remembrances slowly began to appear. Yes, Youssef remembered the spot they frequented, and he remembered still the fish twisting on the line and the way he and Jason leaped with joy at their catch, watching anxiously as Costas removed it from the hook and placed it in their basket. Yes, he was remembering a great deal . . . a new world was opening up to him. Costas used to build a fire and cook the fish there on the shore. And the twins would eat the delicious food and lick their fingers, and then they would all set out with the rest of their catch for home, tired and happy after their joyous afternoon. Youssef began to remember those days, the feeling of contentment known only by children; warmth flooded his heart . . . and nostalgia swept over him. He asked to see more, and Costas took him everywhere. They covered every narrow pathway of the village, every stream and rivulet, every hill and valley in the surrounding area. Youssef walked on this Greek soil he had forgotten these many years and breathed the Greek air so many men had died for. And in a few days he knew every spot in Zagora, and he begged Allah to let him see Helena again so that he might tell her of his new discovery. There was only one thing he had not seen, and he thought it strange that Costas should not have taken him there first. Perhaps he was saving it as the crowning pleasure. He did not question Costas about it, but waited, wondering why he had not mentioned Helena's home in Zagora. And then, at the end of the second day—it was nearly twilight—Costas turned to Youssef somberly.

"There is one more thing you must see . . . the house where you were born . . . the house where your mother lived until they took you away."

Youssef looked at him anxiously, smiling his approval.

"And your father . . . do you remember your father?"

The blood drained from Youssef's face.

"No . . . and I have no desire to see this man you say is my father. . . . The house, yes, I would like to see the house . . . but the man, no. . . ."

"Joseph, listen to me . . ." Costas pleaded, "he's

old and he's sick . . . in fact the villagers say he came back to die."

"He's not old . . . he's useless. . . ." Youssef had heard the stories in Chios. Although Helena never discussed her husband with him, Joanna had gathered bits and pieces from their cousins and often spoke of him to Youssef. He was ashamed of this man who had abandoned his wife and sons, never caring for them all those long years.

"They told me he went back to Chios to see my brother and *Kyra* Helena . . . just before the massacre . . ." Youssef said slowly, "and they sent him away."

Costas did not know what to say.

"I'm glad they sent him away. . . ." He turned, embarrassed. And then his face brightened for a moment. "You came from Skyros, didn't you? You were fishing near these waters."

"Yes . . ." Costas eyes looked far away. ". . . And I met your mother and both of you boys. . . ."

"And you didn't have the heart to leave . . . you left your safe island to come here, with the Turks breathing down your back. . . ." A light seemed to come on in Youssef's mind. He was ashamed of his father, and he had lost the trust of Mahmud, who was the only father Youssef ever knew. But now, suddenly, as though a miracle . . . he had found someone else—Costas, who cared for them, who had sacrificed a part of himself for him.

"I never regretted it, Joseph . . . not for a moment," Costas said and embraced the young man.

"Will you see your father . . . for my sake?"

"Where is he?"

"He's waiting at the house to see you."

"I don't really want to see him."

"He's not old in years, Joseph, but he's old in spirit—the flesh, too."

A sudden thought struck Youssef. His mother had remarried—that meant she was told that Stratis was dead—Helena would never have considered divorce. He feared for her now, wondering what she would say to this discovery. He told Costas, who set his mind at ease.

"I'm sure the Church has straightened it out for her, Youssef," he assured him. "The Greek Orthodox faith grants divorces in such cases, don't worry about it."

Youssef hoped this was true, otherwise Helena's marriage to Captain Petros was not legal. Even now, the man destroys, Youssef thought, and hated him at this moment. Strange, he had never thought of his father before, never wondered where he was. And now this sudden hatred awoke within him and began to grow.

"He's been asking for you."

"I can't..."

The two men talked until night fell, and nothing Costas could say would persuade Youssef to visit the man who had harmed Helena. He had no wish to see him . . . he feared that anger would overcome him if he did, and he might do something he would later regret, and that possibly would have serious repercussions for Costas. After all, he was with the Greeks now, and he could not act as he wished. They were interrupted by a knock at the door, and Costas's wife hurried to open it. Youssef turned to look at what was once a tall bulwark of a man now somewhat bent, but trying vainly to stand up straight. His hair was all gray and his beard and mustache too, and there was something familiar in his face. Youssef looked up at him curiously. Costas rose and went to the man, took his cape, and brought him to the table where Youssef sat brooding. The man tried again to pull himself to his full height and Youssef smelled the heavy scent of *raki*.

"Joseph, this is your father . . . Stratis Delipetros," Costas said.

Youssef froze in his chair, his eyes looking at the man with blank expression, inwardly fighting the pounding of his heart that was so loud he was certain everyone would hear it. He said nothing, and Costas came to his side. Youssef finally stood up. Stratis offered his hand . . . Youssef ignored it. Stratis coughed nervously and smiled.

"Well, well, well"—he slapped Youssef playfully on the back—"if it isn't my young Turk . . . my Janissary son . . . how are you, young man?"

Youssef disliked him on sight.

"I am well." He looked angrily at Costas, then turned back to his father. "I . . . I hope you are well, too. . . ."

No, I don't hope you are well, he said inside, I hope you are ready to die, give up the precious space your carcass is taking up. He was surprised at his own intensity regarding a man who had never mattered to him. It was Jason, he realized; this man had hurt Jason . . . and Helena . . . and for this, Youssef suddenly hated him. Youssef looked at the two men again, shrugged his shoulders, and sat back down . . . he would not bother to care one way or the other.

Costas's wife hurried with some wine and tidbits and Costas tried to break the uncomfortable silence, but, for the first time in his life, he was tongue-tied.

As the woman set the wine bottle down, Stratis let out a shout.

"Come now, my good woman, take the wine away and bring us some good, pure *raki*." He slapped Youssef on the back again and laughed. "Eh, boy? You're a Turk . . . no sweet wines for you . . . me neither . . . I'm a *raki* drinker from way back."

How crude he is, thought Youssef, and remembered the dignity of Helena. He wondered if Stratis were always like this . . . Helena was better off that he had left her.

Stratis's stare became hazy and his words began to slur—the days of constant drinking had taken their toll and the man could not hold his liquor any longer. Disgust came over Youssef but he sat quietly watching him.

"Drink up, my boy," Stratis said as he downed several cups in a row. "You're a man, a Janissary, eh? Well, we'll take care of that part later. At least you're not like your brother Jason . . . Virgin Mother! That boy, no drink, no women . . . a man to be ashamed of!"

Youssef leaped from his chair and clenched his fists to avoid slapping the cup from Stratis's hand.

"Don't you speak my brother's name . . . you're not half the man he was . . . and you never will be. . . ."

"Well now, you're touchy too, I see." He turned to Costas. Obviously he did not know Jason was dead. "How do you like that? One son a sissy, another a Turkish bastard who thinks he's better than his own father."

Youssef turned white and bit his lips until the blood came. He wanted to pummel this man to the ground, and barely controlled himself from doing

239

just that. All he could see was Helena struggling alone while this drunken sod found his pleasures elsewhere, not caring what happened to his wife and children. And then to return to Chios after twenty years and degrade Jason as he had done . . . it infuriated Youssef. Xenophon had told him of that terrible confrontation between father and son. Stratis had expected Jason to welcome him with open, loving arms after his desertion. But twenty years was too long . . . it had hurt Jason too deeply. And Stratis, not knowing how to handle the situation, made the ultimate of blunders to his sensitive son. He suggested their reconciliation be celebrated by taking two whores to their beds—like two adult friends, he'd said laughingly. Jason had felt revulsion and shame, and the infuriated Stratis sarcastically offered to bring his son a *hanoumaki*, a young boy the Turks used for sexual pleasure. It was the final insult against Jason, who stormed out of the room and out of his father's life. Hated and rejected by both Helena and his son, Stratis left Chios never to be seen again.

And now Stratis was here to gloat again, to take Jason's name in vain, to humiliate them all. How Youssef hated him. Deserter . . . deserter . . . the small voice inside him cried out to the older man. And then that same voice asked Youssef softly, like you, Youssef? Deserter . . . like you?

No . . . no, it was not like that with him. Youssef had not deserted Joanna and little Jason. Joanna had died . . . he had loved his wife but she had died, leaving him empty, alone. The child . . . the children, he suddenly remembered the infant in Constantinople . . . he had not really deserted them, either. He would take care of them. He would go back. Allah, help me go back to them, he pleaded silently as he looked up at the ceiling, his fists clenched, a ray of hope entering his being. He did not want to end up like this man, alone and sick, his conscience blurred, unwanted and hated. Oh, yes, Youssef would take care of his children, both his brother's son and his own. He would find a way . . . he would take little Saki to Helena. The thought of his mother filled him with warmth, a pleasure he clutched in this moment of confusion.

Costas was sorry he had forced the issue, but the news of Youssef had traveled quickly in the village and Stratis had begged Costas to bring him. When he did not, Stratis, who never accepted refusal, set out to meet his son. And as always, he could not express what really lay in his heart. His flippant attitude and his flaunting of responsibility always worked against him, blocking him from those he wanted to impress, those he wanted to love. And Costas did not have the heart to tell him now that Jason was dead, knowing that in his present fury he would react more wildly than ever. Oh, Jason, thought Costas, and his heart turned over, you are gone . . . and a part of me has died knowing this.

Stratis struck his fist on the table. "Damn it," he shouted, "damn it to hell . . . I'm your father, you Turkish bastard and don't you forget that."

"You sired me . . . and nothing more," Youssef answered calmly, "like a dog . . . except that dogs stay around awhile to watch their pups grow . . . before leaving."

He looked at Costas, embarrassed, and then back to Stratis, fighting to remain calm.

"I can see why my brother walked away from you

. . . and now if you will excuse me . . . I will do the same."

"Don't you walk away from me . . . you Turkish pig," Stratis shouted, turning red, as though a blood vessel would burst in his head. And at that moment . . . it did. He gasped, clutched his chest, and fell to the ground. Youssef looked down at him, unmoving, as Costas and his wife frantically tried to revive him.

"The wheels of the gods grind slowly, but they grind exceedingly fine." Youssef spoke the words softly, almost to himself, as he had read them in a Mohammedan volume long ago. He was glad . . . Helena had been avenged. It was as though he had taken a sword and slaughtered this man, his father, himself. Justice had prevailed . . . he felt relief, a cleansing of his soul. Youssef walked to the adjoining room and closed the door behind him.

The townspeople were not shocked by the news. They had known since Stratis arrived a few years ago, that he had come home to die. And he had not stopped his drinking and attempts at carousing in spite of what people thought . . . or said. He often cursed, however, the loss of his former strength—ah, the sexual games he had played in his time. But just as the villagers predicted, when he was too old for bedplay, the women he had frequented no longer wanted him. Luckily, the gold pieces from his mother's land had seen him through these last years in Zagora. Costas pleaded with Youssef and he finally agreed to attend the funeral, managing to stand calmly through the short service. He felt he was living a scene from a dream . . . as though this were not really Youssef, in this strange place that was his homeland . . . among people who remembered him as a child, and now watched his father, his sire, being laid in the ground. He wished he could spend a few minutes with Helena when this was over, to lay his head on her shoulder, to have her soft voice whisper, My son, my beloved son, in all her compassion and understanding. And he realized that from this very moment, he was indeed beginning to change. The transformation had been slow and silent, so subtle that he had not recognized it . . . until now. Now, facing the Greek man who had fathered him, he had cause to be ashamed of his Greekness, but he was not ashamed at all. The wall between him and the Greeks fell with Stratis, crumbled with the remains of a useless man. Perhaps he was not so useless after all, Youssef thought suddenly. Perhaps he had his purpose, in the end— to take with him the hatred and bitterness that lay within his own son. How blind we are, Youssef thought as they walked home after the funeral—oh, how blind we can be. And when they sat over cups of coffee, and Costas tried to ease the turmoil Youssef must surely feel, the young man told him that now, indeed, he understood many things.

"I *am* an Ottoman, you know, Costas." He said finally, "It's very hard to deny . . . and . . . I don't think I will ever deny it . . . but somehow, for the first time today . . . I don't know . . . it's strange . . . I wonder how it can be that the death of this man, this stranger, would be the opening of a dark curtain."

Guilt swept over him, not for Stratis, but for having betrayed the only father he knew . . . Mahmud . . . and yes, perhaps for having killed the father he had suddenly despised. But he had found a new father here—Costas . . . so all was not lost. He was not really alone after all.

"Don't try to find an explanation just yet," Costas replied, "let it rest for now. Go and sleep it away. Tomorrow we begin preparing for the trek south. You're going to see more of Greece and your people."

CHAPTER 20

THE NEIGHBOR'S ROOSTER crowed at dawn and Youssef opened his eyes and listened to the sounds of morning. He heard footsteps from the kitchen—Costas's wife was up and about, preparing the dough for her weekly baking. Soon Costas, too, moved about. Youssef listened contentedly to the sounds of life on the other side of his door. How strange, he thought. I have just met these Christians and yet I feel close to them, a part of them. They were so kind, so good to him, giving him their bed, insisting on sleeping in the kitchen to make their guest comfortable. It did not enter their minds to look upon him with suspicion or distrust, for after all, he was their enemy.

He closed his eyes, trying to fathom the meaning, the reason for all this. He smiled and looked around the room, and his thoughts were of Helena . . . she would be so happy to learn that Costas was alive, that he had found Youssef and that they were sharing these days together. Youssef felt the clock had turned back—the faint memories, what he believed were merely dreams, were now real. He had seen this village in his mind so often, but he had thought it was elsewhere, near the Turkish border where the Greeks had supposedly killed his parents. All these years he had believed the tale they had impressed on his child's mind . . . that he was an Ottoman by birth, and that he must avenge the killing of his parents by the Greeks. They had lied to him . . . and yet he did not hate the Ottomans. How could he? They were the only people he had known . . . had belonged to. They did what they did for a reason . . . he would not judge, not try to unravel the reason. Instead he was bitter at Fate, who played such ironic games with him . . . and he wondered what he had done to deserve this punishment. Yet it was not only he who was being punished; everyone who loved him was touched by tragedy, or death— Helena, who had suffered so on his account . . . his brother Jason who was killed the day of their meeting . . . Joanna his young, beautiful wife . . . Olga, the woman who taught him about life and love. And Selina? What had happened to her? She did not appear in his dream any longer . . . the nightmare had vanished the day he left Constantinope. He wondered if this were an omen. Had Selina vanished too? He was uneasy, wondering how he could learn news of her and the child. When this is over, he thought—and surely it soon will be—when it's over, I will return and try to pick up my life again. But what would he do with Selina? He could not take her as his wife . . . he truthfully did not want to. Yet the thought of deserting little Saki gnawed at him . . . he thought of Stratis and secretly swore he would never be like his father. He would find some way, some solution to take care of both children. It was too confusing now, too complicated a problem to solve. Perhaps Helena might help him. He looked forward to the day he would be reunited with her. There was so much he understood now . . . so much he wanted her to know about his new feelings, his new understanding of it all.

He lay there for a long while, nurturing these thoughts, and finally rose and dressed. When he entered the kitchen, the table was set for the breakfast meal and Costas was sitting there, waiting for him. He smiled when he saw Youssef and bade him take his seat. Costas's wife poured the warm milk and brought out goat's cheese and several kinds of olives with the peasant bread. The smell of the dough rising in the corner of the room filled Youssef's nostrils, and he took a deep breath, enjoying it all.

They set out early, the leaders and nearly a hundred men, and they trekked south, passing Volos with its olive trees and orchards, down to the gulf where the blue waters languished in serenity, knowing nothing of wars and battles, of bloodshed and exhaustion. The gulf spread out in all its blue-green splendor, and the men stopped at the shore to rest.

"Ah, to lie on Greek soil and let the Greek sun shine down on you . . . this is paradise." Andrikos sighed and lay on the warm sand.

The men sprawled everywhere, some on the beach, others on the slopes in the shade of bushes and trees that grew in abundance in this fertile area. When they had eaten their noonday meal—a meal of bread, olives, and cheese, the staples of all fighters, they slept a while, minutes, and woke refreshed, ready to move on. They were heading southwest for Lamia, where they would be joined by the great chief, Captain Kolokotronis.

Youssef wondered why they had allowed him to go along, since they knew his position . . . he was surprised that they were not wary or suspicious of him. After all, he was a Janissary of the Sultan, and it was well known that most of them denied their Christian heritage even when it was eventually revealed. But Costas knew there was no danger . . . he knew it in his heart, and he staked his life on the fact that Youssef would not betray them. At first he had trouble convincing the other men who were not as understanding as Anthos, but Costas did not give up—he pounded away, pleading, bargaining, guaranteeing Youssef with his own life. And as the hours of their journey passed, he knew that he was not wrong. He saw the slow change, the light of understanding that came over Youssef—asking questions, searching, looking for the truth, wanting to believe, but waiting and weighing everything he heard with everything he had been taught. Youssef knew that both sides were not above reproach, but he admired these men. Costas told him of the long years of slavery and despair, of a humbled and humiliated people stripped of human dignity.

"And that is the worst, Youssef," Costas said somberly, "for how long can man continue to live without dignity?"

"The Chiotes suffered nothing like this," Youssef told Costas. "They were free in almost all respects. They have their own government, their own schools . . . and yet they joined the revolt."

"Freedom, my boy, is to live without a yoke—without even a loose one, and the Chiotes were never really free men. Don't blame them . . . after all, they refused to join the revolution at the start. But they soon learned that they, too, must take up the banner and join the fight."

"Yet they're still not free . . . and it looks as though they won't be for a long time."

"Twice now, they turned away the men who were sent there to free them. ..."

"The Chiotes are not fighters, Youssef," Costas tried to reassure him, "they're merchants and educators ... we know that."

"The Hydrans aren't fighters either, but they hired mercenaries and freed their island long before now."

Costas smiled ... Youssef was clever ... he knew his facts. He did not want to embarrass him with further comments on Chios and decided not to reply.

Youssef laughed. "All right, Costas, why don't you say it? They're not only nonfighters ... they're also ..." He did not want to say it, and he was surprised at his sudden sense of loyalty to his mother's people.

"They're ... thrifty, shall we say?" added Costas amused.

"Let's be honest, Costas. They could have financed a dozen ships and hired men to do their fighting for them ... but money was too precious for such things ... isn't that so? Just between us, now. ..."

Costas grinned and slapped Youssef's shoulder.

"Yes, my boy, that's just between us. ..."

And they hurried off to catch up with the others.

Dusk had fallen when they entered Lamia, and the men scurried to the hillside where they gathered wood for the fire. Their guides had returned with freshly caught game, and some of the fighters had managed to pick up fresh fish from one of the villages along the way. Darkness began to settle around them and the two cooks set to work preparing the men's supper. Youssef watched them curiously from the rock where he rested, and for a moment he could have sworn he saw a faint roundness inside their shirts. He stared awkwardly at them, and sensing this, they hurried about their work, keeping their backs to Youssef. Were they effeminate boys, he wondered? He approached the fire as the younger one stirred the pot, and when he looked into the large brown eyes that turned quickly away from his gaze, he realized it was a girl—they were both girls. He said nothing but turned and walked casually back to where Costas lay on the thick grass. He lay down beside him and whispered quickly.

"Did you know those two are females?"

Costas sat up. He was silent a moment ... then he nodded.

"Yes, they're Bousgos's sisters." He pointed to one of the men cleaning his musket. "He's the captain from Livadia ... he was once second in command to Diakos, the great hero, back in '21 when the revolution first started."

"But what are his sisters doing here?"

It was unheard of, two women roaming the hills with a band of men.

"It's a long story, Youssef, and a good one ... later, I'll tell you about it later. . . . Just don't pay attention to them ... they can rip your heart out with a knife very easily."

Youssef was intrigued and the look on his face made Costas laugh.

"Oh, not because you're a Janissary, no ... not that, Youssef. . . . They'd tear out your heart no matter what side you were on, if you tried to lay a hand on them. No one has dared yet."

And then Costas decided to tell Youssef a bit

more. "Rosa, the oldest, was the betrothed of Athanasios Diakos, the hero of '21—he's a legend, a symbol of our cause. Some people call him a myth, but we know better . . . we have Rosa to prove it. She's never been the same since his death, so stay away from her. The other one, the younger sister Katerina, is a hellion too, but she's all right . . . she doesn't have the nightmares that rattle the brain of the other one."

The wind blew softly and the scent of the stew cooking in the pot filled the air. To the left, white coals gleamed in the darkness as Andrikos turned the small goat over the spit.

"Ah, what a smell," called out Andrikos. "Catch that smell, friends. I tell you this is food for the gods."

Youssef's eyes followed the movements of the two girls who went about their work quietly, looking up at times, eyeing Youssef with curiosity. When the food was ready, the men gathered around the fire and ate with gusto.

"What stew . . . ah, Rosa and Katerina, health to your hands . . . what delicacies you prepare."

The men joined in their praises, smiling and nodding at the two girls who were gruffly pleased. Youssef noticed a furtive look in the older girl's eyes— from time to time she would start, as though frightened. She kept glancing to the side, into the thick bushes as though someone would suddenly leap from the darkness.

"It's all right, Rosa," the other girl assured her as she put her arms around her. "There's no one there except our own men. The Turks are gone . . . gone from Roumeli, and Thessaly, too. . . ."

"She's frightened," Youssef whispered to Costas.

"Why do they bring her along if the girl's so terrified?"

"She won't stay behind . . . besides, she's not always like this," replied Costas. "It's just once in a while this fear comes over her. At other times she's a tiger. . . . I tell you, she's a whiz with the rifle . . . shot down over twenty Turks. She got this way since Diakos's death . . . ah, what a story to tell our grandchildren. . . ."

Youssef's curiosity was aroused . . . a story for their grandchildren? He began to watch every move the girls made. And he caught the younger one looking up shyly at him from time to time, a half-smile on her face. When, for a moment, their eyes met, she flushed and turned quickly away . . . and Youssef felt his heart beat faster. He shook his head, amused at himself . . . this rough, unkempt figure had caught his fancy. He wanted to laugh out loud . . . after all the beautiful, feminine women he had known, that he should even look twice at such a figure! He could barely discern her body through the thick fighter's clothing, but he looked at her again, and the reflection of the firelight made her eyes gleam—dark eyes, wide and penetrating. He noticed the contour of her eyebrows, thick and curved, and the hair piled under her cap, black wisps falling from it. He felt a turmoil inside him and he wanted to get up and walk into the brush, but he knew he could not do that . . . he was not above suspicion. He nudged Costas and they both rose as the others scattered to make ready for the night's encampment.

They walked awhile and Youssef turned to Costas. "Do you mind, Costas, I would like to be alone." He was embarrassed. "Will there be any problem? You know I won't leave. . . ." And he walked off.

He stood there alone for a long while, watching the valley below. The moon was high—it was a full moon—and myriad stars decorated the heavens. It was so beautiful, so peaceful that he held his breath. He felt good . . . he expected something wonderful to happen . . . the release of his shackles . . . the moment of breathing free . . . he knew it was near. All the sadness of the past years welled up inside him and came out in a deep sigh, and he felt relieved, as though the great burden he carried for so long was being lifted from him. How strange that he should feel this way in foreign territory, with these strangers. But they are not strangers, his little voice whispered inside . . . no, Youssef, these are not strangers, and this is not foreign territory, you are home . . . home . . . home. The word reverberated in his insides, echoing in his brain. He closed his eyes and turned up to the heavens.

"Allah . . . Allah," he whispered, and then shyly he added, hesitantly, questioningly, "My God, my God!"

It was the first time he had used the word *God* and he was a little frightened . . . was it wrong of him? He kept his eyes closed as the thoughts intertwined in his mind.

"What are you doing here?" the female voice interrupted his reverie. "Why aren't you with the others?"

It was Katerina eyeing him with suspicion.

"What are *you* doing here? You should be back with your sister . . . don't you know it's dangerous out here?"

"Dangerous? For me?" Her eyes lit up with anger. "Ha! You think I'm afraid of you?" She pulled out a knife from her belt and held it poised. "I could cut you down before you knew what was happening."

Youssef looked at her surprised, with amusement, unable to believe the sight before him. He could have knocked her down with one mild sweep . . . and yet she dared to stand before him threatening him with a knife. He could not help himself and burst out laughing . . . it infuriated her.

"How dare you laugh at me . . . you . . . you renegade!"

He stopped laughing and the color flushed on his face. She was sorry she said that, for she had heard his story from her brother and from Costas. She knew it was unfair to lash out at him like this . . . but she wanted to hurt him for laughing at her.

He came forward and she thought he was going to strike her . . . but she did not move. She deserved to be struck and she would take it like a soldier. She was not prepared for his arms grabbing her and crushing her body against his. And when his lips came down on hers she thought she would faint . . . she had never been kissed like this. She had only experienced hasty pecks from the village boys at festivals when they drank wine and danced the *syrto* . . . when she was barely fifteen. But this . . . this was a kiss she'd heard about in fairy tales. The years of her blossoming had been spent in the hills fighting the Turks. In all this time she had tried to forget she was a female, forcing all her emotions against the enemy, until the day would come when they were free. Then and only then, she had pledged, she would turn to thoughts of love, of a man, of marriage—what every girl dreamed of. It was a vow some considered foolish, but it was her choice and she had kept it all these years. And now, suddenly, this Turk had turned her whole life inside out in a day . . . from the moment he walked into their camp. It was insane. One kiss from a stranger had turned her to jelly . . . she was so ashamed. . . . she was dizzzy now and she would have fallen if Youssef did not hold her up. When he finally let her go, she saw him only blurrily before her, and had to steady herself. Frozen with embarrassment, she watched his amused look. And then she began to cry . . . angry tears. My God, she thought, I've killed men in battle . . . I've been fighting in the hills like a maniac and I'm crying because this silly, barbaric Janissary kissed me. But the tears would not stop . . . until he bent over her and kissed her again . . . again . . . until the heavens opened up for her and bells rang on that hillside. Her brother's voice cut into the darkness . . . and the magic.

"What in the hell are you two doing out here?"

It was dark, and Youssef's back was to Bousgos.

"Katerina!" her brother shouted, "Katerina, are you crazy?" He pulled out his saber and turned to Youssef just as Costas appeared from behind a bush.

"We were looking at the stars . . ." Costas said smiling, ". . . enjoying the night. And I was explaining things to Joseph here . . . he's been gone so many years . . . there's a lot to catch up with. . . ."

Youssef noticed that Costas referred to him as Joseph but said nothing. Bousgos looked at his sister's tear-streaked face. "Is that why she's crying?"

He nudged Joseph. "What have you done to my sister?"

"For God's sake, Bousgos, I was here all the time," Costas cried. "We were telling her how the Turks abducted Joseph when he was a child . . . that's why the girl's crying."

"No matter how strong females seem . . . battles or no battles, they are still females," Youssef said softly, looking at Katerina. "And their hearts are kind and compassionate."

She blushed again, and her heart pounded wildly. He is so handsome, she thought as she eyed him secretly, looking at her brother with an innocent stare.

"I'm sorry, Vassili, I did not mean to upset you," she said. "I just went for a little walk and I ran into . . . the two men . . ."

"Went for a little walk . . . at night. . . ." He was surprised at his sister, this was not like her. "What business did you have to stop?" He was angry again.

"We did nothing wrong . . . we only talked," she replied, hoping her voice did not betray her.

Ignoring the two men, Bousgos took Katerina's arm and led her away; Costas and Youssef breathed a sigh of relief and sat down on the cool ground.

"That was a close one, my friend," Costas said.

"Were you behind that bush all the time?" Youssef was embarrassed . . . had Costas witnessed the amorous scene?

"I must say you're quite a ladies' man . . . but then you're a handsome one, my boy." He slapped him on the back. "Ah, to be young again . . ." he sighed, recalling his youth and the years he had waited for Helena, only to lose her. "But that was not too wise a move, Joseph. . . . Don't play around with Greek females, not this kind, anyway—you could get your head lopped off."

He was surprised at the somber look on Joseph's face . . . could it be he was really interested in this hoyden?

"Well, now, if you're going to get serious about the girl, that's a different story."

"Serious? Now? Under these conditions? I'd have to be mad . . . I don't know if I'll live from one day to the next."

"Don't protest so strongly, my boy, I believe you," Costas said and added, "life goes on . . . it goes on, Joseph, in spite of wars and trials. . . ."

They lay down, closed their eyes, and with the stars as their blanket, fell into a deep sleep.

CHAPTER 21

"HE'S COMING . . . HE'S here. . . ." The voice woke them a little after dawn, and the men scrambled from their makeshift beds to greet the chief.

"It's Kolokotronis . . . Kolokotronis is here!"

The men ran to greet the riders galloping toward them. They reached the slope of the hill and quickly dismounted.

"It's over . . . it's all over. . . ." one of Kolokotronis's men shouted, laughing and slapping those who came to get him. "Greece is free . . . at last we're free!"

A cry of joy came from the men who had gathered, and Kolokotronis hurriedly called a council meeting of the leaders. And then he told them the news. Except for scattered guerrilla warfare in some of the areas of Morea, the revolution had been called to a halt, with the Greeks winning their long-sought independence. Shouts of joy and screams of laughter filled the morning air . . . even the songbirds joined in the festive cries. The sun was shining and a faint breeze cooled the hot rays that fell upon the joyful crowd. It seemed that Nature, too, rejoiced along with these brave men.

"Four hundred years, men . . ." Kolokotronis spoke suddenly, looking each man in the eye. "Four hundred years . . . and at last we're free . . . praise God."

A silence fell over the men . . . a somber, holy silence that spoke more than any words could . . . yes, their dream of freedom had been realized. The banner which rose at Saint Laura on March 25, 1821, had finally brought the beginning of a new nation—of men who had lived under the Turkish yoke for so long that freedom was an untouchable, unreachable dream. The priest, Father Fotios, rose now, and offered prayers of thanks as the men knelt to receive his blessings.

"Glory to God in the highest," the holy man said. "Praise the Lord . . . thank the Lord . . . peace to all men."

He made the sign of the cross and the men followed suit, tears streaming down some of the faces. There was not a man there who was not choked with emotion.

"Now we must sit down . . . we must prepare for what is to follow," said Kolokotronis, and the leaders gathered around him waiting for his next words.

Youssef looked anxiously for signs of the girls, and when he saw Katerina he sighed in relief . . . the day was brighter now . . . he had wanted to share in her joyous moment. She was embracing her sister, and the two women quickly set about making coffee for the men, and distributing bread and olives. When Katerina brought Youssef his share, he smiled and she lowered her eyes, embarrassed, but not before he caught an answer in them . . . a reply that only Youssef understood. His heart beat faster . . . yes, it was a happy day for him, too. He was glad for the Greeks . . . glad they had reached their goal . . . and he felt somehow grateful that someone had come his way who might erase the unpleasant, painful memories that haunted him. Beneath the heavy clothing and the dust and dirt of the hills that covered Katerina was the promise of softness, of passion . . . yes, and perhaps of love. The world looked bright again, and Youssef was filled with optimism. He wanted to talk to Katerina, to be alone with her, but how, how, in this Godforsaken hill, with all eyes upon them? He must find a way . . . he would. Costas's eyes looked into Youssef's, telling him that he suspected his thoughts, and Youssef bit his lip in frustration. How could Costas tell? Costas smiled . . . ah, young love, he thought, not missing a thing.

The fighting units who had gone ahead of the Greek leaders had met Kolokotronis and he had relayed the news to them. They were instructed to turn back since there would be no more fighting. Kapodistrias, the President who had been serving the newly freed territory of Greece for several months now, was in council with representatives of the foreign powers. But a ship had arrived from Constantinople with a message from the Sultan withdrawing representation from the conference table. There were also instructions for Vizir Kayam and Youssef to return to Constantinople immediately. Kolokotronis looked around the circle of men, pausing when he saw Youssef who sat by anxiously listening to him.

"Word has it from Turkish sources that Mahmud is out for Youssef's life. He has given orders to kill him on sight . . . and to ship his head to the palace as confirmation."

He looked closely at Youssef and added, "It

seems this former Janissary has betrayed the Sultan...."

Costas held his breath as the men fell silent, eyeing Youssef intently. They were relieved—now they could indeed trust him. They let out a yelp and rushed to Youssef's side, slapping him on the back, embracing him and welcoming him officially to their group.

"Once a Greek, always a Greek ... eh, friend?" Andrikos cried. "And to think I wanted to cut your heart out."

He waved his knife as he leaped in the air.

"Long may you live, Christian brother."

Youssef sighed in relief, and then in guilt ... guilt not only for his betrayal of Mahmud, but for now ... here. These men thought he had betrayed the Sultan because of his sympathies with the Greeks ... if they only knew it was over a woman! He felt shame, and he wished there were a way he could prove himself to these trusting men. Costas knew the story and understood—Youssef had told him much of his past in the short time they were together. He nodded to him now and whispered encouragingly.

"It's all right, Joseph, it's all right...."

But Youssef's heart was heavy. The palace was closed to him forever ... now he had nowhere else to go.

Kolokotronis walked up to Youssef and the young man rose to his feet. The captain offered him his hand.

"Welcome, brother," he said to the embarrassed Janissary. "Welcome to Greece, and to your home ... your country needs you. We hope you will stay and help us build our new nation . . . it's going to be hard work."

And then he turned to the men to make his last comments before his departure, hoping to prepare them for what lay ahead.

"Men," he said, "we won a tough victory, but the real battle begins now . . . in the peace. Remember this is a time of awakening. We must unite to go forward in creating the new Greece."

Yet even as he spoke, misgivings swept over him—bickering among the egotistic Greek leaders had increased. Bitterness and jealousies had reared their ugly heads, muting the hope and excitement of their new venture as free men. Kolokotronis was determined to do all in his power to inspire his men in peace as he had done in war, leading his men to victory through unsurmountable odds. Now they must face the fight from within.

"We have made a beginning," he continued. "We are the first of the Christian people to revolt. And we have a duty to create a national identity—a national awakening for others to follow. And there will be others . . . men, other Christian provinces will rise against the Turk. We must pledge ourselves to work in peace and harmony as the first of these free nations."

The men were silent . . . not a sound was heard. Even the winds stopped their whistling. The birds sat on the branches watching quietly, as though they, too, understood the enormity, the seriousness of Kolokotronis's words.

"I see a vision . . . a new way of life," he said. "Soon the great powers, our allies, will help us draw up our boundaries . . . our boundaries, men! Do you realize . . . Greece will live again!"

A shout came from the men as they leaped up in excitement and the air filled with cries of joy.

"But wait . . . there is one thing more, one last thing I want you to think about carefully."

Silence came instantly and the men sprawled on the grass again, waiting with attention at the great captain's next words. Youssef cast a quick glance at Katerina, at her dark, chiseled features, the strength of her face, the proud tears in her eyes, and felt a strange sensation. But then the men, too—the rough, unshaven fighters of the hills—had difficulty controlling their emotions. To be so close to freedom was almost more than they could bear.

"We must remember one thing, men," continued the captain. "We conquered the Turks, yes, but now we must fight the enemy within us, our own pettiness and resentments, our tendencies to drift apart and turn against each other. Because the Turk will be waiting . . . oh, yes, he will come back . . . he will strike again when we are weak . . . weak from our own failings . . . and he will conquer us again."

The men nodded their heads. They, too, knew the dangers that lay ahead. They had known of the disunity that had spread the last few years of the war, disunity that threatened to destroy all they had won these eight years of fighting. At last Bousgos spoke.

"Captain, sir, your words show good sense, but then you're known not only for your bravery but for your wisdom as well. I think I speak for every leader here when I say that we will follow your advice . . . we promise that we will do everything we can to bring unity and keep it among our people."

"If everyone believes this and exercises it within his own jurisdiction, then nothing can stop us," the captain said.

The men cheered in agreement and shouted their support to Kolokotronis, as he prepared to depart. The men gathered their packs and made ready for the trip back home, while Captain Kolokotronis prepared to ride south to join the heads of the Peace Committee. But what the captain did not know was that the foreign ambassadors had no intentions of consulting with the Greek leaders or with the temporary Greek Assembly with regard to the form of government to be selected for the new Greek state. Nor, for that matter, on the issue of the tribute taxes to be paid to Turkey. The peace conference set to meet on the island of Corfu had been transferred to Poros, off the eastern coast of Peloponnesos. And further, the allied powers were undecided about the frontiers of Greece. One suggestion was to stop at Morea, creating a small Greece that would be completely independent. But others said the probability of Turkish hostility necessitated a strong, defensible frontier, preferably near Salonica or even southward at Lamia. It was Britain's Canning who rejected a small Greek state—a large one would suit Britain better, for only a large Greek state could move away from Russia and into English influence. The conference would begin, and the French and British ambassadors would be bogged down in discussions and queries. They would send requests to President Kapodistrias for various information, but even when the President would supply all the answers, the discussions would bring no progress . . . they would go on and on . . . and on. . . . Indeed, it was the beginning of a new Greece—a Greece founded by foreigners to be manipulated by them.

"And so, you are one of us now," said Costas to Youssef when the meeting had ended.

"I guess I have no choice . . ." Youssef replied, smiling sadly, for he knew well he could never go back to Constantinople. He wondered about Selina . . . was the dream fulfilled completely now? He had the premonition of death. Surely the Sultan would not have spared her after learning of their betrayal. And the child, Saki, what had become of him? Would he see him again? He felt in his heart that the child was alive. But he knew that as long as Mahmud lived Youssef would never set foot in the palace. His heart turned, and then it nearly stopped. . . . He would not be able to return to Chios either! Chios was still under Ottoman occupation, and it was not to be included in the new Greek state, of that they were all certain. He pulled himself out of his momentary shock and forced himself to believe all was not blackness . . . he would find a way—he must. He saw Katerina watching him anxiously and felt suddenly optimistic. Yes, a new courage, a new will to survive, to live again, rooted within him.

They made ready for their trip back. Youssef found himself with Bousgos—had Katerina manipulated it—and tried to edge as closely to him and his sisters as possible. When noon came and they stopped for rest and food, he followed the path the girls took, making ready to build a fire. Within moments he found himself in a small clearing and paused a moment to ponder his whereabouts—he was cut off from the others, but was not too far away, for he could hear the sound of their voices. Suddenly the bushes parted and Rosa stepped forward—had she been hiding there? She smiled at him, and there was a calm, loving expression on her face.

"Thanasi!" she cried out with joy, "Thanasi Diakos, you've come back!"

She ran and put her arms about Youssef.

"Thanasi Diakos?" he asked, laughing, "you're mistaken, my girl."

"I'm not mistaken," she insisted. "Would I forget my own betrothed? Where have you been, Thanasi? I've been looking everywhere for you."

And as Youssef tried to untangle himself from her, she bagan to cry. "My darling, don't you recognize me? I know"—she touched her face sadly—"I've aged these past seven years . . . but it's because of you . . . ever since they took you away, I've not been able to sleep or eat or think properly."

She caressed his hair and touched his face. "Oh, my dear, my dear one . . . you're back."

Youssef looked around in confusion. Costas had told him the girl was a bit light-headed . . . By Allah, she was mad . . . he was certain of this when he saw the anger that suddenly came over her. She flew into a rage.

"Please, please . . ." he said, trying desperately to appease her.

At that moment Katerina came running toward them.

"Thank God I found you . . ." she said and took Rosa's hand, trying gently to lead her away.

Rosa twisted her arm free.

"How dare you?" she shrieked at her sister. "How dare you try to take me away from Thanasi?" She turned and looked at Youssef and her manner softened. "Oh, Katerina, look at him, he hasn't changed a bit . . . look how handsome he is."

She hugged herself in her madness and smiled.

"I'm so lucky to be marrying such a handsome, brave man . . . my Thanasi Diakos. . . ."

Just then Bousgos appeared, and the rough, hardened fighter became gentle and soft-spoken as he took his sister by the shoulders. "Come now, Rosa, Thanasi will see you later . . . we have so much to do now—he and I—to make preparations."

"Oh, of course, dear brother, you do . . . you do," the mad girl said. "My dowry . . . you must discuss my dowry. . . . He doesn't want very much, brother, he's so proud, so loving . . . so good. . . . Don't worry about the dowry . . . when will the wedding be?"

"Soon, my dear, just as soon as we go back home . . . then we can plan the wedding."

By Allah, Youssef thought, she seemed fine earlier . . . what a state, poor girl. He stood rooted to the spot, watching Bousgos and Katerina lead Rosa away. Katerina turned to Youssef, and seeing his ashen face, motioned for him to remain there. He nodded, wondering if Katerina would be foolish enough to risk her brother's wrath by returning to meet him.

Rosa's crying jag passed and she was calm now. They laid her on the grass and soothed her with words of love, humored her, promising her she would see Thanasi soon. And when she closed her eyes, exhausted from the ordeal, sleep came quickly.

Katerina turned to leave quietly, hoping Bousgos would not see her.

"Where are you going?" he hissed. "Have you no shame? How dare you run after that man?"

"Please, brother, don't be harsh with me. . . ." She had to return to Youssef, nothing would stop her . . . but she did not want to anger Bousgos. "Nothing will happen to me . . . I want to talk to him . . . I want to tell him about Rosa . . . and Thanasi. He should know . . . now that he has found his way back to his own people."

"What concern is that of yours?" Bousgos was furious with her. "Since when have you been appointed spokesman for Rosa and Thanasi . . . ?"

Katerina looked at him silently, and what he saw in her eyes—she was pleading—softened his heart . . . and his countenance. But he was strict, and he was protective of his sister . . . this was against his principles, and should have been against hers, he thought with annoyance.

"Listen, Katerina," he said patiently, "we took you with us to the hills to fight, to help out, not to cavort with men."

She was hurt at his words but she knew well there was just cause for it. "Have I ever taken up with anyone," she asked her brother, "all these years . . . can you truthfully say I have not been an honorable girl?"

Bousgos knew that Katerina had kept herself pure for the man she would one day marry according to the custom of their people. And he could not deny that temptations were great. All this time in the hills among men, Katerina had carried herself in an exemplary fashion. She was respected by all . . . but she was a hellion that men feared, too, for she had clawed several who had made the mistake of misjudging her position. Bousgos knew of his sister's vow . . . he knew she had kept it. Not until Greece was free would she let her heart out of its self-imposed prison. He was proud of her. He smiled now . . . this Youssef was from Zagora, of a good mother . . . an educated young man, regardless that he had been with the Ottomans—he had been duped. Yes, perhaps Youssef would make Katerina a good husband. He was a Greek who returned to the fold—otherwise Bousgos would have ripped his heart out . . . and Katerina's too. The Greeks had not shed their blood to have their women join their lives with the enemy—it would be the ultimate disgrace. He hesitated a moment, then with pretended anger said, "Go on . . . go and talk with him . . . but I warn you . . . if anything happens . . ." He looked up at the sky. "Be back soon . . . it looks like a storm is brewing."

She kissed him hurriedly on the cheek.

"I promise . . . thank you . . . oh thank you, Vassili," and she ran off.

Youssef sat on a large rock on the hillside, looking down at the fields . . . pondering the happenings of the last few weeks. He could not believe where Fate had brought him . . . he had been swept by the winds to many corners of the earth, only to return to the place of his birth, a place he thought he hated, and a people he once despised. But all the bitterness and hatred of the past dissolved now . . . and even some of his frustrations began to fall away with this new emotion he had discovered here. And he wondered, was man's fate determined for him at birth? Did the Fates decide, the moment the infant came into the world, what his life would be—where the winds would take him? His reverie was broken by the sound of falling earth and he turned to see Katerina, who had slipped on a rock, tumbling down on him. He leaped to her side and grabbed her, breaking her fall, and they stopped there, his arms around her, both breathing heavily. Her cap had fallen off and for the first time Youssef saw the cascades of black hair falling over her shoulders. She was embarrassed, and she started to draw away from him, but he held her. She was covered with dust and there were smudges on her forehead and her cheek. But the large olive-dark eyes that stared deeply into his own were clear and sparkling and there was a softness in her strong face. He felt her body beneath her shirt and when he held her away from him to admire this dust-covered woman, he noticed that her top button had come open. He saw smooth, dark skin and the size of her breasts. . . . She smelled of earth and grass and he wanted her that moment—he wanted her very much. He pulled her to him again and kissed her fully on the mouth, and she clung to him, helpless as she had never been before. It was the most beautiful, most passionate communication she had ever known. He sensed it and would not let her go. She wanted to remain there with him, to forget everything—the war, Rosa, her long years of aloneness. Oh, God, she thought, don't let him go . . . don't let me lose him. I want this man . . . he is the only one for me.

She pulled away, finally, and tried to appear angry, but failed miserably, for she knew she had instigated this. After all, she had asked him to wait for her. What must he think? Oh, God, she thought, if he thinks I'm indecent, I'll die.

"I almost killed a man once, for trying that," she said, and looked into his eyes. What was he thinking? Something gnawed inside her.

"You wanted this as much as I did . . . don't try to hide it," he said softly.

"I don't want you to think I do this with other men."

"I know you don't."

"How do you know?"

He looked at her somberly, deep into her eyes. By Allah, he thought, by Allah and all the prophets in paradise, I really like this wench. . . . I not only want her, I like her. But he was afraid to commit himself again, even in his thoughts.

"Katerina . . ." He pulled her down to the grass. "Katerina, let's just say sometimes a man knows about a woman."

He looked at her anxious face and his heart went out to her. He wanted to seize her, to lay her down on the green earth and make love to her . . . wild, passionate love . . . here, without the silks and luxuries of a palace, without the comforts of a bed, without music or dancing, or *raki*. He wanted to to take her here in the midst of Nature, to love her openly, honestly. He smiled to himself as he realized he would be taking his first virgin. . . . He knew she was a virgin, he believed it, and it gave him a strange sense of superiority. The thought of virginity had never entered his mind before—none of the women he had loved or made love to, were virgins. He smiled bitterly. What did it matter? And yet, he wanted, for the first time in his life, to take a woman who had never belonged to another man. To have her completely his, from the very beginning of her awakening. He moved toward her and she sensed his intention. Tears flashed in her eyes and she jumped up angrily.

"Another conquest for the handsome Janissary?" she cried out. "Someone to add to your harem?"

She wanted him to love her, to ask her brother for her hand . . . to belong to him honorably, the right way. She felt ridiculous expecting all this from someone so alien to her ways. And then she saw the look of confusion, surprise in his eyes and hated herself for lashing out at him. My God, what have I done, she reprimanded herself, he isn't like that at all . . . I should have known. Her tone softened.

"I'm sorry . . . I didn't mean that," she said, half smiling, pleading for forgiveness. "I know it's my fault . . . it's all my fault. What else could I expect after the way I've acted since I first saw you?"

She was so afraid she had lost him now, but she could do nothing else. She felt ridiculous, this fighting hellion, who had shot Turkish soldiers and slapped off Greek hands that attempted any caress, felt like a silly schoolgirl now. She did not know what to say as her cheeks flushed. She finally offered her hand to him.

"Let's be friends . . . let's pretend this didn't happen. . . . I really came here to talk to you, about something you should know."

He shook her hand, again resisting the urge to crush her against him, dust and all. Underneath her fighter's uniform he knew there was a soft, passionate body aching for his touch, waiting for him to awaken it. And he would . . . this would not be the end of it. He looked at her now, controlling his rising passion, urging his body to relent, to be patient.

He felt good—a sense of well-being came over him and he sighed. Yes, Katerina would be his . . . soon. There were no obstacles here—no Sultan, no Baron to stand in his way. She sighed, too, and smiled thankfully as she prepared to tell her story. For it was an important story—it was something Youssef must know, to cling to, to feel a part of. For she knew, through her feminine instinct that Youssef was groping to find himself.

"They say he is a legend . . . only a myth . . . this Athanasios Diakos, Thanasi, as Rosa called him, and his friends too."

Youssef was intrigued by the mystery of this man. He listened, waiting for what sounded so important, so sacred . . . so relevant to him.

"But he was real, Joseph, he was as real as you and I . . . and he did what he did for a reason. . . ."

She took a deep breath as they both sat down facing each other . . . and Youssef forced his hands to remain still, forced himself not to take her in his arms again. He waited, listening and her words were to hypnotize him.

"He was from Livadia, and he had entered the monastery to become a priest. A tall, handsome, beautiful man that all the girls sighed over. What a pity that such a man should close himself in a monastery, they all said. And then, when the first skirmishes of rebellion broke out in '21—before the official uprising in Saint Laura—he left the monastery . . . he could not stay there any longer. Though he was a deacon, he put aside his religious vows and came down to his people . . . to join the fight for freedom.

"Oh, Joseph, if you could have seen him then, so

young, so daring. He quickly became a leader and his men loved him . . . they would die for him. He never asked them to do anything he would not have done himself. He led his fighters into battle after battle, and they were victorious in every one . . . because there was a fire that burned inside them . . . why, they freed every village they passed. The name Thanasi Diakos rang in the hills and the valleys; wherever men gathered to talk of freedom or to prepare for battle, the name Diakos was heard. And my sister, my sister Rosa, fell in love with him . . . like so many girls did. Except that in her case, he loved her too . . . and he decided he would not return to the monastery after the fight. He would stay here when it was over and marry Rosa. We were all so happy . . . it was such a glorious time . . . even with the fighting, it was new and exciting, and everyone was eager and unafraid. We would gladly have died for the cause . . . I was fourteen then but I took up the rifle too. . . . We all grew up fast . . . so fast."

Katerina paused and looked at Youssef. He smiled at her and nodded, urging her on.

"There was no bickering then," she continued. "The leaders were all organized and their men followed them loyally, trusted them. And now . . ." Her voice drifted off and she was silent a moment.

"You don't know what it's like to live under occupation, Joseph. . . ." She tried to explain, to make him see their lives as they were, to give him reason for the bloodshed of the past seven years. "If the Greeks were lucky enough to have a Turkish Governor who was kind and compassionate, then somehow life became a little more bearable. But some . . . some were no better than animals. They stripped us of our pride, Joseph, of our dignity. And when people lose that, there's nothing . . . you leave them nothing. They don't live, they exist. I remember my father having to get off his mule when a Turk rode by on a horse—we weren't allowed to ride horses, you know. He would get off the horse and bow down, on the ground in front of the Turk. I remember the look on his face when he finally rose, dismissed by the ones who called themselves our protectors . . . protectors?"

She paused, unable to continue and Youssef waited patiently, nodding to show he understood.

"I remember my father paying tribute so that we would stay alive. To pay, Joseph, to have to pay your hard-earned money—gold—so that your head is not cut off! That is living? That is being one's protectors?"

She fought to stop the tears, and she succeeded. "Do you see why we could not go on?"

Youssef felt pity, compassion . . . he began to understand, a little, the reason for the ferociousness of the infidels, the *giaours,* as the Ottomans called all Christians.

"And so we finally rebelled . . . and slaughtered, too," she continued, "and we killed and raped and burned Turkish neighborhoods. But we did it because the blood had risen up to choke us . . . we could not bear the indignities any longer. An eye for an eye—isn't that what the Bible says? What else can you say after four centuries? Four centuries of being strangled . . . all we asked was the right to breathe free air—to govern ourselves, to own our own schools, to study our own language, to be allowed to travel, all the privileges they had taken away from us as free people. But you can't degrade a human being forever . . . not forever, Youssef. . . . One day he will rise and cut you down . . . as we have done the Turks."

She looked at him carefully, hoping he understood.

"I didn't mean to preach . . . or to get overly sentimental. It's just, I wanted you to know how it is . . . how it has been for us. . . ."

There was an embarrassing silence. Youssef did not know what to say. What could he say? He had been a part of this so-called inhumanity, and though he felt empathy for her people's plight, he could not completely erase his side of the slate. There was a reason for all this . . . there was the Ottoman's side to the story. . . .

"What about Diakos?" he finally said. "You were going to tell me about Diakos."

"Yes . . . I was carried away . . . but then the very mention of the name Diakos brings to mind all these other things. You see, that's what he stood for . . . and died for. . . ."

His heart went out to her, she was trying so hard to convince him. And yet, it did not really matter. What was done was done. She took a deep breath, and her eyes looked into the distance . . . and the clock turned back nearly eight years . . . and it was 1821 in the area of Lamia, in the village of Zitouni.

The cry echoed in the hills and valleys of Lamia—"They caught Diakos! They captured Diakos at the pass!" Nineteen men against Omar Vrionis's hordes . . . they fought to the last man and now lay strewn in pools of blood. All but Diakos, who had stood facing the enemy, raised his sword and aimed it at his own heart. Never, never would they take him alive, to torture him, to gloat in his final humiliation. Thank God Bousgos, his second in command, had not returned from the scouting mission. He had been sent to look for the other Greek forces who had not showed up to meet Diakos's men. They had been cut off, elsewhere, and now Diakos and his men stood near the spot where Leonidas and his four hundred had fought the Persians in ancient days. Diakos wanted to die fighting, like Leonidas . . . but the Turks were too quick for him. Vrionis admired this mad Greek fighter as he watched him from atop his horse, gloating at thoughts of the rich reward for this prized captive. For months the Turks had hunted Diakos, long after all their efforts to bribe him into submission had failed. You fool, thought the Turkish General, what a leader you would have made for us . . . and what position and wealth you would have had, like me . . . but you chose to fight for these inconsequential ants.

They marched Diakos into the village—fifty soldiers ahead of him and fifty behind—and brought him before Hassan Agha, the Governor of the region. The Agha sighed with relief . . . at last the slippery eel was caught, perhaps now his region would have peace again. His followers would surely give up when Diakos was out of the way. He looked at Diakos for a long while.

"If only you had given up your foolish idealism and lived in the real world, Diakos, the world of the Ottomans . . . what a pity."

Diakos merely smiled. "You warned me, Agha . . . I chose my way."

The fool had ignored the Agha, now he would

pay. "Get the girl," he shouted, "get his betrothed ... the Rosa woman ... have her witness his final humiliation."

Aha, he thought, the ultimate punishment for a traitor.

"I did indeed warn you, Diakos," the Agha said with smugness. "I offered you power, position ... all I asked of you was that you lay down your cursed musket and live in peace with us."

"I don't want your charity." Diakos's voice was soft, calm, hardly that of a rebel fighter.

Ah, you actor, thought the Agha, behind your soothing voice lies a tiger. "I offered to make you leader of all the Turkish and Greek forces in my jurisdiction ... what more did you want?"

"Freedom." Again, the voice was calm.

"Freedom is only a word, fool. You people are free. Who stops you? You marry, have children, worship your god, hold your festivals ... what the devil more do you want?"

"Life is more than getting married and having children. . . . What good are children when we don't know when they'll be torn from our arms? It's more than festivals and churches, too, Agha."

"You're hopeless," the Agha murmured, and sighed. He did not want to see Diakos burn at the stake. He did not want to create a hero. "Why? Why?" he almost pleaded.

"I gave my word to fight for the liberation of my people."

"What is a man's word as opposed to his life? Life, Diakos, life! To live and breathe and love!"

"You wouldn't understand."

"I understand that you're a fool ... there would be no trouble if you Greeks learned to obey...."

"Ah"—Diakos half smiled—"now that's one of the problems, Agha . . . *if* we learn to obey, you say. And why must the Greek obey the Turk?"

The Agha went into a rage. "Because we are superior, imbecile." He raised his fists as the blood rushed to his head. And yet he knew Diakos was far from an imbecile. The man was immovable, fearless. The Agha did all he could to control himself as he stormed through the door into his private quarters to face General Omar Vrionis who languished on the Agha's silken pillows as he drank *raki* and smoked his *nargile*. Vrionis ignored the Agha's presence by staring calmly at the smoke rings he blew into the air. The gurgling of the water in the *nargile* was the only sound in the room.

"I turn him over to you, my Pasha," the Agha said. "You'll take care of him, by Allah! Diakos is a dog, a miserable dog . . . he's tormented me, ruined me. All these months I've had little sleep. Torture him . . . and that girl . . . make him pay."

Omar remained silent, still avoiding the Agha's eyes.

"I won't sleep until he's dead," the Agha ranted on, "dangling from a stake. . . ."

"You Aghas sleep too much."

The Agha's mouth fell open.

"Of course he's your prisoner, *effendi*"—he tried to ignore the insult—"and you will decide his punishment."

"Is the girl here?" Vrionis did not bother to look at the Agha as he addressed him.

"Yes, she's outside . . . with him."

"Good!" Vrionis finally turned to the Governor. "Now . . . what is your name again?"

How dare he humble me this way, the Agha

bristled, how dare he. These generals have gotten out of hand.

"I am Hassan Agha," he replied, "Governor of the region of Livadia, area of Lamia."

"Oh, yes, of course." Vrionis turned to the guard. "Bring Diakos in."

Vrionis stared at his cup of *raki*.

"Hassan Agha, I'm an Albanian," he said, "and we Albanians fight for a living. Do you know what it means to fight for a livelihood? To do battle? To stand beside death every day?"

The Agha said nothing.

"That is precisely what I do . . ." Vrionis continued, and the Agha wondered what he was leading up to. "I earn my living doing battle."

He emphasized the last words and continued to stare at his cup. "And because of this I respect anyone who battles death, no matter who he is."

Vrionis paused and looked at the Agha, who began to cough nervously. "Did you ever see Diakos fight?"

"No, but what does it matter? He's a rebel . . . a traitor."

"Aha! But I was a rebel too, Agha . . . you didn't know that?"

"No."

"My family were Christians. In fact, one of my uncles was a priest . . . when I was a child I used to ring the church bell in our village. Then when I was twelve I was taken to Ali Pasha . . . and I changed my faith. . . ."

At that moment Diakos was brought in. His hands were tied and blood was caked on his body, while fresh blood oozed from the wound in his arm. He stood before the two Turks defiantly. Two Greek

Elders of the village stood to the side as witnesses . . . the Ottomans were fair in their judicial proceedings.

"One bows before a Pasha, my friend . . . and before a General," Vrionis said, "why don't you bow?"

Diakos remained silent, not moving.

"I'm the General who defeated you, Greek. Your life hangs by a thread . . . a thread I hold in my hand."

The Agha leaped for Diakos. "Pig . . . traitor," he shouted, "I'll tear you to pieces myself."

"Stop, Agha," Vrionis shouted; then turning to Diakos he said, "Ignore him, he's an Agha. The only thing Aghas are good for is eating, drinking, and sleeping." He turned to the Agha who was stunned at the humiliation of Vrionis's words. "Leave us alone . . . go order us some coffee."

The Agha left the room cursing and muttering under his breath. This was the ultimate insult . . . but what could he do? Vrionis was the most powerful, most beloved General of the Sultan.

"All right now, Diakos, sit down." Vrionis noticed the blood on the Greek's arm. "You're wounded . . . why haven't they taken care of that?"

He motioned to one of the servants. Diakos waved him off.

"What difference does it make . . . I'm going to die anyway."

"Well now, I don't know about that . . . I don't want to have to kill you, Diakos." Vrionis looked sternly at the Greek and Diakos saw truth in the Turk's face.

"I don't want to kill you but I have others above me who are screaming for revenge. They'll go to the

Sultan if I let you go without . . . without justifiable reason."

"I'm not asking you to save me . . . my men died, and I must die, too."

"But it's a waste . . . a waste, my friend."

"All right . . . what is your price?"

"A very small one . . . and I should know. . . ." He looked deep into Diakos's eyes. "Renounce your faith and take ours."

"Ha! Is that all?" Diakos spit on the floor and the Agha, who had just entered with the servants bringing coffee, shrieked at the sight.

"Kill him this instant, *effendi*, kill him!"

Vrionis remained calm. "I have faith in you, Diakos . . . and patience. Listen to me. . . ."

The mild Diakos was calm no longer—a transformation had taken place.

"I listen to nothing your filthy mind is planning," he said, pronouncing every word carefully. "You'll never drag me to your level, Vrionis . . . I know who you are, who you were. . . . You betrayed your family and your faith . . . you killed Christians, your own people. You're even worse than the others . . . at least the Turks did it for their Empire. But you, Vrionis, you did it for profit . . . for power and profit!"

He paused only to catch his breath. His arm was throbbing . . . the pain made him squint.

"Well, you've got it all now, Pasha . . . and I have none of it . . . but I know that in your heart you despise yourself . . . and in my heart there is peace."

"That's enough, Diakos." Vrionis's voice was steel.

"In your heart you're a coward, Vrionis!"

"I said that's enough!"

Diakos removed his cap. He stood tall before Vrionis. "You see this cap? I know that the greatest insult to Moslems is to remove your cap and toss it before them. I will not only do that, I will trample it as well."

"No you won't . . . because if you do, you must die."

"Have you anything else to say?" asked Diakos.

"Yes, curse you, yes! May the devil take you and carry you away from here. . . ."

He motioned for the guards, and they began to tie him up.

"Tie me up all you want, Vrionis, I will always be free!"

Vrionis was determined . . . he would make one last effort. "Wait!" he shouted to the guard, "untie him. Listen, Diakos, damn you and your faith. All right . . . go . . . I will set you free. You don't have to change your faith . . . just give me your word that you'll leave here, that you'll go to the islands . . . anywhere . . . just leave the mainland and promise you won't stir up any trouble with the rebels."

"Ah, but I will . . . that's the one thing, the only thing I will do if I'm freed." He removed his cap and stood before Vrionis unafraid, taunting him. "And as for your faith . . . and your friendship, Omar Vrionis . . . I trample them both." And with that he tossed his cap to the floor and stomped on it.

Only then did Vrionis lose his calm. He raised his hands and screamed. "Take him away . . . take him away and burn him at the stake." And he collapsed on the pillows.

"Damn you, Diakos," he sighed, "one hour with you and I've aged five years."

They led the prisoner away and it was proclaimed throughout the region that Diakos would be impaled at noon the next day. But first he would be paraded through the streets with trumpets blaring and drums beating—that the other Greeks would see what happens to obstinate, treacherous infidels.

"Go find the heads of his fighters!" Vrionis shouted. "Go to the pass and bring them back and strew them around his carcass."

Vrionis was a patient man . . . he was fair and just . . . he had given Diakos ample opportunity to save his life . . . but Diakos was a foolish idealist, and now he had added insult to injury. . . . Vrionis had no other choice . . . he must save face.

The hours passed and Vrionis remained alone, drinking and smoking his *nargile*, wanting no one to witness his personal defeat. For he knew he had not really won . . . that foolish idealist wanted to die— he had begged for death—the thought made Vrionis's blood boil. Yes, Diakos wanted to be a hero . . . a dead hero, the ass! Yet he knew in his heart that Diakos was neither a fool nor an ass . . . and Vrionis admired him for his courage. He leaned back on the pillows and felt nauseous. . . ."

"Curse this whole mess . . ." he whispered, "damn it all!"

The next morning, at sunrise, the Turks set about preparing for the ritual of the impaling. Hassan Agha was pleased that his enemy, the enemy of the Ottomans, would at last be disposed of. Surely then the others would spread the word, and peace would reign over the region again. The Agha hated war and battles and all the confusion that disturbed his comfortable life. Now he could look forward to better times, and certainly a commendation from the Sultan himself. After all, he was host to the brave Turkish General, the great Omar Vrionis, who had captured Diakos. But the General woke in a foul mood and was unfit for conversation. The Agha tried to stay out of his way, for Vrionis cursed everyone and everything that crossed his path.

When the sun was at its peak, and the villagers had gathered, silently, morosely, to witness the impalement of the Greek, the Agha stood by in full authority, wondering why Vrionis did not come to witness the event. If he wanted to shut himself away at this important moment, let him. Vrionis was a fool . . . and good riddance . . . he would be on his way by tomorrow morning.

They brought Diakos and laid him on the ground. Impalement was a delicate operation . . . it was important to make just the right opening in the body and to insert the rod in such a way that the intestines would not be pierced, nor the heart or lungs. In this way they could keep the prisoner alive to feel the torture he had earned. Diakos was silent, biting his lips as the first incision was made—he must not cry out, he would not give them this satisfaction. As he lay face down on the earth he turned and saw, to the left, the head of Nikos, the young shepherd who had followed Diakos's band of fighters. It lay on the ground and he shuddered at the staring eyes, the bloodied edges where it had been severed from the body.

"Oh, God, my God," Diakos moaned softly,

smothering the cry of pain that tried to escape his body.

The women began to whimper, both Greeks and Turks, and a murmur rose from the crowd as Rosa came running forward. The rod was pushed through the body and came out to the side of Diakos's neck. His head jerked and the eyes rolled, but he was still breathing. He clenched his teeth so he would not cry out from the excruciating pain . . . and he prayed, he prayed with all his being, that it would end quickly. Dear God, please don't let me die in disgrace . . . don't let me cry out, make it quick. . . .

His mind was clouded now, and the horizon whirled around him, twisting like a tornado, passing over weeping faces, stern soldiers, the green landscape. And then, in his stupor, he heard Rosa, faintly, as she ran screaming to him. A guard tried to stop her but the Agha ordered him to bring her closer.

"Let her see what happens to rebels who betray their protectors. . . ."

The crowd sighed . . . a deep, giant sigh, as though it were one person . . . the whole world.

The Agha turned to them. "Look upon this man and see the consequences of rebellion. We have been kind and benevolent to you . . . and there are those who repay us with treason, forcing us to retaliate in such unpleasant ways."

His eyes scanned the crowd and fear rooted inside him as he noticed that there was not one young man in the midst—there were only old people and young girls. And he suspected what Vrionis knew would come to pass. Not one young man remained in the village . . . they had all taken to the hills to join the rebels. They had obeyed Diakos's command:

"Leave your village and go carry on for me. This is the only way to avenge my death . . . and liberate your people!"

Diakos had spoken to Bousgos when, in a monk's disguise, he was allowed an hour alone with him. And he, in turn, had made the others see that Diakos's death would do more for Greece than all the fighting, all the leadership he could offer. For it was a time of moral enlightenment, a time for heroes . . . of spiritual growth for the Greeks. It was a time long forgotten but now reborn, like the Phoenix rising from the ashes. They all knew and they abided by Diakos's wish that he not be saved. He must die . . . it was the only way the flame he helped light would burn to its full consummation.

They tied Diakos's feet and his body to the stake and placed it in the ground, standing the body up in a Christlike manner—except that his arms were not outstretched, they were tied behind him over the stake, like a lamb to be skewered over coals.

Rosa reached him at that moment and fell at his feet, crying, "My love, my love . . . why did you do it? Nothing is worth all this, nothing . . . no country, no honor, nothing!"

Diakos's lips moved for a moment. It was merely a twitch, for the pain was unbearable. A faint, rasping sound came from his lips.

"It *is* . . . oh, Ro . . . sa . . . it *is*. . . ."

And the head bowed in its final breath.

She screamed and leaped on the body, trying to clutch the still-warm flesh, the wounded body slowly draining of blood. Hassan Agha signaled a guard who pulled her away slowly, gently, pity smothering him. And yet he kept a cool composure, like a true Ottoman, trying to reassure himself that Diakos deserved his end. What would happen if all such rebels were spared. Better to use one as an example . . . perhaps then others would be saved . . . there is always a rational explanation for all atrocities, after all. He led the girl away, but she suddenly began to flay her hands, screaming and kicking like a wild animal. Another guard ran and helped subdue her.

Vrionis viewed the scene from the terrace . . . he would not, could not come down. But he had ordered that the carcass not be burned . . . it was sufficient that Diakos was impaled, there was lesson enough in that for all Greeks. Now he turned his back on the unpleasantness of his task. Damn Diakos, the stubborn fool, he had spoiled Vrionis's day, his triumph, He settled down on his pillows only to be interrupted again as the guards brought Rosa inside.

"Why in cursed hell did you bring her here?"

"We thought she is your prisoner, *effendi.*"

"Get her out of here . . ." He waved his hand and turned away, unable to meet the glazed look in the girl's eyes. She was quiet now, too quiet to suit Vrionis.

"Leave me at peace . . . in the name of Allah, let me be . . . send her back to her family."

She jerked herself free from the guards and came forward slowly. Vrionis motioned the guards to let her be. Ah, these Greeks would be the death of him.

"You caught Thanasi Diakos?" she asked in a calm voice. "Foolish man, you can't catch Diakos . . . no one can catch Diakos . . . or hold him. . . ."

Vrionis looked at her silently, cursing the feeling that came over him.

"Diakos is like the wind," she continued, tilting her head playfully and smiling. "Who can catch the wind, great Pasha? No one . . . no one can catch the wind. . . ." And she began to laugh . . . louder and louder . . . and the sound bounced on the walls and struck Vrionis, almost breaking his eardrums, piercing his heart. It was a horrible, tormented laugh . . . he put his hands to his ears to shut out the mockery of it.

"Take her away I say . . ." he shouted, "send her to her home!"

They led her away . . . and Vrionis settled back again on the soft, silken pillows, to his *raki* . . . and his water pipe. And as he took another long-drawn puff and watched the bubbles dancing in the water, he thought of Diakos . . . and of his own family in that small Greek town of his childhood. He puffed harder . . . and drank more *raki* . . . and tried to kill the gnawing pain inside his gut.

"He's buried just a way's down," Katerina said. "Rosa was coming from there when she saw you."

Katerina watched Youssef's face carefully, waiting for his reaction. He was drained of color and she realized he was moved . . . and pained, by her story. Yes, Youssef felt pain, the pain she felt, that her people felt, transferred to this stranger, this young man who was not really a Greek or even a Turk. He was a human being, and compassion was alive in him. At this moment, she felt a bond with him, and he felt it too. All the while she was talking, the years in between had suddenly come together for Youssef . . . the little boy and the young soldier had met and become one. He looked at Katerina now, not knowing what to say . . . wanting to put his arms around her, to share her sorrow. But he did not want her to see him in a weak moment, so he merely lowered his head.

"And you know, Joseph, Diakos did not really die . . . he was with us all those years of fighting. He was a symbol that held us together, that gave us courage when we were ready to quit. He kept us from falling back to what we were those centuries ago, when we suffered and waited for the great moment to come."

A momentary silence followed . . . all they could do was look at each other.

"Rosa never recovered . . . as you can see," Katerina finally said and tears filled her eyes. "But she is harmless . . . we keep her with us, always . . . and now that it's over, perhaps we can settle down to a peaceful life. . . ."

He noticed that her tears had receded . . . she was a fighter and she would not cry for long. Youssef thought of Helena and smiled . . . ah, you strong women, he thought with admiration.

"Yes, you must put all that aside, behind you." It was as though he were talking to himself, "Think of the future, now."

He was shaken by her story . . . her people were strange, obstinate, but they were admirable. Helena's bloodline was one to be respected . . . and he felt proud, proud to be Helena's son, proud that the blood of these people mixed with his. And yet, what does it matter after all, he thought as he looked at this girl beside him, what does all this matter? He was a Turk . . . a Greek . . . a man—deep inside he felt pain and hunger, and sorrow and joy, like all men. Ah, Youssef, that little voice inside him said, but all men are not the same—yes, they all feel, but they feel differently, they behave differently, they have different degrees of emotion. These people differed from his own . . . perhaps because they had been deprived of their birthright. He wondered how he would have felt if he were in their position. And then he thought of Jason . . . his brother must have felt this fire inside, this fierce desire to drive away the "protectors" of his people.

Katerina watched him somberly, waiting for his next move. He smiled . . . he was young and his body was alive, desiring, wanting the female. The world will always go on fighting, killing, conquering, he surmised, as the flesh goes on fighting, conquering, glorying in its moments of ultimate triumph. He wanted to take Katerina in his arms, to hold her, to weep with her for her people as well as for his own.

"Diakos is dead . . ." he said softly. "No, they were right . . . he will never die."

He was moved by the Greek leader's courage, by his obstinacy in holding on to what he believed. But his greater sympathy leaned toward Omar Vrionis, the Greek turned Turk. Youssef understood him . . . and pitied him. For in the final stage, Diakos was the victor—he would live on as the symbol of man's desire for freedom—while Vrionis, the triumphant, wealthy Turkish General, the great Vizir, was a sad, lonely man, belonging to no country and to no people. Youssef pondered this as Katerina watched him anxiously. Perhaps Vrionis was important too . . . Youssef smiled ironically . . . perhaps he was necessary to all this in creating the legend of Diakos. Fate has a way of dealing with matters in the way she considers best. But best for whom, he wondered. He would never know, never be able to clear this in his mind. Katerina touched his hand,

and Youssef put his arms around her and held her for a moment. He kissed her lightly on the forehead, checking what rose inside him these past weeks. She clung to him silently and he felt her love penetrating his body . . . touching his insides . . . and he was surprised. This girl loved him. They hardly knew each other and yet he knew that something had begun, a spark had caught fire and he must feed it slowly lest it flame too quickly and die. . . . He thought of Joanna and Olga and even Selina, figures that flashed sadly in his mind. He kissed Katerina on the mouth, gently . . . and the three figures disappeared . . . there was only Katerina now.

No other man had touched her . . . she had waited for Youssef all her life. I love you, Joseph . . . I love you, her heart cried silently, voicing what her lips were too embarrassed to say.

They sat on the ground together, silently, but their hearts were speaking. Youssef felt a strange peace . . . as though there were nothing in the world to disturb him now. He had found something he never knew existed. Perhaps this was what he was searching for, all these years. Here, on this foreign hillside beside a stranger, an unadorned female in fighter's clothing who carried a musket and killed Turks. He felt that this was perhaps where he belonged. And he knew Olga would be happy for him, and Joanna too, for he had loved them both, truthfully, with all his heart. He realized now that the more love one gives, the more there is to give . . . and he wondered if this were what life was all about, after all.

He turned to Katerina and thought he saw fear in her eyes. What was she afraid of? His intentions were honorable. He would live by her code, her customs . . . he did not know if he would like it, but at least he would try. For he respected these strange, mad people who dared do what they had done.

"Will you go back with us to our village?" She asked hesitantly.

"Yes . . . yes, I will, Katerina," he replied. "As soon as all this is settled I will speak to your brother . . . it will be all right."

Dusk settled around them, the wind began to blow, and he thought of the fierce winds of Chios, and subsequently of Helena, his mother. She will be pleased, he thought, and a bittersweet pain went through him—would he ever see her again? He took Katerina's hand in his, and slowly they walked back to the camp.

EPILOGUE

Chios . . . 1828

THE DECEMBER SUN shone brightly and the winds of winter were gentle, quieted . . . until spring again, when the *meltemi* would sweep fiercely over the island. It was a cool wind, but it felt good against Helena's face as she walked out of the chapel of the Prophet Elias with Captain Petros and little Jason. She had lit a candle to thank the Prophet for the letter she had received, the news that Joseph was alive and well.

They stood on the hilltop near the chapel now and glanced down at the villages below. Past Thymiana they saw Kambos, the rich fertile plains where the orange and tangerine groves were in full bloom this time of year. Petros would have a good crop—his men would be setting about to cut the ripe fruit in January. They stood there, the three of them, silently for a moment, and the child touched the piece of paper in Helena's hand as though to make certain it was real.

"Will my father be coming home soon?" Jason asked, his eyes wide, hopeful. He missed Joseph, wanted him back . . . soon . . . now!

"Not right away, my darling," Helena replied and

tears came to her eyes. "But one day . . . one day. . . ." She tousled the child's hair and held him against her.

The letter was brief and not too clear, for Joseph was afraid it might fall into the wrong hands. But it was enough to tell her he was well . . . that one day he hoped to see her . . . that he had married a Greek girl she would like very much, and that he was looking forward to their reunion. From one of the sailors on the ship who brought the note, Petros had gathered additional news—information that was safer not put into writing. Youssef could not return to Turkish-occupied land, at least not yet, not while Sultan Mahmud was alive . . . there was a price on his head.

Petros tried to soften the new pain that was meant for Helena. Chios was still under the Ottomans and would be for a long time.

"At least he's alive, my dear, he's alive." He put his arms around her and she felt comforted, more hopeful in his protective love.

Yes, she must hope . . . and pray . . . she felt instinctively that this time Fate would not be cruel, that she would bring them together one day. They might even sail to the mainland and find her son . . . when the sporadic fighting was finally over . . . when it was safe. At least the frontier boundaries of Greece had been settled. Helena looked at Petros, fondly touched his face, and he pressed her hand and smiled, his love shining in his eyes.

The three stood together breathing in the cool, winter air, basking in the warm rays of the sun. Helena waved the letter in her hand with tears of relief . . . joy . . . hope. . . . Indeed, she could hardly believe the words she had read. Though it was simple and brief, the letter contained a hidden message ... the message she had hoped and dreamed of hearing all these years.

It began, *Dear Kyra Helena,* but it ended with *I embrace you ... and kiss your hand.*

Your son,

Joseph.

About the Author

ATHENA G. DALLAS-DAMIS was born in Baltimore, Maryland, and grew up in Weirton, West Virginia. Her parents were immigrants from the Greek island of Chios, which is the setting of her first novel, *Island of the Winds*, and its sequel *Windswept*. A journalist and translator of Nikos Kazantzakis (*The Fratricides, Three Plays, Buddha*), she now lives with her husband in Bayside, New York. Their son Peter Dallas, who is a free-lance writer based in Manhattan, recently completed his own first novel.